Understanding Econometrics

Jon Stewart

Senior Lecturer in Econometrics,
University of Manchester

Hutchinson

London Melbourne Sydney Auckland Johannesburg

Hutchinson Education

An imprint of Century Hutchinson Ltd

Brookmount House, 62-65 Chandos Place, London WC2N 4NW

Century Hutchinson Group (Australia) Pty Ltd
16-22 Church Street, Hawthorn, Melbourne, Victoria 3122

Century Hutchinson Group (NZ) Ltd
32-34 View Road, PO Box 40-086, Glenfield, Auckland 10

Century Hutchinson Group (SA) (Pty) Ltd
PO Box 337, Bergvlei 2012, South Africa

First published 1976
Reprinted 1979, 1982
Second edition 1984
Reprinted 1986

Set in 10/12 point Press Roman by Allset Composition, London

Printed and bound in Great Britain by
Anchor Brendon Ltd, Tiptree, Essex

British Library Cataloguing in Publication Data
Stewart, Jon
  Understanding econometrics. – 2nd ed
  1. Econometrics
  I. Title
  330′.028   HB139
ISBN 0 09 156401 8

Understanding Econometrics

Jon Stewart

Jon Stewart was born in 1944 and educated at Manchester University. In 1966 he gained a first class honours degree in Econometrics, and was awarded the Cobden prize. From 1966–8 he worked as a research assistant in Econometrics at Manchester, and in 1968 he took his MA with distinction. He subsequently lectured in Economics for a year at the New University of Ulster, before returning to Manchester, where he is Senior Lecturer in Econometrics. Jon Stewart is married with four children.

Contents

Preface to the first edition

I have written this book in the belief that it is possible to present the methods of econometrics to a relatively wide audience. The topics covered are those that one would expect to find in a comprehensive introductory course, but very little mathematics is assumed and a prior knowledge of statistical method is not essential.

The key features of the presentation are as follows. First, it is necessary to explain what an economic model is and why such models are used. It is then necessary to explain why random disturbances are introduced and to show how this is achieved. In the course of this discussion a statistical survival kit is provided, containing those components which are essential to an understanding of the nature of econometric methods. The various ideas can then be applied in the context of the two variable regression model, and the extension to multiple regression is achieved by interpreting a multiple regression coefficient as a coefficient from a simple regression on adjusted data. This interpretation allows a full discussion of the use of the single equation linear model, and topics such as the use of restrictions, specification error and multicollinearity are included. The later chapters cover disturbance problems, the use of lags, dynamic models and simultaneous equation methods.

It is explicitly recognized that the application of econometric techniques does require the use of a computer and, where possible, the calculations necessary under various extensions of the basic linear model are expressed in a form which is suitable for the application of a program designed for ordinary least squares estimation. Details which are more appropriate to hand calculation are not given and matrix algebra is not required. The emphasis is on understanding why particular techniques are used, and this is always very carefully explained.

To all those who have helped with the production of this book, I extend my thanks. I received valuable comments from a number of people, but I would like to make special mention of the contributions made by Bill Farebrother, Ray O'Brien, Stuart Moore, George

Hadjimatheou, Michael Parkin and Martin Timbrell. Nina Roach made a really excellent job of the typing and Anne Bennett gave invaluable help in the preparation of diagrams. My wife and children had to endure both my presence and my absence during long days of writing: to Christine and the boys, my thanks once more.

Jon Stewart
August 1975

Preface to the second edition

I consider it to be of crucial importance to maintain the distinctive features of the original edition of this book. However, the teaching of econometrics has undergone significant changes in the last few years and it seemed to me that alterations in both content and emphasis were necessary to reflect this fact. The student coming to a first course in econometrics is typically somewhat better prepared, and this has enabled me to rewrite certain sections in which the extended verbal presentation did become rather tedious and in which a small increment in formality should serve to clarify rather than obscure. I have also added some material which seemed too 'technical' for inclusion in the original edition: experience has shown that such exclusions can be a considerable nuisance in teaching. Finally, there is discussion of a small number of completely new topics and new examples, based on published data for the UK economy. It is my hope that these changes will offer definite improvements for classroom use, without disappointing those who so kindly encouraged me by their reception of the first edition as a genuine attempt to explain econometric methods to a wider audience.

My wife, Christine, typed the revised manuscript with considerable patience, and my Apple computer cleverly produced numerous off-prints at various stages in the production. Given my dependence on both participants, I would not dream of omitting thanks to either.

Jon Stewart
July 1983

1 Introduction

1.1 The nature of econometrics

Econometrics is a discipline embracing aspects of methodology from economics, mathematics and statistics. The econometrician is simply an economist who, in trying to understand the working of economic systems, makes use of techniques which are based primarily on the methodology of statistics and which are often communicated in the language of mathematics. This formal background to the subject is sometimes a deterrent to those who would like to understand the nature of econometrics, and this book represents an attempt to explain how and why econometric methods are used in a way which does not assume that the reader is already familiar with the mathematical and statistical concepts involved. Although the ideas introduced are precise and do have to be carefully used, formal derivation and proof is not always necessary and an explanation of why a particular result is likely to hold can often provide an adequate alternative.

1.2 Economic models

Before any progress can be made, it is necessary to understand exactly what is meant by an *economic model*. Economic systems are undoubtedly complex, and the idea of using a model arises because of this complexity. A model is an abstraction from reality, drawn in such a way as to reveal the major features of the system. Clearly, there can be 'good' and 'bad' models. If the abstraction is taken too far, the model may have little to say about the corresponding real system. If, on the other hand, the abstraction is not taken far enough, the model may be so complicated that one is unable to isolate those aspects of the real system that are of crucial importance.

Models exist in many forms. The analysis of any system must be based on a model, but the model need not necessarily be explicit. Economic journalism provides many examples of analysis which is obviously based on a set of assumptions — sometimes explicit, often not so — which represent an underlying model. It is clearly advantageous to those wishing to evaluate the analysis if the model can be given some explicit form.

The models with which the econometrician is typically concerned are expressed in mathematical form, but this is not true of explicit models in general or of economic models in particular. For example, a diagram showing the flows of goods, services and finance in the economy is a model. However, a model must be appropriate to the questions which the economist wishes to ask and, if he is concerned about the relationships between the flows, the flow diagram is unlikely to be sufficient on its own. In this case, the level of abstraction is taken too far.

The discussion in the remainder of this chapter is based largely on the example of a postulated relationship between consumers' expenditure and personal disposable income at the macroeconomic level. The assertion that such a relationship should exist is a model, but one which is insufficiently precise to answer questions concerning the magnitude of the changes in consumption that occur as a response to changes in income. To make progress, the relationship must be given some explicit form. One way in which this can be done is to make the relationship as simple as possible, until such time as there is evidence, from observation of a real system, that the simple form is inadequate. This is a useful approach for an introductory text, but the reader should not jump to the conclusion that all modelling exercises start with very simple relationships or that the ability to reproduce observed behaviour is the only test of model adequacy that one might use.

1.3   A simple model

Suppose that, for a hypothetical economy, there exists a relationship between consumers' expenditure C and personal disposable income D that can be expressed as

$$C = 50 + 0 \cdot 8D \qquad (1.3.1)$$

In this equation, C and D are variables which can take different values at different points of observation of the economic system. The numbers 50 and $0 \cdot 8$ are constants. To fix ideas, suppose that consumption and income flows were observed for each of two time periods. Then, whereas consumption and income would generally take distinct values in each period, the existence of a fixed relationship would imply that the numbers 50 and 0·8 remain the same. Although the values of the variables change, the relationship between the variables does not.

The graph corresponding to equation 1.3.1. is shown in Figure 1.

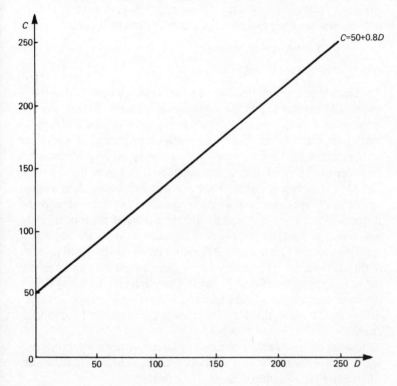

Figure 1

It can be seen from the graph that the equation represents a straight line. If consumer behaviour in the (hypothetical) economy is described by this equation, each pair of consumption and income values represents a single point which would lie on the straight line. A more general representation for a straight line or *linear* relationship between C and D is:

$$C = \alpha + \beta D \qquad (1.3.2)$$

where α and β are described as *parameters* of the relationship. In our hypothetical economy, $\alpha = 50$ and $\beta = 0·8$. In a second case there might again be a linear relationship, but with different parameter values.

Parameter α is called the *intercept* and parameter β the *slope*. The intercept represents the value of consumption which, according to the equation, would hold if income were zero. The slope represents the change in consumption resulting from a unit change in income. If this is not obvious, use equation 1.3.1 with income levels of 0 and 1:

$$C = 50 + 0 \cdot 8(0) = 50$$
$$C = 50 + 0 \cdot 8(1) = 50 \cdot 8$$

The increase in consumption for a unit increase in income is thus $0 \cdot 8$, and this is the value of β in the hypothetical economy. Because the relationship is linear, the effect of a unit change in income is always the same, irrespective of the point from which the unit change takes place.

If equation 1.3.2 is interpreted as determining the level of consumption for a given level of income, consumption is said to be the *dependent variable* and income is said to be the *explanatory variable*. In economic terminology the relationship would be described as a linear version of the *consumption function*, and β would be the *marginal propensity to consume*. The marginal propensity to consume is simply the slope of the consumption function, but it is important to realize that it is only in the case of a linear function that the slope is a constant and does not depend on the values taken by C or D. The graph corresponding to a *nonlinear* relationship would be a curve rather than a straight line and, in the case of a curve, the slope does change as the values of the variables change.

In what follows we shall concentrate largely on linear relationships, and it is important, in several distinct contexts, to be able to recognize when a given relationship is linear. The equation

$$5C = 250 + 4D$$

does represent a linear relationship, because division by 5 on both sides gives

$$C = 50 + 0 \cdot 8D$$

which is in the standard linear form. In contrast, the equation

$$C = 20 + 10\sqrt{D}$$

is nonlinear in the variables C and D: a graph of C against D produces a curve rather than a straight line, and the equation cannot be expressed in exactly the same form as equation 1.3.2. At the risk of complicating the argument we should add that the last example is linear in the variables C and $\sqrt{D}$: if one were to draw a graph marking values of $\sqrt{D}$

on the horizontal axis, instead of values of D, the equation drawn would be a straight line. But a graph of C against D would produce a curve. This is illustrated in Figure 2.

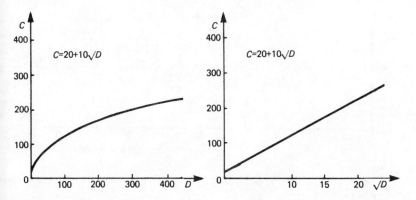

Figure 2

If it were true that there existed an exact linear relationship between consumption and income then, by observing the flows for two periods of time, plotting the two pairs of values on a graph and joining the two points, the relationship would be known. That is, the values of α and β would be known and, by using the graph or the equation with the appropriate values of α and β written in, it would be possible to calculate the level of consumption for any given level of income. But if, for any real economy, one were to take figures for consumption and disposable income over a number of years and plot more than two points on the graph, it would not generally be possible to find a single straight line to pass through all the points. One might then consider the use of an equation which represents a curve rather than a straight line. In fact, it is always possible to draw some curve through a given number of points, but inevitably, on taking an additional observation, one would find that it did not fall exactly on the chosen curve. Although the linear form is not always appropriate, choosing ever more complex curves is not the answer.

Figure 3 shows a plot of consumers' expenditure at 1975 prices against personal disposable income at 1975 prices, based on data for the UK economy for the period 1970–80. Since it is apparent that it is not possible to draw a single straight line through all these points, it

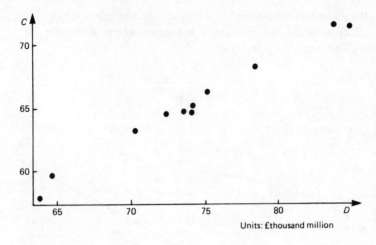

Figure 3

is clearly unreasonable to have a model which suggests that such a possibility exists. It is presumably true that there are links between consumption and income in the real system, but the model representing these links has to be changed. It is therefore assumed that a satisfactory model can be provided by an *inexact* linear relationship. This is written as

$$C = \alpha + \beta D + u \tag{1.3.3}$$

where u represents a *disturbance* to the relationship between C and D.

Given the present specification for the main part of the model, the disturbance represents every error, whether avoidable or not, that is inherent in using the equation $C = \alpha + \beta D$ as the underlying economic hypothesis. If there are other important influences on consumption, these could simply be left as part of the disturbance, but it would presumably be more satisfactory to extend the list of explanatory variables so that important influences are explicitly included in the main part of the model. The method for doing this is described in Chapter 3. There may, however, be other factors, which are not individually important and which cannot easily be measured. Since no other representation is possible, the disturbance is a convenient and legitimate device for including these factors. The implication is that equation 1.3.3 would be acceptable if income were the only major influence on consumption, but it would not be acceptable if there were other important influences which had been omitted from the main part of the model.

With this in mind, we shall impose a set of conditions on the disturbance term. These conditions are chosen in such a way that they are not likely to be satisfied unless the main part of the model does contain all the major influences on consumption. The main part of the model has also to be acceptable in other respects. It has been argued that choosing an alternative to the linear form will not remove the need to have a disturbance term. But the conditions on the disturbance are unlikely to be satisfied unless a linear relationship is a reasonably good approximation to the links which exist between consumption and income in the real system.

The conditions to be imposed on the disturbance term are obtained by applying the concept of modelling to the process by which disturbance values are determined. The model used is similar to that which can be applied to a game of chance. A game of chance is described as such because it is impossible to determine, in advance, what the outcome of the game will be. This description actually implies a model: since it is very difficult to understand why a particular outcome occurs, the outcome is said to be determined 'by chance'. This does convey a vague impression of outcomes being chosen in some quite arbitrary way but, for our purposes, it is necessary to construct a much more explicit form of model. The modelling of a game of chance is not, in itself, of direct interest, but it will serve as a useful vehicle for introducing ideas which can then be applied to modelling the disturbance term in the consumption function.

1.4 A model for a game of chance

Consider a game consisting of a single throw of a six sided die, marked with the numbers 1 to 6. The possible *outcomes* of this game would be the distinct values 1, 2, 3, 4, 5 and 6. The essential characteristic of an outcome is that only one outcome can actually occur in a single play of the game. Outcomes are therefore said to be *mutually exclusive*. It is also possible to think of sets of outcomes which are said to constitute particular *events*, such as that described by obtaining a number greater than 3. This event would take place if one of the outcomes 4, 5 or 6 were to occur. It is quite possible to define two events which can take place simultaneously. If one event is defined as the occurrence of a number greater than 3 and a second event as the occurrence of a number less than 5, both events would occur if the number shown on the die is 4. So outcomes are always mutually exclusive, but events may or may not be mutually exclusive.

When a die is thrown, there is presumably a reason, however complex, for obtaining a particular outcome. But, because the real mechanism is likely to be very complicated, it is much easier to think of the game in terms of a model. According to the model, each outcome is associated with a measure to represent the chance or odds for that particular outcome. More generally, such a measure is also associated with any event made up of the individual outcomes. This measure is the *probability* of an event, and the measure has the following characteristics:

1   The probability of an event is greater than (or equal to) zero.
2   The probability of an event which must take place is one.
3   For mutually exclusive events, the probability that one or other will occur is given by the sum of the individual probabilities.

From these axioms of probability, all other properties of the measure can be deduced. But all that we really need to know, to give an interpretation to the concept of probability, is that it is a number between 0 and 1 in value, and that the higher the probability the more likely it is that the event will occur.

A complete description of the model for a single throw of the die would consist of a list of possible outcomes, together with the associated probabilities. A particularly simple version could be based on the assumption that all outcomes are equally likely, in which case the properties of the probability measure would dictate a probability of 1/6 for each outcome. One outcome must occur and so the probability of obtaining 1 or 2 or 3 or 4 or 5 or 6 must be 1. But outcomes are mutually exclusive, so the probability of obtaining 1 or 2 or 3 or 4 or 5 or 6 is equal to the sum of the probabilities of the individual outcomes. It follows that the sum of the individual probabilities must be 1, and if it is also assumed that each outcome has equal probability, this common probability must be 1/6.

The list of possible outcomes, together with the associated probabilities, is known as a *probability distribution*. It is possible to express the outcomes as the different values that can be taken by a variable V. This variable can take as many distinct values as there are distinct outcomes. Hence, for throwing a die, the values are $V = 1$, $V = 2$, $V = 3$, $V = 4$, $V = 5$, $V = 6$. For each value there is a corresponding probability, assumed to be 1/6. A variable whose value is determined according to the rules of a probability distribution is said to be a *random variable*.

So our model for throwing a die is based on the assertion that a variable representing the possible outcomes can be thought of as a random variable.

The example given above does seem fairly straightforward. The number of possible outcomes is small, it is very reasonable to assume that the individual probabilities are equal and, on this basis, it is easy to determine a complete probability distribution. We shall use similar principles in constructing a model for disturbances to the consumption function, but there are certain properties of random variables which are best introduced in the context of a relatively simple example. So, for the moment, we shall continue to discuss the die throwing game.

As a first step, consider the *expectation* or expected value of a random variable. To obtain the expectation, each possible value of the random variable is multiplied by the corresponding probability and the resulting products are then added together. For a random variable V, the expectation is written as $E(V)$. So, for throwing a die,

$$E(V) = (1/6)(1) + (1/6)(2) + (1/6)(3) + (1/6)(4) + (1/6)(5)$$
$$+ (1/6)(6)$$
$$= 3 \cdot 5$$

The value $3 \cdot 5$ can never actually occur as an outcome to the game. A single play will result in one of the outcomes $V = 1$ to $V = 6$. What the expectation represents is a theoretical average score, which is not obtained by actually throwing a die and recording the results, but by considering all possible outcomes from a single throw and the associated probabilities. We are able to compute a value for the expectation because we have assumed a certain probability distribution. The expectation is described as a theoretical concept because there is no way of knowing, with complete certainty, that the assumptions embodied in that distribution are appropriate for a given real die.

The expectation of a random variable is sometimes described as the *mean* of the corresponding probability distribution: the two descriptions refer to exactly the same concept and are interchangeable. It is important to realize that $E(V)$ is not itself a random variable: $E(V)$ is a constant value which conveys a certain amount of information about the random variable V. It is also very important to distinguish between an expectation (or mean of a probability distribution) and a *sample mean*. The word *sample* refers to a set of observations taken from a real system. In the die throwing example, observations would be obtained by actually throwing a die and recording the results. The sample mean is the arithmetic average of such a set of observations. Some information on the calculation of sample statistics is given later in Section 1.6. Here we simply note that any measure computed from a set of observations on a real system is conceptually distinct from a measure which relates to a probability distribution.

Now consider the concept of *variance*. As used here the variance is also a theoretical measure, which relates to the spread of possible outcomes around the expectation. To illustrate this point, note that one could mark each face of a die with the number 3·5. Although there would still be six faces on the die, the random variable representing scores could now take only one value, namely 3·5, with a probability that must be equal to 1. The expectation would still be 3·5, but there would be no variation at all in individual outcomes. In contrast, the original game does involve distinct outcomes and there are differences between the possible scores and the expectation. In this case, the random variable does exhibit variation and it is the extent of this variation that is measured by the variance.

For a random variable V, the variance is written as var (V) and defined as

$$\text{var}\,(V) = E([V - E(V)]^2) \tag{1.4.1}$$

In the original version of the die throwing game, $E(V) = 3·5$, and so $V - E(V)$ can take the values

$$1 - 3·5 = -2·5; \quad 2 - 3·5 = -1·5; \quad 3 - 3·5 = -0·5$$
$$4 - 3·5 = 0·5; \quad 5 - 3·5 = 1·5; \quad 6 - 3·5 = 2·5$$

According to equation 1.4.1 these values are now squared to give

$$6·25,\ 2·25,\ 0·25,\ 0·25,\ 2·25,\ 6·25$$

The probabilities associated with the six values shown are exactly the same as those associated with the original outcomes: although $[V - E(V)]^2$ is a distinct random variable, the probabilities can be deduced from the distribution of the original random variable V. Since we now know the probabilities for the random variable $[V - E(V)]^2$, we can compute the variance of V by computing the expected value of $[(V - E(V)]^2$:

$$\text{var}\,(V) = E([V - E(V)]^2)$$
$$= (1/6)(6·25) + (1/6)(2·25) + (1/6)(0·25)$$
$$+ (1/6)(0·25) + (1/6)(2·25) + (1/6)(6·25)$$
$$= 2·917$$

The calculation above shows that, for the original version of the die throwing game, var $(V) = 2 \cdot 917$, but it is still not entirely clear what this value tells us. In exercise 1.1, the reader is asked to consider two variants of the game. In the first, the faces of the die are marked with the numbers 7, 8, 9, 10, 11 and 12. In this case the expectation is increased but the variance does not change, since the spread of values is no greater than in the original game. In the second variant, the scores are 2, 4, 6, 8, 10 and 12. In this case both the expectation and the variance are increased. This illustrates an important point. We may compare the variances obtained for two different random variables or we may compare the variance of one random variable with some other measure, but we do not usually consider the variance in isolation. It is not the number 2.917 that is important in itself: it is the comparison between this number and some other quantity that will usually tell us something of interest.

For some purposes it is convenient to measure the spread of a probability distribution by the square root of the variance. This measure is known as the *standard deviation*. It has the advantage that the units of measurement are the same as those for the original random variable, whereas the variance is measured in squared units. If the notation sd ( ) is used to denote standard deviation, then

$$\text{sd} (V) = \sqrt{\text{var} (V)} \qquad\qquad (1.4.2)$$

Now suppose that the game consists of two throws of the die. The outcomes for a two throw game can be represented in terms of two random variables V_1 and V_2. The value taken by V_1 represents the outcome from the first throw and the value taken by V_2 represents the outcome from the second throw. This means that there are now two probability distributions, but since there is no reason to believe that the mechanism in the real system would be different as between the two throws, we could assume that V_1 and V_2 have the same set of outcomes and the same set of probabilities. The two distributions would then be said to be *identical*. Among other things, this means that both random variables have the same expectation and that both have the same variance. And, in the real system again, there is no reason to believe that the value obtained on the first throw would have any influence on the value obtained on the second throw. This is reflected in the model by the assumption that the distributions are *independent*. We shall not give a precise technical definition of the concept of independence, but we shall note an important implication. In analysing the behaviour of two independent random variables we can specify a distribution for each variable, and this provides a complete description. There is no need to consider the interaction between the two variables, for independence implies that no such interaction exists.

For some purposes it is useful to express the lack of association between two random variables in a somewhat different way. The *covariance* between random variables V_1 and V_2 is defined as

$$\text{cov}(V_1, V_2) = E([V_1 - E(V_1)][V_2 - E(V_2)]) \qquad (1.4.3)$$

In order to evaluate $\text{cov}(V_1, V_2)$ directly, it would be necessary to specify the joint probability distribution for V_1 and V_2: in the die throwing example, the joint distribution would assign a probability to each of the 36 possible outcomes from a two throw game. But if the random variables are independent, one knows without further calculation that the covariance is zero, since independence implies zero covariance. The sole motivation for introducing the covariance, when the random variables are independent, is that it is sometimes easier to use the implied condition of zero covariance than it is to use the technical condition for independence.

The extension to a game consisting of n throws is immediate. The model would involve a set of n random variables $V_1, V_2, \ldots, V_n$, each having the same distribution and each distribution being independent of all other distributions. There is an important reason for this extension. All that we have said so far relates to a theoretical model for throwing a die, but one could obviously take observations from the corresponding real system by actually throwing a die and recording the results. Having collected these data, one would have a set of observations from the real system and a model which attempts to 'explain' those observations. The model for a single throw would not be of much use, because the corresponding observation on the real system would be the result of a single throw and it is doubtful whether this would tell us much about the real system. It is much more likely that one would take a set of observations and, if comparisons are to be made between a model and the real system, it is the model representing the generation of a set of observations that is needed.

Technical note 1

When V_1 and V_2 are such that $\text{cov}(V_1, V_2) = 0$, the random variables V_1 and V_2 are said to be *uncorrelated*. Although independent random variables are always uncorrelated, uncorrelated random variables are not always independent. Thus independence implies zero covariance, but zero covariance does not necessarily imply independence.

We now have a model which is similar, in many respects, to that which will be used for the disturbance term in the consumption function. There is, however, a small problem of interpretation. As we shall see from the discussion in the next section, the data taken from the real economic system consist of a set of observations on consumption and income, usually relating to different periods of time. The natural representation for n observations on consumption is $C_1, C_2, \ldots, C_n$. But we shall also find that, according to the model, each observation on consumption is just one of the values that could have been assumed by a corresponding random variable. The crucial distinction here is between the use of the terms *variable* and *random variable*, and a possible confusion arises from the use of the term variable in the discipline to which the probability model is applied. Thus consumption is a single economic variable, but one can have a model which implies that each observation on consumption corresponds to a different random variable. To avoid a completely unworkable system of notation, the symbols $C_1, C_2, \ldots, C_n$ are used to represent a set of n observations on consumption, but they are also taken to represent a set of random variables, just as $V_1, V_2, \ldots, V_n$ is a set of random variables in the model for throwing a die. Having made this point, no confusion need arise, and it should be obvious from the context what is intended. If the symbols $C_1, C_2, \ldots, C_n$ appear in a formula giving instructions for a calculation to be performed on observed data then, when the calculation is carried out, the symbols would be replaced by the values actually observed. But, in discussing the theoretical implications of the model, we may also take $C_1, C_2, \ldots, C_n$ to represent a set of random variables.

1.5   Random disturbances

The ideas developed in the previous section are now applied to the disturbance term in the consumption function. The model suggested in equation 1.3.3 is

$$C = \alpha + \beta D + u \qquad (1.5.1)$$

In practice the model will be applied to a specific set of observations on consumption and income. Often these values relate to aggregate consumption and income measures for a single economy in different periods of time, and this does assume that the consumption function remains the same over a certain time horizon. Alternatively one might be prepared to assume that a number of different consumers have the same consumption function, and one could then take observations relating to different consumers at the same point in time. In either case, a set of n observations on consumption can be written as $C_1, C_2, \ldots,$ C_n, or more concisely as $C_t; t = 1, 2, \ldots, n$. The corresponding observations on income can be written as $D_t; t = 1, 2, \ldots, n$. The model applied to these observations would then be

$$C_t = \alpha + \beta D_t + u_t; t = 1, 2, \ldots, n \qquad (1.5.2)$$

This indicates that the model holds, for some constant α and β, for the n time periods identified as $t = 1$, $t = 2$ and so on. We shall generally refer to time periods, but it should be understood that the argument could equally well apply to any other type of observation. A set of observations relating to a single unit in different periods of time is called a *time series*. A set of observations relating to different units at a single point in time is a *cross-section*. In different contexts these units might be households, firms, industries, regions or countries. But, at least in macroeconomics, time series are the most frequently used observations, and the discussion is continued on this basis.

It is now assumed that the disturbance in each time period behaves as though it were generated according to the rules of a probability distribution. In the simplest case, it is also assumed that the distributions are identical and that they are all independent. There is thus a clear analogy between the model for a set of n disturbances and the model for n throws of a die. The same probabilities govern each throw of the die, and the result of any one throw has no influence on the results obtained from the other throws. Similarly, the same probabilities apply to the generation of the disturbance value for each time period, and the value obtained in one period has no influence on the values obtained in other periods. Unfortunately the analogy is not complete, because the disturbances are generally considered to be *continuous* random variables whereas the variables in the die throwing game are *discrete*. The distinction here is between the six possible outcomes for the die throwing game and the very large number of outcomes that are conceptually possible for a random disturbance. According to our model, the value of consumption in any time period depends partly on the value of a random disturbance. Although there is a limit to the accuracy with which consumption can be measured, this still leaves a very large number of values that could be observed and, because consumption is supposed to be partly determined by the random disturbance, the disturbance must also be capable of assuming many different values. Since it is impossible to say initially which values might occur, we would usually treat the set of possible outcomes as being equivalent to the set of real numbers. This does raise certain conceptual difficulties, because there is no limit to the number of distinct real values that exist in any interval defined on the real line. If a disturbance can take any real value, the probability of finding one of those values must be extremely small; in fact, in the case of a continuous random variable, we do not refer to probabilities in this way. Instead of talking about the probability of a point value, we consider the probability of finding a value within a certain interval. Thus we can refer to the probability of finding a value greater than 0, or a value between 0 and 1, but it is not meaningful to consider the probability of obtaining a value precisely equal to 1.

It should now be obvious that we cannot represent the probability distribution for a continuous random variable as a list of outcomes, together with associated probabilities. Instead we use the *probability density function* (pdf), from which one can obtain the probability of finding a value of the random variable in any given interval. Figure 4 illustrates the pdf for a *normal distribution*, which is the type most commonly used in the representation of disturbances. In fact, we need only consider a single typical disturbance, written as u, with no qualifying subscript, because it has already been assumed that the individual disturbances are independently and identically distributed.

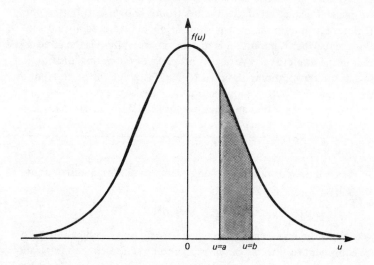

Figure 4

In Figure 4, the horizontal axis represents the possible values of u. Above the horizontal axis is a curve, which captures the idea that values in an interval under the centre of the curve are more likely than values in an equal interval well away from the centre. The height of the curve is certainly connected with probability, but it does not give the probability of the corresponding point value on the horizontal axis. The curve is actually the graph of the pdf, which is denoted as $f(u)$. The probability of finding a value between any two points on the horizontal axis is given by the area contained between the curve, the horizontal axis and vertical lines drawn through the two points in question. This is illustrated in Figure 4: the shaded area corresponds to the probability of finding a value of u between the points $u = a$ and $u = b$. The reader with some knowledge of calculus will recognize that this area corresponds to the definite integral of $f(u)$, evaluated between $u = a$ and $u = b$. Fortunately, for the most frequently used distributions, there are tables which enable one to obtain probabilities without having to evaluate the integrals. The use of such tables is discussed further in Sections 2.6–2.8, 3.7, 4.3 and 4.5.

A normal distribution is not completely defined until one specifies values for the expectation and variance. In this context, the expectation and variance are said to be parameters of the distribution. As in the case of a discrete random variable, the expectation is a theoretical average over the values that could occur and the variance is a measure of spread. Calculation of these values from a known distribution now requires integration rather than summation, but we need not pursue this point. What is important is that the interpretation is the same as that in the discrete case. A further property of the normal distribution is that the expectation falls under the highest point on the graph of the pdf, so the distribution shown in Figure 4 has an expectation equal to zero. Remember that an exactly equivalent statement is that the

---

Technical note 2

If u is a continuous random variable which has a normal distribution, the pdf is

$$f(u) = (2\pi\sigma^2)^{-1/2} \exp\left[-(u - \mu)^2/2\sigma^2\right]$$

where π is the mathematical constant $3 \cdot 1415\ldots$, μ can be shown to be equivalent to $E(u)$, σ^2 can be shown to be equivalent to var (u) and exp [ ] represents the exponential function. Knowledge of the form of this pdf is not essential to the discussion which follows.

mean of the distribution is zero. The assumption that the expectation is zero reflects the fact that the disturbance is supposed to represent many small influences on consumption, which cannot be built into the main part of the model. There is no reason to believe that such influences would increase or decrease consumption in a systematic way and, if this belief is correct, the assumption of zero expectation is quite reasonable.

After a considerable amount of preparation, it is now possible to state a complete specification for the consumption function model. It is assumed that

$$C_t = \alpha + \beta D_t + u_t; t = 1, 2, \ldots, n \tag{1.5.3}$$

where the disturbances can be thought of as a set of random variables which are initially assumed to have identical and independent distributions. If the distributions are identical, they have the same expectation and the same variance and the common expectation is assumed to be zero. Typically, the disturbance distributions are also taken to be normal. An important implication of this model is that each observation on consumption must be thought of as representing a single value taken by a corresponding random variable because, according to the model, each value $C_1, C_2, \ldots, C_n$ is determined in part by the corresponding disturbance. To illustrate this point, take a single consumption term, say C_1, and consider what would have happened if the income value D_1 had remained the same but the disturbance value u_1 had been different. The answer is that C_1 would have taken a different value. We know that, in practice, only one value of C_1 is observed, but this does not matter: the model is an abstraction and it is perfectly feasible to describe what would happen, in terms of the model, in a situation which cannot occur in practice.

So, in discussing the theoretical properties of the model, each observation on consumption is treated as being a single value taken by a corresponding random variable. But the model does not necessarily imply that the same is true of the observations on income. In fact the model does not explain how the income values are determined, and it is convenient to assume, wherever possible, that the explanatory variable observations are fixed nonrandom quantities. One could think of disposable income as being fixed by policy decision, although this is rather unrealistic. The alternative is to interpret the present analysis as being partial and conditional on income values determined elsewhere. In either case, $D_1, D_2, \ldots, D_n$ can be considered to be nonrandom and, since the expression $\alpha + \beta D_t$ does not involve any random variables, this can be described as the deterministic part of the model.

It is very important to note that we do not know the values of α and β for which the model is valid. Indeed we do not know whether the model is valid at all. We therefore have two crucial objectives. The first is to find a method which will produce *estimates* of α and β. One possibility is to plot the observed values for consumption and income on a graph and to choose a straight line which looks as though it passes reasonably closely through the observed points. The intercept and slope of this line would then be estimates of α and β respectively. But there is more to estimation than simply producing a pair of numbers. The rather elaborate theoretical structure that we have developed does provide a model for the relationship between consumption and income, but it also makes it possible to say something about the behaviour of the estimates, at least for certain standard methods of estimation.

It is fairly obvious that any method of estimation would make use of the observed values of consumption and income. Now, according to the model, the observations on consumption correspond to random variables. A different set of disturbance values would imply a different set of consumption values and hence a different value for an estimate calculated from the consumption values. It follows that the estimate actually obtained is just one of the values that could have arisen. The rule defining a method of estimation, usually expressed as an algebraic formula, is called an *estimator*. Replacing elements in the formula by the values actually observed gives a particular value of the estimator, and this provides a more precise definition of what is meant by an estimate. Our argument suggests that an estimator defines a random variable and that an estimate is a particular value taken by that random variable.

In the consumption function model, both α and β are unknown, and we would therefore need two estimators. The estimators are random variables and therefore have probability distributions, and it is usually possible to deduce these distributions from assumptions concerning the disturbances. Some rules which will help us to do this are given in Sections 2.3–2.5. If one can obtain distributions for the estimators, it is possible to make probability statements about the closeness of the estimates to the unknown 'true' parameters. However, the validity of such statements depends on the truth of the underlying assumptions, and this brings us to the second important objective. In subsequent chapters, we shall develop methods of testing some of the assumptions embodied in the model, to see whether these assumptions are consistent with observations taken from the real system. We shall also consider various extensions of the model, to allow for more realistic representation of highly interdependent economic systems.

1.6   Sample statistics

In the literature of statistics, a model of the kind that we have introduced would be described as a *two variable regression model*, and the twin problems of estimation and testing would be described as problems of *statistical inference*. According to the model, each observation on consumption is just one of the values that could have arisen and, in this sense, observation of the real system provides incomplete information about the model. Statistical inference is the process of trying to discover something about the model on the basis of this incomplete information. The set of observations actually obtained is a sample: we have one sample but, according to the model, there are many different samples that might have been obtained.

A measure computed from a set of observations is a *sample statistic*. In this section we introduce the sample mean and the sample variance, but it is perhaps obvious that estimates of α and β would also be sample statistics. The distinction between a sample statistic and an estimate is that one can always compute a sample statistic, regardless of whether or not there is an underlying probability model. If there is such a model, one may use the value of a sample statistic as an estimate of the value of an unknown parameter. If there is no underlying probability model, the sample statistic has a purely descriptive interpretation: it is simply a number which conveys some information about a particular set of observations and has no relevance beyond that set of observations.

There is a very useful shorthand device which is used to write down formulae for sample statistics. Suppose that we have a set of n observations on some variable X. The observations are written as $X_t; t = 1, 2, \ldots, n$. The operation of forming a sum of the observations can be written as

$$\sum_{t=1}^{t=n} X_t$$

which means 'add all the values of the variable, in this case X, starting with X_1 and finishing with X_n'. Often it is obvious from the context what the range of summation should be and, if so, one of the shortened forms $\Sigma_t X_t$ or ΣX_t is used instead. It is convenient to be able to carry out algebraic manipulation of expressions which involve the summation notation, and the following rules are useful in this respect:

1 If c is a constant,

$$\sum_{t=1}^{t=n} c = nc$$

2 If c is a constant and X is a variable,

$$\Sigma(cX_t) = c\Sigma X_t$$

3 If X and Y are two variables,

$$\Sigma(X_t + Y_t) = \Sigma X_t + \Sigma Y_t$$

By putting these rules together, we can manipulate more complex expressions. Thus, for example, if c and d are constants

$$\Sigma(cX_t + dY_t) = c\Sigma X_t + d\Sigma Y_t$$

Note, however, that it is not true that $\Sigma(X_t Y_t)$ is the same as $\Sigma X_t \Sigma Y_t$. Each of these statements can easily be verified by inventing a few numerical examples (see exercise 1.3).

Given the summation notation, the formula for the *sample mean* of a set of observations on X is

$$\bar{X} = \Sigma X_t / n \tag{1.6.1}$$

This represents a simple average of the observations, and $\bar{X}$ is a conventional notation for the sample mean of the variable written underneath the bar. The *sample variance* is written as s_X^2 and defined as

$$s_X^2 = \Sigma(X_t - \bar{X})^2/n \tag{1.6.2}$$

The reader with some knowledge of elementary statistics may wonder why the sample variance is not defined with a divisor of $n-1$ rather than n. The answer is that if the sample variance is used in a purely descriptive way, there is no reason to do anything other than average the squared deviations. For reasons best explained later, there is a purpose in using $n-1$ when the sample variance is used as an estimate of an unknown variance, in the context of a certain type of probability model. It is also worth noting that, for descriptive purposes, the sample standard deviation may be a more effective measure of spread than the sample variance. The *sample standard deviation* is the square root of the sample variance:

$$s_X = \sqrt{[\Sigma(X_t - \bar{X})^2/n]} \qquad (1.6.3)$$

The advantage of this quantity is that the units of measurement are the same as those for the original sample.

Although there are obvious analogies between the measures relating to a probability distribution and those relating to a sample, there are also some crucial differences. The expectation and the variance are theoretical concepts and they can only be evaluated by making some assumption about underlying probabilities. The sample mean and sample variance can be calculated directly from a given set of observations. A more subtle difference is that the expectation and variance of a random variable are not themselves random, but the formulae for the sample mean and sample variance could each define a random variable. According to our model, this would be true of the measures for a sample of consumption values, because observations on consumption are considered to be values taken by a set of random variables. But it would not be true of the corresponding measures for income, because the observations on income are taken to be fixed nonrandom quantities. In this case, the sample measures would be purely descriptive.

The discussion in this chapter has covered a number of important ideas, and it is useful to present a brief summary. It has been argued that an exact relationship between economic variables will not generally correspond to what is observed in the real system, and so disturbances are added to the model. Since the model is designed to explain the behaviour of the dependent variable, a necessary preliminary is to have some 'explanation' of how the disturbance values are generated. This is achieved by constructing a probability model for the disturbances. To follow up the implications of the probability model, it is necessary to have some basic ideas of statistical method. To the reader who has not previously encountered statistical arguments, the range of ideas covered in this chapter might be somewhat daunting. However, we have now covered some essential elements of a statistical survival kit, which should be quite sufficient to enable the reader to understand the arguments which follow.

1.7   Exercises (solutions on p. 273)

1.1 Consider two variants of the die throwing game, in which the values marked on the die are
   (*a*)   7, 8, 9, 10, 11, 12
   (*b*)   2, 4, 6, 8, 10, 12.

In each case, find the expectation and variance of a random variable representing the outcome of a single throw. Can you suggest, for each case, a rule which links the expectation of the modified random variable to the expectation in the original game? Can you also suggest rules for the variance?

1.2 Temperature F in degrees Fahrenheit is related to temperature V in degrees centigrade by the linear relationship

$$F = 32 + 1 \cdot 8V$$

For a given month and location, it is known that $E(V) = 15$ and $\text{var}(V) = 9$. Extend the rules developed in the previous exercise to find values for $E(F)$ and $\text{var}(F)$.

1.3 The variable X takes the values 1, 2 and 3, the variable Y takes the values 2, 4 and 6, and c is a constant equal to 10. Use these examples to demonstrate the validity of the rules of summation given in Section 1.6.

1.4 The following data consist of observations on consumers' expenditure C and personal disposable income D, in £ thousand million at 1975 prices, for the UK economy over the years 1970–80. For each variable, calculate the sample mean and sample standard deviation.

Year	t	C_t	D_t
1970	1	57·81	63·74
1971	2	59·72	64·54
1972	3	63·27	70·21
1973	4	66·33	75·06
1974	5	65·05	74·05
1975	6	64·65	74·00
1976	7	64·71	73·44
1977	8	64·52	72·29
1978	9	68·23	78·26
1979	10	71·60	83·67
1980	11	71·55	84·77

Source: Economic Trends, annual
supplement, 1983 edition

2 The two variable linear model

2.1 The least squares principle

In Chapter 1 the consumption function was used to illustrate the nature of the two variable regression model, but very little was said about how parameter estimates could be obtained. We now start on a more systematic discussion of the use of the model, and the first step is to introduce a general notation. The convention adopted is that Y represents the dependent variable and X the explanatory variable. Hence, in this general notation, the linear model becomes

$$Y_t = \alpha + \beta X_t + u_t; t = 1, 2, \ldots, n \qquad (2.1.1)$$

If a line is estimated, perhaps by plotting points on a scatter diagram and choosing a line to go through the points, any given value X_t can be used to generate an estimated or predicted value of the dependent variable. The algebraic representation of this would be

$$\hat{Y}_t = \hat{\alpha} + \hat{\beta} X_t; t = 1, 2, \ldots, n \qquad (2.1.2)$$

where $\hat{\alpha}$ and $\hat{\beta}$ represent estimates, as distinct from the true values α and β, and where $\hat{Y}_t$ is a predicted value of the dependent variable, as distinct from an observed value Y_t. Any point $(X_t, \hat{Y}_t)$ will lie on the estimated line, whereas a point (X_t, Y_t) may be close to the estimated line but will not, in general, lie exactly on the line. So, for each observed point, there is a *residual*

$$e_t = Y_t - \hat{Y}_t; t = 1, 2, \ldots, n \qquad (2.1.3)$$

which corresponds to the vertical displacement of the observed point from the estimated line. This is illustrated in Figure 5.

By combining equations 2.1.2 and 2.1.3, one can express the residuals in terms of the estimates $\hat{\alpha}$ and $\hat{\beta}$:

$$e_t = Y_t - \hat{\alpha} - \hat{\beta} X_t; t = 1, 2, \ldots, n \qquad (2.1.4)$$

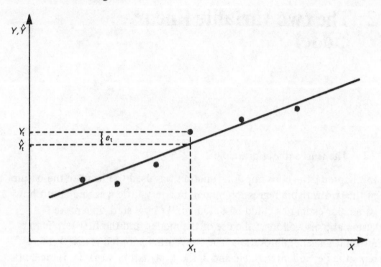

Figure 5

The residuals must be carefully distinguished from the disturbances, used in writing down the model, which are

$$u_t = Y_t - \alpha - \beta X_t; t = 1, 2, \ldots, n \qquad (2.1.5)$$

Since the true values of α and β are unknown, and since it is highly improbable that a particular pair of estimates would coincide exactly with the true values, it follows that the disturbance values cannot be observed and that it is highly unlikely that they would be the same as the residuals defined in equation 2.1.4.

It would be very inconvenient to have to actually draw a scatter diagram to estimate the line, and so we consider a method which allows estimates of the intercept and slope to be obtained from algebraic formulae. It is obviously desirable that the estimated line should pass as closely as possible through the observed points, and this means that the residuals $e_t; t = 1, 2, \ldots, n$ should be made as small as possible. To achieve this, the residuals corresponding to each point have to be taken together in some way, and this collective measure has then to be set as close as possible to zero. One could consider taking the sum of the residuals, but for any estimated line passing through the scatter of points, some observed points would be above the line and some would be below. Hence some e_t values would be positive and some negative, and there are actually many lines for which the sum of residuals is zero. We therefore consider the sum of squared residuals, which is a sum of non-negative quantities. The *least squares principle* states that the line (and hence the parameter estimates) should be chosen so as to make the sum of squared residuals as small as possible. Formally, this can be expressed as

$$\text{choose } \hat{\alpha} \text{ and } \hat{\beta} \text{ to minimize } \Sigma e_t^2 = \Sigma(Y_t - \hat{\alpha} - \hat{\beta}X_t)^2 \qquad (2.1.6)$$

There exists a well defined procedure in calculus for solving a problem such as 2.1.6. What the calculus does (see exercise 2.3) is to show that the values of $\hat{\alpha}$ and $\hat{\beta}$ that satisfy the minimization condition are those values that satisfy a pair of equations, known as the *normal equations*:

$$\hat{\alpha}n + \hat{\beta}\Sigma X_t = \Sigma Y_t \qquad\qquad (2.1.7)$$
$$\hat{\alpha}\Sigma X_t + \hat{\beta}\Sigma X_t^2 = \Sigma X_t Y_t$$

In these equations, $\hat{\alpha}$ and $\hat{\beta}$ are unknowns and $\Sigma Y_t, n, \Sigma X_t, \Sigma X_t Y_t$ and ΣX_t^2 are all known in the sense that, for any given set of data, a value can be calculated for each quantity. There are many values of $\hat{\alpha}$ and $\hat{\beta}$ which would satisfy one of the equations, but the least squares principle implies that the correct choice of estimates would be the particular values of $\hat{\alpha}$ and $\hat{\beta}$ which satisfy both equations.

This is one of the contexts in which it is important to be able to recognize linearity, for if two unknown quantities have to satisfy two linear equations, the only possible solution is a pair of values which define a point lying on both straight lines. Since two distinct straight lines can only cross at a single point, there can only be one value, for each unknown, which satisfies both equations. The only cases in which this conclusion does not hold are (1) when the two lines are parallel or (2) when the two equations represent exactly the same line. In the first case, no solution is possible and the equations are inconsistent. In the second case, there is really only one equation and any point on the corresponding line would be a solution: but such a solution is not unique and, to fit a single estimated line to observed points, we do need a unique solution. An example of this second case is provided by the equations

$$10\hat{\alpha} + 50\hat{\beta} = 100$$
$$50\hat{\alpha} + 250\hat{\beta} = 500$$

Division by 5 on both sides of the second equation would reproduce the first equation exactly: it seems, at first, that there are two equations, but in fact there is only one distinct line.

Equations 2.1.7 are linear in $\hat{\alpha}$ and $\hat{\beta}$, and it would usually be possible to obtain a unique solution. We do not need to worry about whether a solution will exist, because inconsistency cannot occur in this context. It is possible that the solution will not be unique, but this will only occur in the highly unlikely case in which X_t happens to have the same value in all time periods. Such a variable is unlikely to be the basis of a successful two variable model.

It would perhaps be useful to have an example at this point. The data in Table 1 are completely artificial, chosen only to make the arithmetic easy. If these values are used in 2.1.7, the equations become

$$5\hat{\alpha} + 150\hat{\beta} = 110$$
$$150\hat{\alpha} + 5500\hat{\beta} = 3690$$

By multiplying the first equation by $150/5 = 30$ and subtracting the result from the second equation, it is possible to eliminate $\hat{\alpha}$, leaving

$$[5500 - 30(150)]\hat{\beta} = 3690 - 30(110)$$

or

$$\hat{\beta} = 390/1000 = 0{\cdot}39$$

Then, using the first equation, it is possible to solve for $\hat{\alpha}$, given the value of $\hat{\beta}$, as

$$5\hat{\alpha} = 110 - 150(0{\cdot}39)$$
$$\hat{\alpha} = (110/5) - [150(0{\cdot}39)/5]$$
$$= 22 - 11{\cdot}7$$
$$= 10{\cdot}3$$

Table 1

t	Y_t	X_t	$X_t Y_t$	X_t^2
1	14	10	140	100
2	18	20	360	400
3	23	30	690	900
4	25	40	1000	1600
5	30	50	1500	2500
$n = 5$	$\Sigma Y_t = 110$	$\Sigma X_t = 150$	$\Sigma X_t Y_t = 3690$	$\Sigma X_t^2 = 5500$

So the estimated line in this example would suggest that Y increases by 0·39 for each unit increase in X and that, when $X = 0$, Y would be 10·3.

The calculation above involves numerical manipulation to eliminate $\hat{\alpha}$, to solve the reduced system for $\hat{\beta}$ and finally, to solve for $\hat{\alpha}$ in terms of the value of $\hat{\beta}$ which has been obtained. It is possible to express this sequence of operations algebraically, to provide explicit formulae for $\hat{\alpha}$ and $\hat{\beta}$. The result would be

$$\hat{\beta} = [\Sigma X_t Y_t - (\Sigma X_t/n)\Sigma Y_t] / [\Sigma X_t^2 - (\Sigma X_t/n)\Sigma X_t] \qquad (2.1.8)$$

and

$$\hat{\alpha} = \Sigma Y_t/n - \hat{\beta}(\Sigma X_t/n)$$

or

$$\hat{\alpha} = \overline{Y} - \hat{\beta}\overline{X} \qquad (2.1.9)$$

where $\overline{Y}$ and $\overline{X}$ are the sample means of Y and X. The formula for $\hat{\beta}$ looks rather complicated, and a more concise version can be obtained by recognizing that the expressions in square brackets in equation 2.1.8 are what are sometimes called 'short cut' formulae for computing sums of squares and products about sample means. If we define

$$y_t = Y_t - \overline{Y} \text{ and } x_t = X_t - \overline{X}; t = 1, 2, \ldots, n$$

then it can be shown (see exercise 2.4) that

$$\Sigma x_t y_t = \Sigma X_t Y_t - (\Sigma X_t/n)\Sigma Y_t \qquad (2.1.10)$$
$$\Sigma x_t^2 = \Sigma X_t^2 - (\Sigma X_t/n)\Sigma X_t \qquad (2.1.11)$$

Equation 2.1.8 can therefore be written as

$$\hat{\beta} = \Sigma x_t y_t/\Sigma x_t^2 \qquad (2.1.12)$$

This formula can be used in conjunction with equations 2.1.10 and 2.1.11, in which case the table of calculations for the numerical example is exactly as shown in Table 1. Alternatively, the data can be adjusted for means prior to the formation of sums of squares and products, in which case the table of calculations is as in Table 2 (p. 38).

Equations 2.1.9 and 2.1.12 represent shorthand expressions for a set of instructions which can be applied to any set of data to produce estimates of the intercept and slope. The formulae define the least squares estimators, and the values obtained from a particular set of data are the estimates for those data. You will notice that, at first, when the

Table 2

t	Y_t	X_t	$y_t = Y_t - \overline{Y}$	$x_t = X_t - \overline{X}$	$x_t y_t$	x_t^2
1	14	10	−8	−20	160	400
2	18	20	−4	−10	40	100
3	23	30	1	0	0	0
4	25	40	3	10	30	100
5	30	50	8	20	160	400
$n = 5$	ΣY_t $= 110$	ΣX_t $= 150$	Σy_t $= 0$	Σx_t $= 0$	$\Sigma x_t y_t$ $= 390$	Σx_t^2 $= 1000$

$\overline{Y} = 110/5 = 22; \overline{X} = 150/5 = 30; \hat{\beta} = 390/1000 = 0.39;$
$\hat{\alpha} = 22 - 0.39(30) = 10.3$

minimization problem which produces the formulae was defined, $\hat{\alpha}$ and $\hat{\beta}$ were used to represent arbitrary estimates for α and β. From now on, this notation refers only to the least squares estimators, or to particular least squares estimates. As a consequence of this redefinition of $\hat{\alpha}$ and $\hat{\beta}$, it should be recognized that the formulae

$$\hat{Y}_t = \hat{\alpha} + \hat{\beta} X_t; t = 1, 2, \ldots, n$$

and

$$e_t = Y_t - \hat{\alpha} - \hat{\beta} X_t; t = 1, 2, \ldots, n$$

now refer to least squares predicted values and to least squares residuals, rather than to predicted values and residuals based on arbitary estimates.

2.2   The correlation coefficient

The least squares method produces an estimated line which is the best fitting of all possible straight lines, at least in the sense of minimizing the sum of squared residuals. But the best line in any particular case may not fit very closely to the observed points and so may not provide a particularly good explanation of the behaviour of the dependent variable. Figure 6 shows two different situations, one in which the observed points would fit quite closely to a straight line and one in which the points would not fit closely to a straight line. In the first case (Figure 6a), there is obviously a strong relationship between Y and X, and an explanation relating the behaviour of Y to the behaviour of X does correspond to what is observed. In the second case (Figure 6b),

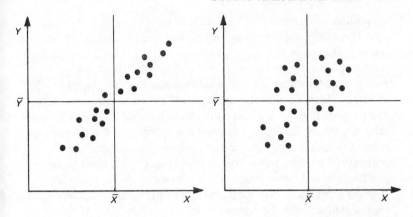

Figure 6

the explanation is poor and the linkage between Y and X is weak, if it exists at all.

To give a precise numerical measure to the strength of the relationship (sometimes called the *goodness of fit*), the *correlation coefficient* is used. This is denoted by r and defined by the formula

$$r = \frac{\Sigma x_t y_t}{\sqrt{\Sigma x_t^2}\ \sqrt{\Sigma y_t^2}} \qquad (2.2.1)$$

As before, $x_t = X_t - \bar{X}$ and $y_t = Y_t - \bar{Y}$; $t = 1, 2, \ldots, n$. To see why this formula does provide a measure of the strength of the relationship, consider again the two situations shown in Figure 6. In both cases the estimated line would actually pass through the point $(\bar{X}, \bar{Y})$, the point of sample means of the variables X and Y. This is a property of the least squares method and equation 2.1.9 shows this directly:

$$\hat{\alpha} = \bar{Y} - \hat{\beta}\bar{X}$$

so

$$\bar{Y} = \hat{\alpha} + \hat{\beta}\bar{X} \qquad (2.2.2)$$

Equation 2.2.2 states that $\bar{Y}$ and $\bar{X}$ are particular values which do satisfy the equation corresponding to the estimated line, and so the point $(\bar{X}, \bar{Y})$ must lie on that line. In the first case, shown in Figure 6a, nearly all the points for which X_t is greater than the mean $\bar{X}$ are also points for which Y_t is greater than the mean $\bar{Y}$, and nearly all the points for which X_t is less than $\bar{X}$ are also points for which Y_t is less than $\bar{Y}$.

So positive deviations $x_t = X_t - \bar{X}$ tend to go with positive deviations $y_t = Y_t - \bar{Y}$, and negative deviations x_t tend to go with negative deviations y_t. Consequently, almost all the terms in the sum $\Sigma x_t y_t$ are the product of two positive numbers or the product of two negative numbers, and in either case the product is positive. In a case like that shown in Figure 6a, the value of $\Sigma x_t y_t$ will therefore tend to be large and positive. In the second case, shown in Figure 6b, there is still some tendency for the deviations to have the same sign, but this is less marked than in the previous case and the sum $\Sigma x_t y_t$ contains both positive and negative terms. Consequently cancellation tends to occur, and $\Sigma x_t y_t$ would take a smaller value than would be the case with a stronger relationship between Y and X. Finally, note that if there is a relationship whereby the value of Y decreases as the value of X increases, the sum $\Sigma x_t y_t$ would be negative.

The expression

$$s_{XY} = \Sigma x_t y_t / n \qquad (2.2.3)$$

defines the sample covariance between Y and X. According to the argument above, the size of this quantity will reflect the degree of association between Y and X, but unless one had some idea of what would happen in the case of a perfect fit to the observed points, it would be very difficult to decide on what constitutes a 'large' value of either s_{XY} or $\Sigma x_t y_t$. It is for this reason that r is defined as in equation 2.2.1 or, equivalently, as

$$r = \frac{s_{XY}}{\sqrt{s_X^2}\ \sqrt{s_Y^2}} \qquad (2.2.4)$$

where s_X^2 and s_Y^2 are sample variances. Both equations 2.2.1 and 2.2.4 involve scale factors to ensure that r lies in the range -1 to $+1$. The additional terms in the formulae do not change the sign determined by the value of $\Sigma x_t y_t$, because these terms are based on sums of squares, which involve only non-negative quantities, and it is understood that positive values are taken for the square roots. A perfect fit based on a positive relationship would give $r = 1$; a perfect fit based on a negative relationship would give $r = -1$; and a situation in which there was absolutely no connection between Y and X would give $r = 0$. However, these are theoretical extremes. In practice one would obtain a value close to but not equal to 1 for a strong positive relationship, close to -1 for a strong negative relationship, and somewhere in a region around 0 for a weak or nonexistent relationship. It is often convenient to use

r^2 rather than r, for then positive and negative slopes are treated in exactly the same way. The fact that r is bounded is not proved here, but the elements of a proof will be found in Section 3.4.

If the slope estimate has already been obtained by means of equation 2.1.12, it is relatively simple to extend the calculation to obtain the correlation coefficient. All that is needed is an extra column for the values $y_t^2; t = 1, 2, \ldots, n$. In the example used in the previous section, $\Sigma y_t^2 = 154$, so that

$$r = \frac{390}{\sqrt{1000}\sqrt{154}} = 0 \cdot 9938$$

The value obtained for r indicates that the artificial data show a strong positive association between Y and X. However, this is a purely numerical illustration, and in practice one would have to be very careful in trying to draw conclusions from as few as five observations.

If one chooses to work with unadjusted data (Y_t and X_t, rather than y_t and x_t), the correlation coefficient can be computed as

$$r = \frac{\Sigma X_t Y_t - (\Sigma X_t)(\Sigma Y_t)/n}{\sqrt{[\Sigma X_t^2 - (\Sigma X_t)^2/n]}\sqrt{[\Sigma Y_t^2 - (\Sigma Y_t)^2/n]}}$$

The terms in this expression are 'short cut' formulae for evaluating $\Sigma x_t y_t$, Σx_t^2 and Σy_t^2: the first two are given as equations 2.1.10 and 2.1.11, and the formula for Σy_t^2 is obviously similar to that for Σx_t^2.

Finally, if one uses a computer program to obtain the least squares estimates, it is quite likely that one will be given a value described as R^2, rather than a value for r. In the special case of the two variable model, the statistic known as R^2 is indeed the square of the correlation coefficient defined above, so that $R^2 = r^2$. In other cases R^2 has a more general meaning, which we discuss further in Section 3.4.

Strictly speaking, the correlation coefficient defined by equation 2.2.1 is a sample correlation coefficient, since it is a quantity computed from a specific set of observations. In practice this description is seldom used, but it is worth noting that r is conceptually different from a correlation coefficient defined for two random variables V_1 and V_2, which is given by

$$\rho(V_1, V_2) = \frac{\text{cov}(V_1, V_2)}{\sqrt{\text{var}(V_1)}\sqrt{\text{var}(V_2)}}$$

The distinction between r and $\rho(V_1, V_2)$ exactly parallels the distinction between the sample variance and the variance of a random variable, or that between the sample covariance s_{XY} and the covariance of two random variables, defined in equation 1.4.3. For the purpose of distinguishing between correlated and uncorrelated random variables, one might just as well use the covariance as an indicator, since $\rho(V_1, V_2)$ is zero if and only if $\text{cov}(V_1, V_2)$ is zero. If we follow this practice there need be no confusion between the two types of correlation coefficient and, from now on, it is to be understood that correlation coefficients are sample measures, despite the usual practice of dropping the word 'sample' from the description of the measure.

2.3   Least squares estimators: expectation

By application of the least squares method, one can obtain estimates for the parameters of any economic relationship which corresponds to the two variable model

$$Y_t = \alpha + \beta X_t + u_t; t = 1, 2, \ldots, n \tag{2.3.1}$$

Remember that the formulae for $\hat{\alpha}$ and $\hat{\beta}$ are described as estimators: these are rules, which can be applied to a given set of data to produce numbers which are the estimates based on those data. In Chapter 1 it was suggested that an estimator defines a random variable and that an estimate is a particular value taken by the random variable. If this is so, it would be misleading to treat estimates simply as point values: we should be able to say something about the quality of estimation and, in particular, about the probability of our estimates being within a certain distance of the true values. To achieve this, it is necessary to establish the type of probability distribution associated with the least squares estimators and to find parameters of that distribution, such as the expectation and variance. The investigation of the statistical properties of the estimators will also provide some further criteria to justify the choice of least squares as a method of estimation. Although, for many economic applications, the two variable model is unduly restrictive, it is a useful vehicle for the discussion of estimator properties and, in terms of the statistical analysis, the extensions introduced in the next chapter, to allow for further explanatory variables, are extensions of detail rather than of fundamental principle.

According to the model, the value taken by Y_t is determined by the value of X_t and by the value of the disturbance u_t. A different drawing from the probability distribution determining the disturbance would imply a different value for the dependent variable, and this is turn would imply a change in the scatter of observed points. Remember that the explanatory variable is assumed to take certain fixed values and that these would not change: the observed points would be different because of a change in the dependent variable values. If the observed points do change, one would expect a slightly different estimated line, which means that the parameter estimates would be different.

This argument should indicate why it is that the estimators are considered to be random variables. The random behaviour can be traced directly back to the random nature of the disturbance terms, and this provides a clue as to how one can derive estimator properties. If all that is known about the disturbances is that they are random, there is nothing that can be said about the probability distributions of the disturbance process, and the relationship between the estimators and the disturbances is of no help in trying to find the distributions of the estimators. If, however, we make certain plausible assumptions about the disturbance process, of the kind outlined in the previous chapter, the dependence of the estimators on the disturbances can be used. The precise nature of this dependence can be shown more concisely by means of an algebraic statement, and the slope estimator

$$\hat{\beta} = \Sigma x_t y_t / \Sigma x_t^2 \qquad (2.3.2)$$

is used to illustrate this. The expression for the estimator contains the dependent variable values, in the form of deviations from the mean

$$y_t = Y_t - \bar{Y}; t = 1, 2, \ldots, n \qquad (2.3.3)$$

and the model states that

$$Y_t = \alpha + \beta X_t + u_t; t = 1, 2, \ldots, n$$

By combining these three pieces of information, it is possible to show that

$$\hat{\beta} = \beta + \Sigma x_t u_t / \Sigma x_t^2 \qquad (2.3.4)$$

The full derivation of this expression is given as the solution to exercise 2.5.

Equation 2.3.4 shows clearly that the estimator does depend on the random disturbances, but it also conveys more specific information about the behaviour of $\hat{\beta}$. The estimator is made up of a nonrandom part, equal to the true parameter value β, and a random part, based on the disturbances. It is clearly important, in trying to assess how well $\hat{\beta}$ performs as an estimator, to establish the connection between the estimator and the true parameter, and equation 2.3.4 provides this link. As suggested above, the equation will also enable us to deduce the expectation, variance and probability distribution of $\hat{\beta}$. The key to these derivations is the fact that $\hat{\beta}$ is a linear function of the random disturbances. In order to show this more explicitly, the rules of summation are used to tell us that the term $1/\Sigma x_t^2$ can be brought inside the summation over the terms $x_t u_t$; $t = 1, 2, \ldots, n$. This is a valid operation because, for the purposes of the summation, $1/\Sigma x_t^2$ is a constant. Hence

$$\hat{\beta} = \beta + \Sigma [(1/\Sigma x_t^2) x_t u_t]$$
$$= \beta + \Sigma (x_t/\Sigma x_t^2) u_t$$

or

$$\hat{\beta} = \beta + \Sigma w_t u_t \tag{2.3.5}$$

where

$$w_t = x_t/\Sigma x_t^2; t = 1, 2, \ldots, n$$

Now consider the following argument. If one has a set of random variables $V_1, V_2, \ldots, V_n$ and a set of nonrandom weights $a_0, a_1, a_2, \ldots, a_n$, an expression of the type

$$L = a_0 + a_1 V_1 + a_2 V_2 + \ldots + a_n V_n$$

is a linear function of the random variables. By writing equation 2.3.5 term by term

$$\hat{\beta} = \beta + w_1 u_1 + w_2 u_2 + \ldots + w_n u_n$$

it becomes clear that the relationship between $\hat{\beta}$ and $u_1, u_2, \ldots, u_n$ is of the same form as that between L and $V_1, V_2, \ldots, V_n$. So if we have general properties for linear functions of random variables, we automatically obtain results for the estimator $\hat{\beta}$. Moreover, the same technique can be used with any linear estimator — that is, with any estimator that can be expressed as a linear function of a set of underlying random variables. Thus, for example, one can show that $\hat{\alpha}$ is also a linear estimator, since it can be written as

$$\hat{\alpha} = \alpha + \Sigma (1/n - \bar{X} w_t) u_t \tag{2.3.6}$$

However, it is important to note that the arguments used do assume nonrandom weights in the linear function. In equation 2.3.5 the weights w_t; $t = 1, 2, \ldots, n$ depend on the deviations $x_t = X_t - \bar{X}$; $t = 1, 2, \ldots, n$, which in turn depend on the original observations X_t; $t = 1, 2, \ldots, n$. The weights are thus nonrandom, because the explanatory variable observations are assumed to be nonrandom. Similarly, the weights in equation 2.3.6 depend on $n, \bar{X}$ and w_t; $t = 1, 2, \ldots, n$, all of which are again nonrandom quantities.

In order to move on to the derivation of the expectation of $\hat{\beta}$, we need an appropriate result concerning the expectation of a linear function. The relevant property can be stated, somewhat loosely, by saying that the expectation of a linear function is equal to a linear function of expectations. More precisely, if $V_1, V_2, \ldots, V_n$ is a set of random variables and $a_0, a_1, a_2, \ldots, a_n$ are nonrandom weights, then

$$E(a_0 + a_1 V_1 + a_2 V_2 + \ldots + a_n V_n)$$
$$= a_0 + a_1 E(V_1) + a_2 E(V_2) + \ldots + a_n E(V_n) \qquad (2.3.7)$$

The validity of equation 2.3.7 is not proved here, but some special cases are illustrated by the solutions to exercises 1.1 and 2.1. To apply the general result to the special case in which we wish to evaluate $E(\hat{\beta})$, we first apply equation 2.3.5 to give

$$E(\hat{\beta}) = E(\beta + \Sigma w_t u_t)$$

We then apply equation 2.3.7 with the term a_0 replaced by β, the terms $a_1, a_2, \ldots, a_n$ replaced by $w_1, w_2, \ldots, w_n$, and the random variables $V_1, V_2, \ldots, V_n$ replaced by the disturbances $u_1, u_2, \ldots, u_n$. This gives

$$E(\beta + \Sigma w_t u_t) = \beta + \Sigma w_t E(u_t)$$

Finally, we need to assume something about the expectation of each disturbance. It was suggested earlier that the disturbances should be represented as random variables with zero expectation. This can be stated formally as

$$E(u_t) = 0; t = 1, 2, \ldots, n \qquad (2.3.8)$$

Hence the complete derivation of $E(\hat{\beta})$ can be summarized as follows:

$$E(\hat{\beta}) = E(\beta + \Sigma w_t u_t)$$
$$= \beta + \Sigma w_t E(u_t)$$
$$= \beta + \Sigma w_t (0)$$
$$= \beta + \Sigma (0)$$
$$= \beta \qquad (2.3.9)$$

Given that the disturbances have zero expectation, we have been able to show that the expectation of $\hat{\beta}$ is equal to the true parameter value β. For some sets of disturbance values the slope estimate would be greater than the true value, and in other cases it could be less. The expectation of $\hat{\beta}$ is a theoretical average over the values of $\hat{\beta}$ that could arise, and equation 2.3.9 states that there is no systematic tendency to either underestimate or overestimate the true parameter value. When the expected value of an estimator is equal to the true parameter, the estimator is said to be *unbiased*. The least squares slope estimator is therefore an unbiased estimator. By a similar argument one can show that $E(\hat{\alpha}) = \alpha$, so the intercept estimator is also unbiased.

2.4   Least squares estimators: variance

Having found the expectation of $\hat{\beta}$, the next step is to consider the variance, which acts as a measure of the dispersion of the individual estimates around the expected value. Just as the expectation of $\hat{\beta}$ is derived from an assumption about the expectation of the random disturbances, so here it is necessary to make an assumption about the variance of the random disturbances. Initially, it is assumed that each disturbance has the same variance. Formally, this can be stated as

$$\text{var}\,(u_t) = \sigma^2\,; t = 1, 2, \ldots, n \tag{2.4.1}$$

where σ^2 represents a value which is unknown, but which is assumed constant for $t = 1, 2, \ldots, n$. It is also convenient to assume that the disturbance distributions are independent, which means effectively that the value taken by a single disturbance has no influence on the values taken by other disturbances. Given this assumption, it is not necessary to consider the interaction between the behaviour of individual disturbances, for independence implies that no such interaction exists. Although one cannot always maintain these assumptions in practice, it is helpful to start with the simplest case. Methods for dealing with a relaxation of the assumptions are described in Chapter 4.

From Section 1.4 we know that independence implies zero covariance and, for the purpose of deriving the variance of $\hat{\beta}$, it is actually easier to use the implied condition of zero covariance rather than the precise technical condition for independence. Our formal assumption is therefore

$$u_t, u_s \text{ independent}; s \neq t; s, t = 1, 2, \ldots, n \tag{2.4.2}$$

This states that each disturbance u_t is independent of all other disturbances u_s (where $s \neq t$). But in the derivation which follows, the condition actually used is

$$\text{cov}\,(u_t, u_s) = 0; s \neq t; s, t = 1, 2, \ldots, n \tag{2.4.3}$$

After these preliminaries, it is now possible to start on the derivation of var $(\hat{\beta})$. The relationship between $\hat{\beta}$ and the random disturbances was shown in equation 2.3.5 as

$$\hat{\beta} = \beta + \Sigma w_t u_t$$

It follows immediately that

$$\text{var}(\hat{\beta}) = \text{var}(\beta + \Sigma w_t u_t) \tag{2.4.4}$$

We have already exploited a result on the expectation of a linear function: what is needed now is a result on the variance of a linear function. In the general case this would involve covariance terms, but if the covariance between the individual random variables is zero (the random variables are uncorrelated), a simple version of the general result is available. If, as before, $V_1, V_2, \ldots, V_n$ are random variables and $a_0, a_1, a_2, \ldots, a_n$ are nonrandom weights then, provided that the random variables have zero covariance between all distinct pairs,

$$\text{var}(a_0 + a_1 V_1 + a_2 V_2 + \ldots + a_n V_n)$$
$$= a_1^2 \text{var}(V_1) + a_2^2 \text{var}(V_2) + \ldots + a_n^2 \text{var}(V_n) \tag{2.4.5}$$

Notice that the term a_0 involves no variation and contributes nothing to the variance of the linear function: exactly the same result would be obtained for the variance of $(a_1 V_1 + \ldots + a_n V_n)$. Note also that the weights are squared on the right-hand side of equation 2.4.5: this reflects the fact that variance is measured in squared units, so that multiplying a random variable by a constant multiplies the variance of that random variable by the square of the constant.

Applying equation 2.4.5 to the evaluation of var $(\hat{\beta})$, and using the same substitutions as before,

$$\begin{aligned}
\text{var}(\hat{\beta}) &= \text{var}(\beta + \Sigma w_t u_t) \\
&= \Sigma[w_t^2 \text{var}(u_t)]; \quad \text{if cov}(u_t, u_s) = 0; \ s \neq t; \\
&\qquad s, t = 1, 2, \ldots, n \\
&= \Sigma[w_t^2 \sigma^2]; \quad \text{if var}(u_t) = \sigma^2; \ t = 1, 2, \ldots, n \\
&= \sigma^2 \Sigma w_t^2 \tag{2.4.6}
\end{aligned}$$

To complete the derivation it is necessary to evaluate Σw_t^2 explicitly, using the definition $w_t = x_t / \Sigma x_t^2; t = 1, 2, \ldots, n$. Since

$$w_t^2 = x_t^2 / (\Sigma x_t^2)^2$$

it follows that the summation over $w_t^2; t = 1, 2, \ldots, n$ involves the constant $1/(\Sigma x_t^2)^2$, which can be taken outside the summation sign.

Hence

$$\Sigma w_t^2 = \Sigma[x_t^2/(\Sigma x_t^2)^2]$$
$$= (1/(\Sigma x_t^2)^2)\Sigma x_t^2$$
$$= \Sigma x_t^2/(\Sigma x_t^2)^2$$
$$= 1/\Sigma x_t^2$$

So instead of writing var $(\hat{\beta})$ as in equation 2.4.6, we may now write

$$\text{var}(\hat{\beta}) = \sigma^2/\Sigma x_t^2 \qquad (2.4.7)$$

An alternative approach to the derivation of this formula is given as the solution to exercise 2.6.

What equation 2.4.7 suggests is that the variance of $\hat{\beta}$ depends directly on the disturbance variance σ^2 and inversely on Σx_t^2, the sum of squares of the explanatory variable observations, expressed in terms of deviations from the sample mean. The direct dependence of var $(\hat{\beta})$ on σ^2 is precisely what one would expect. The estimate of the slope is determined in part by a particular choice of disturbance values, and changing the disturbances would alter the value of $\hat{\beta}$. If the disturbances do show considerable variation, the effect on $\hat{\beta}$ of choosing a different set of disturbances is likely to be greater than would be the case if the disturbances show relatively little variation. The other term in equation 2.4.7 is Σx_t^2. It is obviously possible to compute a sample variance for the observations on X, as a purely descriptive device, and this would give

$$s_X^2 = \Sigma(X_t - \bar{X})^2/n = \Sigma x_t^2/n$$

Division by n is simply a means of scaling, and the essential information about the variation in the values of X is contained in the expression Σx_t^2. Equation 2.4.7 states that the variance of $\hat{\beta}$ depends inversely on Σx_t^2, so that a relatively wide spread of values of the explanatory variable produces a relatively low variance of $\hat{\beta}$.

The logic of the inverse relationship between the estimator variance and the spread of the X values can be illustrated by considering an extremely simple case, in which there are just two observations on X. In Figure 7a the observations correspond to widely separated points on the X axis, whereas in Figure 7b, the observed values of X are close together. In each case two lines are drawn which are intended to show the effect of changes in the disturbances. These happen to be in opposite

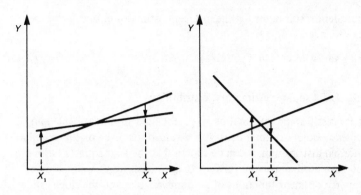

Figure 7

directions, so that the observed point corresponding to X_1 is moved
upwards, whereas the observed point corresponding to X_2 is moved
down. Obviously the diagrams represent an extreme case, but they do
illustrate the fact that a given degree of variation in the disturbances
will lead to much less variation in the slope estimator in the case in
which there is a relatively wide spread of X values.

Given that the estimator variance acts as an indicator of the extent
to which individual estimates are dispersed around the expected value,
it is clearly desirable that an unbiased estimator should have as small a
variance as possible. By using the assumptions concerning the common
variance and independence of the disturbance distributions, it can be
shown that the variance of the least squares slope estimator is at least
as small as that of any other linear unbiased estimator of the slope
parameter. The significance of linearity, in this context, is that $\hat{\beta}$ can
be expressed as a linear function of the disturbances (see equation
2.3.5). By changing the definition of the weights it would be possible
to generate other linear unbiased estimators for the slope parameter,
but the result quoted here enables us to say something about least
squares as a method of estimation, without actually having to specify
a list of alternatives. If any estimator has a variance which is always less
than that of some other estimator, the first estimator is said to be the
more *efficient*. An estimator which is at least as efficient as any other
estimator of a given type is said to be the *best* estimator of that type.
So our result can be stated by saying that the least squares slope estimator is best linear unbiased. An alternative and perhaps more explicit
statement is that $\hat{\beta}$ is a minimum variance linear unbiased estimator. An

equivalent result holds for the intercept estimator $\hat{\alpha}$, but in this case the variance is

$$\text{var}\,(\hat{\alpha}) = \sigma^2(1/n + \overline{X}^2/\Sigma x_t^2) \tag{2.4.8}$$

2.5   Least squares estimators: distribution

There is still some information to be obtained about the behaviour of the least squares estimators. If it is assumed that each disturbance has a normal distribution, it can be shown that the least squares estimators also have normal distributions. Once again, this result is based on a property of linear functions of random variables and the slope estimator is used to illustrate the argument. If the random variables $V_1, V_2, \ldots, V_n$ have independent normal distributions, the linear function $a_0 + a_1 V_1 + \ldots + a_n V_n$ has a normal distribution. To apply this result to the distribution of $\hat{\beta}$, recall that $\hat{\beta}$ can be written as a linear function of the random disturbances, as shown in equation 2.3.5. So, if each disturbance has an independent normal distribution, it follows that $\hat{\beta}$ must be normal. Since expressions for the expectation and variance of $\hat{\beta}$ have already been established, a complete statement can now be made, embracing the expectation, variance and normality of $\hat{\beta}$. A concise form of this statement is

$$\hat{\beta} \sim N(\beta,\ \sigma^2/\Sigma x_t^2) \tag{2.5.1}$$

where the symbol $\sim$ means 'is distributed as', $N(\ )$ signifies normality, β is the expectation of $\hat{\beta}$ (or the mean of the probability distribution of $\hat{\beta}$) and $\sigma^2/\Sigma x_t^2$ is the variance of $\hat{\beta}$.

By an argument similar to that used above, it can also be shown that the intercept estimator, $\hat{\alpha}$, has a normal distribution. We should perhaps mention in passing that the normal distributions associated

---

Technical note 3

Independence is not a necessary condition for the normality of a linear function. If the random variables $V_1, V_2, \ldots, V_n$ have a joint distribution which is multivariate normal, the linear function $a_0 + a_1 V_1 + \ldots + a_n V_n$ has a univariate normal distribution, regardless of whether or not $V_1, V_2, \ldots, V_n$ are independent. If, however, $V_1, V_2, \ldots, V_n$ are independent, then we need only assume univariate normality for each random variable, since independence plus univariate normality implies multivariate normality.

with $\hat{\alpha}$ and $\hat{\beta}$ are not independent and, in general, cov $(\hat{\alpha}, \hat{\beta})$ is not zero. This need not concern us too much at this stage, although we shall have something to say about the covariance between individual estimators in the context of a model with several explanatory variables.

In principle, we have now satisfied the objectives set at the beginning of Section 2.3. If the mean and variance of a normal distribution are known, it is possible to use normal distribution tables to make probability statements about the random variable in question. In the next section, we shall show how this idea is applied to the slope estimator $\hat{\beta}$. The other objective was to provide some further criteria to justify the choice of least squares as a method of estimation and, to satisfy this objective, it has been argued that $\hat{\alpha}$ and $\hat{\beta}$ are best linear unbiased estimators. It is very important to understand that there are many ways of estimating an unknown parameter, but that there are certain criteria that an estimator should satisfy if it is to be acceptable. On the basis of the criteria that we have discussed, the least squares estimators do have desirable properties, but this conclusion depends crucially on the specification of the model, which includes the form of the relationship and the additional assumptions that are made.

The assumptions made play such an important role that it is worth restating the specification of the model in full. The dependent variable is assumed to behave as though the observed values are generated by the relationship

$$Y_t = \alpha + \beta X_t + u_t; t = 1, 2, \ldots, n$$

where each X_t is considered to be nonrandom and where the disturbance values are assumed to be adequately represented as drawings from a set of n independent normal distributions, each having a mean equal to zero and a variance equal to σ^2. The complete model can thus be stated as a list of six assumptions:

(A) $Y_t = \alpha + \beta X_t + u_t; t = 1, 2, \ldots, n.$
(B) X_t is nonrandom; $t = 1, 2, \ldots, n.$
(C) $E(u_t) = 0; t = 1, 2, \ldots, n.$
(D) var $(u_t) = \sigma^2; t = 1, 2, \ldots, n.$
(E) The disturbance distributions are independent.
(F) The disturbance distributions are normal.

Given this list of assumptions, it is possible to obtain the following properties for the least squares slope estimator:

1 $E(\hat{\beta}) = \beta$, indicating unbiasedness.

2 var $(\hat{\beta}) = \sigma^2/\Sigma x_t^2$.

3 $\hat{\beta}$ is a best linear unbiased estimator of β.

4 $\hat{\beta}$ has a normal distribution.

A similar set of properties can be listed for the intercept estimator, $\hat{\alpha}$, but now

$$E(\hat{\alpha}) = \alpha \qquad (2.5.2)$$

and

$$\text{var} (\hat{\alpha}) = \sigma^2(1/n + \bar{X}^2/\Sigma x_t^2) \qquad (2.5.3)$$

An alternative form for equation 2.5.3 is

$$\text{var} (\hat{\alpha}) = \sigma^2 \Sigma X_t^2/n\Sigma x_t^2 \qquad (2.5.4)$$

There is one final problem to consider. There may eventually be enough evidence, from observation of the real economic system, to contradict one or more of the assumptions listed above. If this happens, it would be useful to know how far the assumptions could be weakened without destroying the individual properties of the least squares estimators. It is difficult to answer this question fully at this stage, but there is one exercise that we can usefully perform. In proving the unbiasedness of the least squares slope estimator, we made use of assumptions A, B and C, but we did not use D, E and F. Since the derivations for the intercept estimator are parallel to those for the slope estimator, it follows that $\hat{\alpha}$ and $\hat{\beta}$ would still be unbiased without D, E and F. By a similar argument, the variance formulae for $\hat{\alpha}$ and $\hat{\beta}$ would still be correct without C and F and $\hat{\alpha}$ and $\hat{\beta}$ would still be normal without C and D. Although we cannot conclude from this exercise that properties which are used are strictly necessary, we can be quite sure that removing an assumption which is not used will not lead to a breakdown of the property in question.

Given an appropriate set of assumptions, the various properties specified above hold for any set of observations, irrespective of how many observations there are. In Section 2.10 we obtain a further set of properties which hold only approximately, and then only when the number of observations is large. In later chapters, when the analysis has to be conducted under rather weaker assumptions, it will be necessary to use some of these alternative properties which an estimator may have.

2.6 Confidence intervals: normal distribution

If a random variable has a normal distribution, with a specified mean and variance, it is possible to find the probability that the variable will take a value within any chosen interval. This idea has already been mentioned briefly, but we shall now consider in detail how the probability statement is used. Our objective is to be able to make probability statements concerning the slope estimator $\hat{\beta}$, but initially we shall consider the general case of a random variable V which has a normal distribution with mean $E(V)$ and variance var (V). For any such variable there exists a standardized form, obtained by subtracting the mean and then dividing by the standard deviation. Using Z to denote this form, we have

$$Z = [V - E(V)] \, / \, \sqrt{\text{var}(V)}$$

or

$$Z = [V - E(V)] \, / \, \text{sd}(V) \tag{2.6.1}$$

The random variable Z has what is known as a *standard normal distribution*, with a mean equal to 0 and a variance equal to 1. For any event defined in terms of the normal variable V, there is an exactly equivalent event defined in terms of the standard normal variable Z. Two events are said to be equivalent if the occurrence of one event implies the occurrence of the other and vice versa. Obviously, the probabilities associated with the two events must then be equal.

To illustrate this point, consider the event that V lies within c standard deviations of the mean, where c represents any positive number. The conditions that V must satisfy, for this event to occur, are

$$V > E(V) - c \, \text{sd}(V)$$

and

$$V < E(V) + c \, \text{sd}(V)$$

These conditions can be written more concisely as

$$E(V) - c \, \text{sd}(V) < V < E(V) + c \, \text{sd}(V) \tag{2.6.2}$$

By subtracting the mean and then dividing by the standard deviation, on both sides of each inequality, we can express conditions 2.6.2 in an alternative form which makes clear the implied conditions on Z. The conditions become

$$-c \, \text{sd}(V) < V - E(V) < +c \, \text{sd}(V)$$

or

$$-c < [V - E(V)] / \text{sd}(V) < +c$$

or

$$-c < Z < +c \tag{2.6.3}$$

It is also possible to reverse the argument to show that the conditions 2.6.3 imply the conditions 2.6.2. Hence the two sets of conditions are identical, the implied events are identical and, using Pr ( ) to denote the probability of an event, we have

$$\Pr(E(V) - c\,\text{sd}(V) < V < E(V) + c\,\text{sd}(V))$$
$$= \Pr(-c < Z < +c) \tag{2.6.4}$$

Now suppose that we wish to construct an interval, consisting of a certain number of standard deviations, on either side of the mean, within which there is some specified probability of finding a value of the random variable V. Such an interval can be written as

$$E(V) - c\,\text{sd}(V) \ \text{ to } \ E(V) + c\,\text{sd}(V)$$

or, more concisely, as

$$E(V) \pm c\,\text{sd}(V) \tag{2.6.5}$$

If, for example, the probability level is set to 0·95, then we require a *critical value, c,* such that

$$\Pr(E(V) - c\,\text{sd}(V) < V < E(V) + c\,\text{sd}(V)) = 0.95$$

The essence of the argument above is that the required critical value is also that for which

$$\Pr(-c < Z < +c) = 0.95$$

Table A (p. 267) gives critical values for a range of different probabilities of the form $\Pr(-c < Z < +c)$. If the probability level is 0·95, the table shows that c must take the value $c = 1.96$. Hence

$$\Pr(-1.96 < Z < +1.96) = 0.95$$

and

$$\Pr(E(V) - 1.96\,\text{sd}(V) < V < E(V) + 1.96\,\text{sd}(V)) = 0.95$$

So when the probability of finding V in the interval 2.6.5 is to be 0·95, the interval must be

$$E(V) \pm 1.96\,\text{sd}(V)$$

If the probability level is increased to 0·99 one would expect the interval to be wider, and this is indeed the case. From Table A the critical value for which $\Pr(-c < Z < +c) = 0.99$ is found to be $c = 2.58$, and so the interval corresponding to a probability level of 0·99 is

$$E(V) \pm 2.58 \text{ sd } (V)$$

Returning now to the case of the least squares slope estimator, recall that $E(\hat{\beta}) = \beta$ and var $(\hat{\beta}) = \sigma^2/\Sigma x_t^2$. The standard deviation of $\hat{\beta}$ would be the square root of the variance. In fact, the standard deviation of the probability distribution associated with an estimator is usually called the *standard error* and, if the notation se ( ) is used to represent this, the standard error of the slope estimator would be

$$\text{se }(\hat{\beta}) = \sigma/\sqrt{\Sigma x_t^2} \tag{2.6.6}$$

The value of Σx_t^2 can be computed from the data, but equation 2.6.6 cannot be used unless the value of σ is known. It is convenient to continue the analysis, just for the moment, on the assumption that the correct value can be assigned to σ, but in practice there is no reason why one should know the variance or the standard deviation of the disturbance distributions.

To make probability statements concerning the slope estimator, one can apply any of the general results obtained earlier to the specific case of the distribution of $\hat{\beta}$. So, for example, there is a probability of 0·95 attached to the event that a single value taken by the slope estimator will fall within 1·96 standard errors of the mean. If this result is expressed by writing down an interval of the type shown in 2.6.5, with $E(\hat{\beta})$ replaced by the true parameter β, we can say that there is a probability of 0·95 attached to the event that $\hat{\beta}$ falls in the interval

$$\beta \pm 1.96 \, \sigma/\sqrt{\Sigma x_t^2}$$

The interval can also be written as

$$\beta \pm 1.96 \text{ se } (\hat{\beta}) \tag{2.6.7}$$

It is very important to understand exactly what is being said here. We know very well that, given a set of data, one would calculate a single estimate of the slope, so that $\hat{\beta}$ would take one particular value. That value either falls in the interval defined by 2.6.7 or it does not. The probability statement merely says something about the chances. If it is helpful to think of the estimation being repeated, for many different sets of disturbances and hence for many different sets of observations on the dependent variable, then one can think of 95 per cent of all the slope estimates which could arise as falling within the interval 2.6.7. But this is an aid to understanding rather than an accurate description of what the probability statement means. It is not necessary, either in theory or in practice, to be able to replicate the estimation.

The interval defined in 2.6.7 is centred on the fixed value β. The random variable $\hat{\beta}$ falls within the interval with a probability of 0·95. This implies that there is a probability of 0·95 attached to the event that $\hat{\beta}$ is no further than 1·96 standard errors from the true value. So if one were to construct an interval centred on the random variable $\hat{\beta}$

$$\hat{\beta} \pm 1.96 \, se\,(\hat{\beta}) \tag{2.6.8}$$

it must follow that this would include the fixed true value with a probability of 0·95. It is this form of interval that is described as a 95 per cent *confidence interval* for the true value β. In this case, one can think of repeated experiments in which the entire interval is moved as the value of $\hat{\beta}$ is changed, with 95 per cent of all such intervals including the fixed but unknown value β. Again, this is an aid to understanding. What actually happens is that one interval is obtained, which either does or does not include β. The probability is known, but the outcome is not.

The confidence interval is actually more useful than 2.6.7, because if σ is known it is possible to replace the remaining terms by numerical values computed from the data. In contrast, 2.6.7 involves the unknown true parameter β and so does not form the basis of an interval to which numerical values can be assigned.

The probability associated with the confidence interval can always be increased, but only at the cost of increasing the critical value, which in the interval above is the number 1·96. If the critical value is increased, the interval becomes wider and so there is a trade off between the probability level and the width of the interval. A 95 per cent confidence interval is simply a convenient compromise between the level of probability and the width of the interval.

2.7   Confidence intervals: *t* distribution

The discussion in the previous section was based on the assumption that the disturbance variance σ^2 is known. This is not likely to be the case in practice. The obvious strategy is to try to form an estimate of σ^2 and then to ask whether this has any effect on the confidence interval. If a parameter of a probability distribution is unknown, it is natural to think in terms of using a corresponding sample quantity as an estimator, but we also know that there could be several possible estimators for any parameter and that the chosen estimator should satisfy certain criteria. In the case of a parameter of the disturbance process, there is an additional difficulty, because the true disturbances $u_t; t = 1, 2, \ldots, n$ cannot be observed. All that one has is the set of residuals, defined as

$$e_t = Y_t - \hat{\alpha} - \hat{\beta}X_t; t = 1, 2, \ldots, n \qquad (2.7.1)$$

A sample variance based on these quantities would be

$$\Sigma(e_t - \bar{e})^2/n \qquad (2.7.2)$$

but this expression has to be modified in two ways. It so happens that the sum of residuals from the two variable model is always zero: this follows directly from the first of the normal equations 2.1.7 and, if the sum of residuals is zero, the sample mean is always zero. The term $\bar{e}$ in 2.7.2 is thus redundant. The second modification is necessary because 2.7.2 does not define an unbiased estimator of σ^2. To achieve the property of unbiasedness the divisor should be $n - 2$ rather than n, and so the appropriate estimator is

$$\hat{\sigma}^2 = \Sigma e_t^2/(n - 2) \qquad (2.7.3)$$

To use this formula, it is not actually necessary to compute each residual e_t prior to the formation of Σe_t^2. A convenient short cut method is provided by the relationship

$$\Sigma e_t^2 = \Sigma y_t^2 - \beta\Sigma x_t y_t \qquad (2.7.4)$$

An alternative version, for use with data that are not adjusted for sample means, is

$$\Sigma e_t^2 = \Sigma Y_t^2 - \hat{\alpha}\Sigma Y_t - \hat{\beta}\Sigma X_t Y_t \qquad (2.7.5)$$

Note that most of the sums of squares and products needed will already be available from the calculation of values for $\hat{\alpha}$ and $\hat{\beta}$.

In equation 2.7.3 the quantity $n - 2$ is known as the *degrees of freedom*. Although this is a purely mathematical concept, it is possible to give an intuitive interpretation, or at least a rule of thumb, to be used in deciding what the degrees of freedom should be. If one were to specify a two variable model based on just two data points, it would be quite possible to have two nonzero disturbances, so that the true line need not go through either of the observed points. But if there are just two observations and the line has to be estimated, it is possible to choose a line passing through both points, giving residuals which are equal to zero and a sum of squared residuals Σe_t^2 equal to zero. As this is obviously the minimum possible value of the sum of squares, the estimates obtained are least squares estimates. In this case, the two degrees of freedom provided by the observations are used in estimating the parameters α and β, and the parameter estimates have to be obtained before the residuals can be found. Extending this idea to more than two observations, it would be argued that, of the n degrees of freedom provided by the data, two are used in the estimation of α and β, leaving $n - 2$ degrees of freedom to be associated with the sum of squared residuals.

At this point we must consider a question of terminology, which relates to the standard error. In any practical situation, the standard error of $\hat{\beta}$ would have to be evaluated from an estimate of the disturbance variance and, from now on, the term standard error will be taken to imply that such an estimate is made. Indeed, some authors only use standard error in the context of an estimate of the standard deviation of the distribution of an estimator. So se $(\hat{\beta})$ is now redefined as

$$se \, (\hat{\beta}) = \hat{\sigma}/\sqrt{\Sigma x_t^2} \tag{2.7.6}$$

and a confidence interval, based on this standard error, would be

$$\hat{\beta} \pm c\hat{\sigma}/\sqrt{\Sigma x_t^2} \tag{2.7.7}$$

where c is some appropriate critical value. The interval can still be written as

$$\hat{\beta} \pm c \, se \, (\hat{\beta})$$

but it must be remembered that se $(\hat{\beta})$ is now based on an estimate of the disturbance variance and not on the true value.

In the previous formulation of the confidence interval, given in 2.6.8, the centre point of the interval was a random variable but the width of the interval was fixed. Since se $(\hat{\beta})$ is now derived from an estimator of the disturbance variance, se $(\hat{\beta})$ has become a random variable, and this means that the width of the interval is now random. One would expect this to have some effect on the probability of finding that the interval does contain the true value, and this is indeed the case. If the critical value c is set to 1·96, the interval defined by 2.7.7, making use of an estimated disturbance variance, is now associated with a probability of rather less than 0·95 and, to maintain the level of probability, it is necessary to have a wider interval. This is achieved by replacing 1·96 by an alternative critical value, taken from the *t distribution* rather than the normal distribution. The critical values from the t distribution depend on the number of observations, or to be precise on the number of degrees of freedom, and in this respect the t distribution is different from the normal distribution. But, unless the number of observations is small, a 95 per cent confidence interval based on the t distribution is not very different from that which one would obtain from the normal distribution, ignoring the fact that the disturbance variance is actually an estimate. To give some idea of the differences involved, the following are 95 per cent confidence intervals, based on the t distribution, for various numbers of observations:

$$n = 7, n - 2 = 5: \quad \hat{\beta} \pm 2 \cdot 57 \text{ se } (\hat{\beta})$$
$$n = 12, n - 2 = 10: \quad \hat{\beta} \pm 2 \cdot 23 \text{ se } (\hat{\beta})$$
$$n = 17, n - 2 = 15: \quad \hat{\beta} \pm 2 \cdot 13 \text{ se } (\hat{\beta})$$
$$n = 32, n - 2 = 30: \quad \hat{\beta} \pm 2 \cdot 04 \text{ se } (\hat{\beta})$$
$$n = 62, n - 2 = 60: \quad \hat{\beta} \pm 2 \cdot 00 \text{ se } (\hat{\beta})$$

The relationship between the t distribution and the normal distribution is actually quite straightforward. Since $\hat{\beta}$ has a normal distribution, with mean β and variance $\sigma^2/\Sigma x_t^2$, the random variable

$$Z = (\hat{\beta} - \beta)/(\sigma/\sqrt{\Sigma x_t^2}) \qquad (2.7.8)$$

has a standard normal distribution. But if σ^2 is replaced by the estimator $\hat{\sigma}^2$, a random variable otherwise equivalent to equation 2.7.8 does not have a standard normal distribution. Instead it has a t distribution with $n - 2$ degrees of freedom, and using t to denote such a variable we have

$$t = (\hat{\beta} - \beta)/(\hat{\sigma}/\sqrt{\Sigma x_t^2})$$

or

$$t = (\hat{\beta} - \beta)/\text{se } (\hat{\beta}) \qquad (2.7.9)$$

Note that se $(\hat{\beta})$ is the new version of the standard error as defined by equation 2.7.6, rather than the original version defined by equation 2.6.6. Whereas previously the critical value for the confidence interval was that value c for which

$$\Pr (-c < Z < +c) = 0 \cdot 95$$

the new critical value is a value c for which

$$\Pr (-c < t < +c) = 0 \cdot 95$$

In all other respects the logic of the confidence interval is unchanged.

So, instead of inserting the value 1·96 in the formula

$$\hat{\beta} \pm c \, \text{se} \, (\hat{\beta})$$

we now insert the appropriate critical value for the t distribution. Table B (p. 269) gives critical values for selected probabilities of the form $\Pr(-c < t < +c)$. Since the critical values now depend on the degrees of freedom (df), the number of distinct probabilities tabulated is limited, but it is possible to check the various 95 per cent values quoted above, remembering that, in this application of the t distribution, df $= n - 2$.

As an alternative to the explicit use of a t distribution table one could have a fixed critical value of 2, recognizing that this would give a rather lower confidence level when the number of observations is small. For $n = 7$ the confidence level would be 90 per cent, for $n = 22$ approximately 94 per cent and, for larger numbers of observations, a critical value of 2 would provide a close approximation to a 95 per cent interval.

To illustrate the ideas discussed above, we have used the data of exercise 1.4 to construct a 95 per cent confidence interval for the parameter β in the model

$$C_t = \alpha + \beta D_t + u_t; t = 1, 2, \ldots, n$$

where C is real consumers' expenditure and D is real personal disposable income. The first step is to estimate α and β, using one of the calculation schemes described in Section 2.1. The working for this stage is given as the solution to exercise 2.2a. The result is the estimated equation

$$\hat{C}_t = 18 \cdot 118 + 0 \cdot 6365 \, D_t; t = 1, 2, \ldots, n$$

It is then necessary to calculate a value for se $(\hat{\beta})$, using equations 2.7.3, 2.7.4 and 2.7.6. The working for this stage is given as the solution to exercise 2.2b, and the result is se $(\hat{\beta}) = 0 \cdot 0246$. The data used consist of 11 annual observations, so $n = 11$ and $n - 2 = 9$. The formula for an exact 95 per cent confidence interval is thus

$$\hat{\beta} \pm 2 \cdot 26 \, \text{se} \, (\hat{\beta})$$

where 2·26 is the critical value for which $\Pr(-c < t < +c) = 0 \cdot 95$, when there are 9 degrees of freedom. The confidence interval obtained is $0 \cdot 636 \pm 2 \cdot 26(0 \cdot 0246)$, or 0·580 to 0·692. If one could be sure that the model is valid and that all the assumptions are satisfied, one would be 95 per cent confident that this interval does contain the true value of the marginal propensity to consume implied by this form of model.

2.8 Hypothesis testing

The two variable model states that Y is linked to X by means of the relationship

$$Y_t = \alpha + \beta X_t + u_t; t = 1, 2, \ldots, n \qquad (2.8.1)$$

If, however, the true value of β is zero, the model reduces to

$$Y_t = \alpha + u_t; t = 1, 2, \ldots, n \qquad (2.8.2)$$

In this case Y varies randomly around a fixed value α, but has no connection with X. The decision as to whether or not β is zero is therefore of some importance. Unfortunately, one cannot conclude that β is different from zero simply by finding a nonzero value for the slope estimator. The slope estimator is a random variable and, even in the case in which the true value β is zero, it is highly unlikely that estimation based on equation 2.8.1 would produce a slope estimate exactly equal to zero. It is therefore necessary to devise a test procedure which attempts to distinguish between a nonzero value of $\hat{\beta}$ that arises purely by chance and a nonzero value that arises because the true parameter is also nonzero.

All we have to go on, in constructing a test, is a single value of the estimator $\hat{\beta}$ and the information that there is a probability of approximately 0·95 attached to the event that the true parameter is contained in the interval

$$\hat{\beta} \pm 2 \operatorname{se}(\hat{\beta}) \qquad (2.8.3)$$

Alternatively, we may say that there is a probability of approximately 0·95 attached to the event that the estimator falls in an interval centred on the fixed parameter. In this case the interval would be

$$\beta \pm 2 \operatorname{se}(\hat{\beta}) \qquad (2.8.4)$$

As it stands, interval 2.8.4 cannot be used because the value of β is unknown. But there is a value which could possibly be the true value and which is of particular interest, namely $\beta = 0$, and one can say something about the probabilities that would hold if this were actually the true value. This is the key to the test procedure. Suppose that we do obtain a value of $\hat{\beta}$ which is more than two standard errors away from zero. This could happen because β is zero and we have observed an unlikely event. On the other hand, although we do have an interest in the possibility that β is zero, we have no particular reason to believe that this is the true value. Thus, instead of concluding that we have observed an unlikely event, we could conclude that what has been observed is not necessarily unlikely, because β is not in fact zero. This rather complicated logic is the basis of the test procedure and it can be hardened into a definite decision rule. This states that if $\hat{\beta}$ lies outside the interval

$$0 \pm 2 \operatorname{se}(\hat{\beta})$$

the conclusion drawn is that β is not zero. If $\hat{\beta}$ lies inside the interval, we are not able to conclude that β is different from zero.

The rule suggested above is an example of a *statistical test*, and there exists a formal framework for statistical testing which can be used in a number of different contexts. It is generally convenient to express the procedure in terms of the calculation of a *test statistic*, which is then compared with an appropriate critical value to enable a decision to be made. In order to compute the test statistic, it is necessary to have a working value of the parameter of interest. Then, after the calculation has been performed, the decision is made as to whether the working value is reasonable, in the light of the observable evidence. The working value is called the *null hypothesis* and, in the example above, the null hypothesis is $\beta = 0$. It may well be that the investigator fully expects the null hypothesis to be rejected, but the test calculation can only be performed on the basis of some such working value. If the null hypothesis is rejected, the conclusion drawn is that β is not zero, and this represents the *alternative hypothesis* for the test. The null hypothesis is often denoted as H_0 and the alternative as H_a (or H_1). Hence the conditions of the test described above can be written as

$$H_0: \beta = 0 \quad \text{and} \quad H_a: \beta \neq 0$$

The decision rule used in testing the null hypothesis that $\beta = 0$ is based on the knowledge that there is a probability of approximately 0·95 attached to the event that $\hat{\beta}$ lies inside the interval

$$\beta \pm 2 \operatorname{se}(\hat{\beta})$$

Alternatively, we may say that there is a probability of approximately 0·05 attached to the event that $\hat{\beta}$ falls outside the same interval. Under the conditions of the null hypothesis, the interval becomes

$$0 \pm 2 \operatorname{se}(\hat{\beta}) \tag{2.8.5}$$

The event defined by $\hat{\beta}$ falling outside the interval 2.8.5 can only occur if the ratio $\hat{\beta}/\text{se}\,(\hat{\beta})$ falls outside the interval -2 to $+2$: this ratio defines the test statistic

$$t = \hat{\beta}/\text{se}\,(\hat{\beta}) \qquad\qquad (2.8.6)$$

Since there is only a small probability of finding a value of the test statistic which is less than -2 or greater than $+2$, if β is zero, one would take such a value as evidence that β is not zero and the null hypothesis would be rejected. If the value of the test statistic lies between -2 and $+2$, the null hypothesis would not be rejected. The critical value here is 2, but if we wished the probabilities under the null hypothesis to be exact it would be necessary to use the appropriate critical value taken from the t distribution.

It is useful to restate the argument leading to the use of statistic 2.8.6 in a slightly different way. Recall, from equation 2.7.9, that the random variable

$$t = (\hat{\beta} - \beta)/\text{se}\,(\hat{\beta}) \qquad\qquad (2.8.7)$$

has a t distribution with $n - 2$ degrees of freedom. Under the null hypothesis $\beta = 0$, this reduces to

$$t = (\hat{\beta} - 0)/\text{se}\,(\hat{\beta}) = \hat{\beta}/\text{se}\,(\hat{\beta})$$

which is identical to equation 2.8.6. It may seem confusing to use the same notation for the variables defined in equations 2.8.6 and 2.8.7, but it is usually clear what is intended. The test statistic corresponds to a random variable that would have a t distribution, if it were true that $\beta = 0$. It also represents a quantity to which a numerical value can be assigned, because unlike equation 2.8.7, it does not involve the unknown parameter β. So equation 2.8.7 defines a random variable which always has a t distribution (so long as our underlying assumptions are satisfied), whereas equation 2.8.6 defines a random variable which has a t distribution if $\beta = 0$ and also provides a formula which enables us to compute the value of one particular realization.

Given that we have already discussed the use of the t distribution for constructing an exact 95 per cent confidence interval, it is quite easy to find the correct critical value for a test in which the probability levels are those suggested in the discussion above. The decision rule is based on the fact that, if the null hypothesis is true, there is only a small probability of finding a value of the test statistic outside a certain interval. This probability is known as the significance level and, so far, it has been assumed that the significance level is set at 0·05. If this is so, the required interval is $-c$ to $+c$, where c is exactly the same critical value as that used for a 95 per cent confidence interval. One could describe this as the critical value for a 5 per cent significance level, but this is only true when the alternative hypothesis is of the form H_a: $\beta \neq 0$ — that is, for a 'two tailed' test. For this reason, we shall adopt the practice of identifying critical values by the associated 'upper tail' probability. An upper tail probability for the t distribution is written as $\Pr(t > +c)$, where t represents any variable having a t distribution. Since the t distribution is symmetric about zero, $\Pr(t > +c)$ is exactly half the probability of finding a value of t outside the interval $-c$ to $+c$ which, in turn, is one minus the probability of finding a value of t inside the interval. Hence, in a two tailed test, with a significance level of 0·05, the critical value c is such that $\Pr(t > +c) = 0\cdot025$. In Table B (p. 269) critical values are identified both by the value of $\Pr(-c < t < +c)$ and by the value of $\Pr(t > +c)$; from now on only the latter description will be used. A rather more explicit notation for the critical value would identify the distribution, the upper tail probability and the number of degrees of freedom: hence we could write $t_{n-2}^{0\cdot025}$ for the critical value from a t distribution with $n-2$ degrees of freedom and an upper tail probability of 0·025.

It is obviously possible to draw the wrong conclusion from a statistical test, and there are two ways in which this can occur. *Type I error* is the rejection of a null hypothesis which is actually true, and *type II error* is the failure to reject a null hypothesis which is false. Type I error can only occur if the null hypothesis is true which, in the test described here, would mean that $\beta = 0$. Since the decision rule was originally chosen on the basis of the probabilities that would apply if β were equal to zero, it is easy to identify the probability of type I error as the probability of finding a value outside the interval $-c$ to $+c$ when β is actually zero. In the discussion above, this probability was described as the significance level, and the level was set at 0·05. Hence the probability of type I error is equal to the chosen significance level.

If type II error occurs it is because β is not zero, and the probability of type II error depends on what the true value actually is. If the true value is close to zero, the probability of type II error will be rather high, whereas if β is well away from zero, the probability of type II error will be low. However, the precise meaning of 'close to zero' depends on the theoretical variance of $\hat{\beta}$. If, for example, the number of observations is small, or the explanatory variable exhibits very little variation in the data period, it may be difficult to show that β is different from zero, even for a true value which is not that close to zero. In practice this is likely to be more of a problem in the context of a model involving several explanatory variables. However, it is worth bearing in mind that, if there is any reason to suspect the adequacy of the data, one would probably wish to experiment further, preferably on a more informative data set, before interpreting a failure to reject the null hypothesis as evidence that β really is zero, or so close to zero that no conceivable change in the explanatory variable could ever have any significant impact on the dependent variable.

Now consider an example of the use of the t test. The data are taken from exercise 1.4 and the objective is to test H_0: $\beta = 0$ against H_a: $\beta \neq 0$, in the context of the consumption function model

$$C_t = \alpha + \beta D_t + u_t; t = 1, 2, \ldots, n$$

Despite the rather complex logic of the test, the calculation is relatively straightforward. At the end of the previous section we obtained the values $\hat{\beta} = 0 \cdot 6365$ and se $(\hat{\beta}) = 0 \cdot 0246$. Hence, from equation 2.8.6, we have

$$t = \hat{\beta}/\text{se}\ (\hat{\beta}) = 0 \cdot 6365/0 \cdot 0246 = 25 \cdot 87$$

As no significance level has been specified, we shall assume a level of $0 \cdot 05$ and, since $n = 11$, there are 9 degrees of freedom. Using Table B, the exact critical value $t_9^{0 \cdot 025}$ is found to be $2 \cdot 26$. The calculated value of the test statistic lies well outside the interval $-2 \cdot 26$ to $+2 \cdot 26$, so the null hypothesis $\beta = 0$ is convincingly rejected. In this case, the slope estimate is said to be significantly different from zero. It would actually have been most surprising if we had reached any other conclusion in the context of this particular model.

Although the most common use of the t test is in connection with the null hypothesis $\beta = 0$, exactly the same logic can be applied to a test of any other null hypothesis concerning the value of β. Suppose that, in the example above, the investigator wished to discover whether the true value of β could be 1. Since the random variable

$$t = (\hat{\beta} - \beta)/\text{se}\ (\hat{\beta})$$

has a t distribution, with $n - 2$ degrees of freedom, the test statistic

$$t = (\hat{\beta} - 1)/\text{se}\ (\hat{\beta}) \qquad (2.8.8)$$

would also have a t distribution, if it were true that $\beta = 1$. From this stage on, the logic of a test of H_0: $\beta = 1$ against H_a: $\beta \neq 1$ is exactly the same as that for a test of H_0: $\beta = 0$ against H_a: $\beta \neq 0$. It is possible to calculate a value for the test statistic and, if this value lies outside the interval $-t_{n-2}^{0.025}$ to $+t_{n-2}^{0.025}$, it is unlikely that β is really 1 and we reject the null hypothesis. In the example above, $\hat{\beta} = 0.6365$ and se $(\hat{\beta}) = 0.0246$, so the value obtained for statistic 2.8.8 is

$$t = (0.6365 - 1)/0.0246 = -14.78$$

The critical value is 2.26 and, as the value obtained for t lies well outside the interval -2.26 to $+2.26$, the null hypothesis $\beta = 1$ is also rejected.

If one had a perfectly adequate data set and yet, as a result of a t test, one failed to reject the null hypothesis that $\beta = 0$, then it could be argued that

$$Y = \alpha + u_t; t = 1, 2, \ldots, n$$

would be the appropriate model to use. In practice it is unlikely that an economist would be satisfied with a form of model which suggests that Y varies randomly around a fixed value, and he would probably search for alternative explanatory variables. It may be necessary to try a number of different models before an acceptable form is found. There is no escaping the fact that such experimentation does take place, but the statistical theory that we have used does not allow for a situation in which a given model may be chosen after a sequence of experiments. Such a sequence can be difficult to analyse from a statistical viewpoint; the best that we can do is to say that, in such a situation, the results given in this chapter are likely to overstate the precision attached to estimation and hypothesis testing.

2.9 Prediction

If the parameters of the two variable model have been estimated and if this form of model is found to be acceptable, the predicted values of the dependent variable can be found by substituting the particular values obtained for $\hat{\alpha}$ and $\hat{\beta}$ into

$$\hat{Y}_t = \hat{\alpha} + \hat{\beta} X_t; t = 1, 2, \ldots, n \tag{2.9.1}$$

Suppose now that one wished to predict a value of the dependent variable which, for some reason, could not be observed. The usual context for this problem is when the data consist of a time series of observations representing the recent past, and the object of prediction is a value of the dependent variable which has not yet been observed, either because the relevant time period is still in the future or perhaps because that period has occurred so recently that no information is yet available. But this is not very different from a situation in which the data are taken from different units in a cross-section: the prediction would then concern a unit for which the dependent variable value was unknown. It is convenient to use time as the context for discussion, but the possibility of using similar ideas in a cross-section must not be overlooked.

We shall assume that the prediction is to be made for period $n + 1$. This naturally suggests the period immediately following the sequence $t = 1, 2, \ldots, n$, and this may be the period for which the prediction is required, but in the discussion which follows, $n + 1$ can be taken to refer to any period not included in $t = 1, 2, \ldots, n$. The value of the dependent variable in period $n + 1$ would be Y_{n+1}, and the obvious method for making a prediction is to apply the estimated equation to this period. If X_{n+1} represents the corresponding value of the explanatory variable, the formula for the prediction would be

$$\hat{Y}_{n+1} = \hat{\alpha} + \hat{\beta} X_{n+1} \qquad (2.9.2)$$

Clearly one has to have a value for X_{n+1} before equation 2.9.2 can be used, and the prediction is therefore conditional on the value chosen for X_{n+1}. If X_{n+1} is known, perhaps because it can be fixed by policy decision, well and good, but the more usual situation is one in which some uncertainty is attached to the value of X_{n+1}. In this case, the best strategy is to assume a set of possible values for X_{n+1} and to obtain a conditional prediction for the dependent variable corresponding to each possible value of the explanatory variable. Although this does not forecast the future in a pure sense, it does at least provide some idea of the range of possibilities that could result from different values of the explanatory variable.

The original specification of the two variable model is

$$Y_t = \alpha + \beta X_t + u_t; t = 1, 2, \ldots, n \qquad (2.9.3)$$

which refers specifically to the data period. Before this can be used as a basis for the prediction of Y_{n+1}, it must also be assumed that

$$Y_{n+1} = \alpha + \beta X_{n+1} + u_{n+1}, \text{ where } E(u_{n+1}) = 0 \qquad (2.9.4)$$

This states that the same form of model is valid in period $n + 1$ and, moreover, that the values of α and β which make the model valid are exactly the same as those for the data period. It is possible that the model could be valid for period $n + 1$, but for different values of α and β. What we require is that it is valid for the same values of α and β, for otherwise the estimates obtained from the data period would not apply to the forecast period. The reason for insisting that $E(u_{n+1}) = 0$ is that, in the absence of this assumption, any change in the values of α and β could be offset by allowing a nonzero expectation for the disturbance in period $n + 1$.

It is important to understand the nature of a prediction obtained from a model of this kind. According to equation 2.9.4, Y_{n+1} has a random component u_{n+1}, and since there is no way of knowing the value that u_{n+1} will take, the prediction equation 2.9.2 has an implicit estimate of that value. In the simplest case, we assume that there is no connection between the behaviour of u_{n+1} and that of the disturbances $u_t; t = 1, 2, \ldots, n$. The best that one can then do is to set the implicit estimate of u_{n+1} to zero. Because of this, one could not expect a perfectly accurate preduction of the value of Y_{n+1}. There is also another source of error, because the method of prediction is based on estimates of the parameters α and β. Equation 2.9.2 states that

$$\hat{Y}_{n+1} = \hat{\alpha} + \hat{\beta} X_{n+1}$$

and, since $\hat{\alpha}$ and $\hat{\beta}$ are random variables, $\hat{Y}_{n+1}$ is also a random variable, known as a *predictor*. If particular values of $\hat{\alpha}$ and $\hat{\beta}$ are used in equation 2.9.2, a point prediction is obtained, but since the predictor is a random variable, the point prediction is only one of the values that the random variable could take. So, even if all the assumptions made are valid, it is highly unlikely that a point prediction would be exactly correct.

It is possible to go a little further in the analysis by looking at the probability distribution associated with the random variable which defines the *prediction error*, the difference $(\hat{Y}_{n+1} - Y_{n+1})$. Equation 2.9.4 states that the random component of Y_{n+1} is u_{n+1} and, since $\hat{Y}_{n+1}$ depends on $\hat{\alpha}$ and $\hat{\beta}$, which in turn depend on the disturbances in the data period, the prediction error depends on the disturbances $u_t; t = 1, 2, \ldots, n$ and u_{n+1}. Although we shall not follow the analysis through in detail, it can be shown that the prediction error is based on a linear function of these disturbances. So if, in addition to the assumptions already made concerning $u_t; t = 1, 2, \ldots, n$, it is now assumed that u_{n+1} has a normal distribution, independent of $u_t; t = 1, 2, \ldots, n$, and with $E(u_{n+1}) = 0$ and var $(u_{n+1}) = \sigma^2$, then it can be shown that the prediction error is also normal with

$$E(\hat{Y}_{n+1} - Y_{n+1}) = 0 \tag{2.9.5}$$

and

$$\text{var} (\hat{Y}_{n+1} - Y_{n+1}) = \sigma^2 [1 + 1/n + (X_{n+1} - \overline{X})^2/\Sigma x_t^2] \qquad (2.9.6)$$

Equation 2.9.5 states that the expected prediction error is zero, so that 'on average' the prediction is correct. Equation 2.9.6 gives the variance of the prediction error, but this involves the unknown disturbance variance σ^2. If σ^2 is replaced by the estimator $\hat{\sigma}^2$, defined in equation 2.7.3, the standard error would be

$$\text{se} (\hat{Y}_{n+1} - Y_{n+1}) = \hat{\sigma} \sqrt{[1 + 1/n + (X_{n+1} - \overline{X})^2/\Sigma x_t^2]} \qquad (2.9.7)$$

Since 'standard error of the prediction error' is a rather awkward description, the phrase *standard error of prediction* is used instead.

There are many similarities between the random variable $\hat{Y}_{n+1} - Y_{n+1}$ and the random variable $\hat{\beta}$. Both are linear functions of underlying random disturbances and, given normality of those disturbances, both $\hat{\beta}$ and $\hat{Y}_{n+1} - Y_{n+1}$ would have normal distributions. In both cases the expectation and variance can be deduced, provided that certain assumptions are made about the underlying disturbances. Finally, in both cases, the variance formula involves the unknown parameter σ^2. If this is replaced by the estimator $\hat{\sigma}^2$ we obtain a standard error which is itself a random variable, and any inference procedures which would otherwise use the standard normal distribution must now use the t distribution with $n - 2$ degrees of freedom.

Provided that all the assumptions are satisfied, it follows from the arguments above that there is a probability of approximately 0·95 attached to the event that the prediction error lies in the interval

$$0 \pm 2 \text{ se} (\hat{Y}_{n+1} - Y_{n+1})$$

But if the prediction error is no more than 2 standard errors away from zero, the unknown true value Y_{n+1} is no more than 2 standard errors away from the prediction $\hat{Y}_{n+1}$, and an exactly equivalent event is that Y_{n+1} lies in the interval

$$\hat{Y}_{n+1} \pm 2 \text{ se} (\hat{Y}_{n+1} - Y_{n+1}) \qquad (2.9.8)$$

Equation 2.9.8 is an approximate 95 per cent *prediction interval* for the unknown value Y_{n+1}. To make the interval hold with a probability of exactly 0·95, one should use the correct critical value taken from a t distribution with $n - 2$ degrees of freedom.

The information on the distribution of the prediction error can also be used as a test of the predictive power of the model, but one can only compare prediction with reality in an *ex post* sense, when the true value of Y_{n+1} is known. Even so, such a test can provide useful information and, for this reason, it is worth keeping one or two of the most recent observations out of the data set used for estimation, at least until the test has been made. The null hypothesis for the test is contained in equation 2.9.4, which states that the model continues to hold in the prediction period with the same values of α and β as those which hold in the data period. When this null hypothesis is true, the expected prediction error is zero and the test statistic

$$t = [(\hat{Y}_{n+1} - Y_{n+1}) - 0]/\text{se}\,(\hat{Y}_{n+1} - Y_{n+1}) \qquad (2.9.9)$$

has a t distribution with $n - 2$ degrees of freedom. As before, one could use 2 as an approximation to the critical value, so that a calculated value of the test statistic lying outside the range -2 to $+2$ would lead to rejection of the null hypothesis and the conclusion that, even if the model holds in the prediction period, it does so with different true values of α and β. Alternatively, one could achieve an exact level of significance by using the correct critical value from a t distribution with $n - 2$ degrees of freedom.

To illustrate the use of the test described above, observations for 1981 are added to the data of exercise 1.4. The new observations are $C_{1981} = 71 \cdot 76$ and $D_{1981} = 82 \cdot 90$. The null hypothesis is that the model is unchanged for 1981 or, equivalently, that the observation C_{1981} could have been generated by the model suggested earlier. The estimated equation obtained from the data for 1970–80 enables us to make the prediction

$$\hat{C}_{1981} = 18 \cdot 118 + 0 \cdot 6365(82 \cdot 90) = 70 \cdot 884$$

Also, from previous calculations, we have

$$\hat{\sigma}^2 = 0 \cdot 2671, \ \hat{\sigma} = 0 \cdot 5168, \ \bar{D} = 74 \cdot 00 \ \text{ and } \ \Sigma(D_t - \bar{D})^2 = 441 \cdot 136$$

Then, using equation 2.9.7 for the standard error of prediction, we obtain

$$\text{se}\,(\hat{C}_{1981} - C_{1981}) = 0 \cdot 5168 \sqrt{[1 + 1/11 + (82 \cdot 90 - 74 \cdot 00)^2/441 \cdot 136]}$$
$$= 0 \cdot 5825$$

Hence

$$t = (70 \cdot 884 - 71 \cdot 760)/0 \cdot 5825 = -1 \cdot 50$$

As 11 observations were used to estimate the original equation, there are $11 - 2 = 9$ degrees of freedom and $t_9^{0 \cdot 025} = 2 \cdot 26$. The calculated value of the test statistic lies between $-2 \cdot 26$ and $+2 \cdot 26$, so we do not reject the null hypothesis in this case. Apparently the model does continue to hold for 1981.

If one rejects the null hypothesis in a prediction test, there are various possible interpretations. Rejection could mean that a given relationship has held in the past, but is now breaking down altogether, so that the model is not appropriate outside the data period. It might even mean that the apparently good fit in the data period is a statistical accident, since a 'good' model should really survive beyond the period for which the parameters are estimated. On the other hand, it may mean that the form of model is appropriate, but that the parameter values have changed. Whatever the reason for the rejection of the null hypothesis, it is serious from the point of view of using the model to forecast outside the data period, and it may also raise fundamental questions about the nature of the model itself. It is perhaps unlikely that α and β remain stable through the data period and then change suddenly. It may be that, because the model is an approximation to some real process, the parameters have to evolve slowly through time. If this is the case, observations at the extremes of the data period may well show the accumulated effects of this evolution. All of this is rather speculative, because rejection of a specific null hypothesis cannot indicate directly what the 'true' situation actually is. But it is useful to be aware of the possibilities, and some form of prediction test should be included in the battery of checks to be applied to any proposed model.

2.10   Asymptotic properties

When the model satisfies the various assumptions laid out in this chapter, the least squares estimators have a set of properties which apply for any number of observations on the variables. But the estimates should improve as the number of observations is increased, in the sense that the true variance of $\hat{\beta}$ decreases. The variance of $\hat{\beta}$ is given by equation 2.4.7, which states that

$$\text{var} \, (\hat{\beta}) = \sigma^2/\Sigma x_t^2 \qquad (2.10.1)$$

As the number of observations is increased, Σx_t^2 cannot decrease and will almost invariably increase, and this does lead to a reduction in var $(\hat{\beta})$. Of course, this depends on the assumption that the model continues to hold for the additional observations. Incidentally, it is not quite as simple as it may seem to prove that Σx_t^2 cannot decrease: each x_t is defined as $X_t - \overline{X}$ and, as new observations are added, $\overline{X}$ would change. So it is not just a case of adding new squared terms to an existing sum of squares. Nevertheless, the result is true.

If the variance of $\hat{\beta}$ does decrease as the number of observations becomes larger, it is reasonable to suppose that at some stage the variance might become zero, in which case $\hat{\beta}$ would be equal to the true value β. Such a result would hold as the limit of a process of adding successively more observations, and a property based on this type of argument is known as an *asymptotic* property. There is no way of knowing how many observations would be necessary for the variance to become very close to zero, but it is likely to be a number greater than that which could be used in practice. In this sense an asymptotic property is a rather weak result, but it may tell us something about tendencies, when the actual number of observations is relatively large and one should not be unduly discouraged by the thought that the limiting case cannot occur in practice. It would not be the first time that we have constructed a theoretical argument on the basis of a conceptual experiment, knowing full well that the experiment could not be performed in the real world.

Any argument concerning the asymptotic properties of an estimator tends to be qualified by a number of conditions, and formal derivation is seldom a straightforward matter. Even the definition of an asymptotic result has to be chosen with some care. Thus, although it is correct to say that the variance of $\hat{\beta}$ might approach a certain limit, it would not be correct to say that the estimator itself approaches a limit. A sequence of values of the variance, based on a progressively larger number of observations, is a sequence of nonrandom quantities, whereas a sequence of slope estimators is a sequence of random variables. So one cannot really say what happens to the value of $\hat{\beta}$, but one can say what happens to probability statements concerning $\hat{\beta}$. If $\hat{\beta}$ is unbiased and var $(\hat{\beta})$ has a limiting value equal to zero, it does follow that $\hat{\beta}$ converges in probability to the true parameter value. An exactly equivalent statement is that $\hat{\beta}$ has a *probability limit* equal to the true parameter. What these conditions say is that the probability of $\hat{\beta}$ being different from β approaches a limit of zero, which is not quite the same thing as saying that there is a limit to a sequence of values of the difference between $\hat{\beta}$ and β. This may seem to be hair splitting, but it does illustrate the type of logical distinction that has to be made in the presentation of asymptotic results.

If the probability limit of an estimator is equal to the true parameter value, the estimator is said to be *consistent*. The probability limit is represented by the notation plim ( ), and so the result that $\hat{\beta}$ is a consistent estimator would be stated as

$$\text{plim } (\hat{\beta}) = \beta \tag{2.10.2}$$

Consistency is often considered to be a weak alternative to the unbiasedness property and, if the assumptions made so far are satisfied, there is really no need to use the asymptotic result. In the discussion above, unbiasedness was used as a condition for consistency, but it is not a necessary condition, and this is the real significance of asymptotic properties. Although the properties are weaker, so are the necessary assumptions and, when the model is modified, there can be situations in which no estimator has properties such as unbiasedness. It may then be necessary to choose the method of estimation on asymptotic criteria. There are two possibilities. The existing method may no longer be the best available, in which case an alternative should be chosen. On the other hand the existing method may still be acceptable, so that essentially the same procedures are used, even though the properties of the estimator and the choice criteria are weaker than before.

To give some idea as to why it may be possible to establish results concerned with probability limits, in a situation in which it is difficult to establish equivalent results for expectations, consider the following properties of the probability limit operator. Suppose that A_n and B_n are random variables derived from a set of n observations, and suppose that, as n is increased, A_n and B_n do converge in probability, to probability limits plim (A_n) and plim (B_n). It can then be shown that

1   plim $(A_n + B_n)$ = plim (A_n) + plim (B_n)

2   plim $(A_n - B_n)$ = plim (A_n) − plim (B_n)

3   plim $(A_n B_n)$ = plim (A_n)plim (B_n)

4   plim (A_n/B_n) = plim (A_n)/plim (B_n); if plim $(B_n) \neq 0$ (2.10.3)

Although equivalent results hold for the expectation of a sum and for the expectation of a difference, the statement

$$E(A_n B_n) = E(A_n)E(B_n) \tag{2.10.4}$$

is only true if $E(A_n)$ and $E(B_n)$ both exist and if A_n and B_n are independent (or at least uncorrelated). The only straightforward result for a ratio is that if $E(A_n)$ and $E(1/B_n)$ both exist and A_n and $1/B_n$ are independent (or at least uncorrelated), then

$$E(A_n/B_n) = E(A_n)E(1/B_n)$$

Returning now to the two variable model, consider what happens when we allow the explanatory variable observations X_t; $t = 1, 2, \ldots, n$ to become random as opposed to nonrandom quantities. As before, the equation used to analyse the behaviour of the least squares slope estimator is

$$\hat{\beta} = \beta + \Sigma w_t u_t \tag{2.10.5}$$

where

$$w_t = x_t / \Sigma x_t^2; t = 1, 2, \ldots, n$$

Whereas earlier equation 2.10.5 was treated as a linear function of the random variables $u_1, u_2, \ldots, u_n$, with nonrandom weights $w_1, w_2, \ldots, w_n$ and an additional nonrandom term β, we now recognize that if the explanatory variable observations are random the weights must also be random. We therefore treat equation 2.10.5 as a simple sum of the random variables $w_1 u_1, w_2 u_2, \ldots, w_n u_n$ to which, again, the nonrandom term β is added. Although it is still true that the expectation of the sum of terms is equal to the sum of expectations (assuming that all the relevant expectations do exist), we can no longer use a result which assumes nonrandom weights to evaluate the expectation of $\hat{\beta}$ directly. Hence we may write

$$E(\hat{\beta}) = E(\beta + \Sigma w_t u_t)$$
$$= E(\beta) + \Sigma E(w_t u_t)$$
$$= \beta + \Sigma E(w_t u_t) \tag{2.10.6}$$

where $E(\beta) = \beta$, because β is the nonrandom true parameter. The problem is to evaluate the expectation of $w_t u_t; t = 1, 2, \ldots, n$.

If each observation $X_t; t = 1, 2, \ldots, n$ is independent of each and every disturbance $u_t; t = 1, 2, \ldots, n$, it follows that w_t and u_t are independent for $t = 1, 2, \ldots, n$. In this case we can apply equation 2.10.4 to give

$$E(w_t u_t) = E(w_t)E(u_t); t = 1, 2, \ldots, n$$

If $E(u_t) = 0; t = 1, 2, \ldots, n$, it follows that $\hat{\beta}$ is still unbiased:

$$E(\hat{\beta}) = \beta + \Sigma E(w_t u_t)$$
$$= \beta + \Sigma E(w_t)E(u_t)$$
$$= \beta + \Sigma E(w_t)0$$
$$= \beta \tag{2.10.7}$$

Note that this result does assume the existence of $E(w_t); t = 1, 2, \ldots, n$. In contrast, if X_t is independent of u_t but some pairs (X_s, u_t) are not independent, for $s \neq t$, then it is not generally possible to show that $\hat{\beta}$ is an unbiased estimator. The reason for this problem is that each weight

$w_t = x_t/\Sigma x_t^2$ involves all the X observations: even if X_t and u_t are independent, w_t and u_t will not be independent, if one or more of the X observations is associated in some way with the disturbance u_t. So unless we make the very strong independence assumption, whereby all X observations are independent of all disturbances, it will not generally be possible to show that the least squares slope estimator is unbiased.

The fundamental difficulty with using expectations in the model above is that although

$$\Sigma w_t u_t = \Sigma x_t u_t / \Sigma x_t^2$$

it is not generally true that the expected value of the ratio is the ratio of expected values. In contrast, if we have a ratio of terms, each of which converge in probability, then the probability limit of the ratio is equal to the ratio of probability limits, provided that the denominator probability limit is nonzero. Thus, if we have the situation in which X_t and u_t are independent, but some pairs X_s, u_t are not independent, for $s \neq t$, it may well be possible to show that

$$\text{plim}\,(\Sigma x_t u_t/n) = 0 \tag{2.10.8}$$

and

$$\text{plim}\,(\Sigma x_t^2/n) \text{ exists and is nonzero} \tag{2.10.9}$$

Alternatively, X_t and u_t may not be independent, but they may be uncorrelated, or uncorrelated in some limiting sense, in which case equation 2.10.8 would still hold. Either way, we would have the result

$$
\begin{aligned}
\text{plim}\,(\hat{\beta}) &= \text{plim}\,[\beta + \Sigma w_t u_t] \\
&= \text{plim}\,[\beta + (\Sigma x_t u_t/n)/(\Sigma x_t^2/n)] \\
&= \beta + \text{plim}\,(\Sigma x_t u_t/n)/\text{plim}\,(\Sigma x_t^2/n) \\
&= \beta + 0 = \beta
\end{aligned}
\tag{2.10.10}
$$

where $\text{plim}\,(\beta) = \beta$, because β is the nonrandom true parameter. Although $\hat{\beta}$ may no longer be an unbiased estimator, it would at least be consistent, under the conditions stated here. Very roughly, we may interpret this as saying that any systematic distortion of estimator behaviour will tend to disappear as the sample size is increased. In contrast, if X_t and u_t are correlated and this correlation persists for all sample sizes, then it would usually be possible to show that

$$\text{plim}\,(\Sigma x_t u_t/n) \neq 0$$

in which case $\hat{\beta}$ will not even be consistent. Examples of the type of model in which this occurs will be found in Chapters 5 and 6 and, in such a case, one would almost certainly wish to consider some alternative method of estimation.

There are two points to note in connection with the arguments used above. The first is that one does not always use division by n to obtain terms which will converge in probability: there are cases in which some alternative scaling is needed. The second point is that it is often possible to prove convergence in probability by showing that the expectation exists and that the variance has a limiting value equal to zero. There is thus a purpose in trying to evaluate the expectation of individual terms in an expression such as

$$\Sigma w_t u_t = \Sigma x_t u_t / \Sigma x_t^2$$

Even though the ratio of expectations is not equal to the expectation of the ratio, knowledge of the expectation and variance is often sufficient to enable one to establish the relevant probability limits and hence to show whether the estimator is consistent or not.

Before leaving this topic, it should be noted that consistency is not the only asymptotic property of interest. What consistency implies is the eventual collapse of the probability distribution of an estimator, to a point equal to the true value of the associated parameter. But one could have two consistent estimators which behave rather differently in a large finite sample and, to the extent that consistency is treated as a weak alternative to unbiasedness, we need equivalent results which tell us something about the variance and the probability distribution in a large sample. This immediately raises a problem, for if the distribution of the estimator collapses to a point, there is no longer any variance and the distribution is degenerate. In order to get around this problem, one would not consider the limiting distribution of $\hat{\beta}$ as such, but rather the distribution of some suitably scaled quantity, such as $\sqrt{n}\,(\hat{\beta} - \beta)$. Because the scaling involves multiplication by $\sqrt{n}$, the distribution of this quantity would not necessarily collapse as n is increased. For example, if we restore the full set of assumptions, except for normality of disturbances, then, given certain conditions on the explanatory variable observations, it would be possible to show that $\sqrt{n}\,(\hat{\beta} - \beta)$ converges to a variable having a normal distribution, irrespective of the distribution of the original disturbances. We can then argue that, in a large finite sample, $\sqrt{n}\,(\hat{\beta} - \beta)$ would be approximately normal and, since we are entitled to change the scaling in a finite sample, in a way which is not legitimate in the limit, one can conclude that $\hat{\beta}$ is also approximately normal, for sample sizes which are large, but not so large that the distribution collapses entirely. It is conventional to refer to the property described above as the *asymptotic normality* of the estimator $\hat{\beta}$, despite the fact that it is a scaled quantity, such as $\sqrt{n}\,(\hat{\beta} - \beta)$, that actually converges in distribution.

A similar approach is used in situations in which it is difficult (or perhaps impossible) to evaluate the variance of an estimator in a finite sample. Suppose that $\sqrt{n}\,(\hat{\beta} - \beta)$ can be shown to have a limiting distribution and suppose that the variance of that distribution is q. It could then be argued that, in a large finite sample, the variance of $\hat{\beta}$ could be replaced by the expression q/n, bearing in mind that this is obtained as the variance of an approximating distribution, rather than as an approximation to the variance of the true distribution. The quantities q and q/n are associated with the concept of *asymptotic variance*, but there is no clear agreement, in conventional usage, as to which of these quantities is most appropriately described as the asymptotic variance of $\hat{\beta}$. The most commonly used formal definition would lead one to conclude that q is the asymptotic variance, but it is also common to find the term *asymptotic standard error* applied to a quantity obtained as the square root of q/n (not q), with any unknown parameters replaced by consistent estimates. For most purposes, it seems sensible to use the term asymptotic variance to refer to the quantity that is used to replace var $(\hat{\beta})$, when large sample results are used: this means that, in the case described above, the asymptotic variance would be q/n, a definition that is consistent with that given for an asymptotic standard error. If a scaling other than $\sqrt{n}$ is used, the definitions would have to be modified accordingly.

Finally, we mention the concept of *asymptotic efficiency*. Suppose that there are two estimators, both consistent and both converging to limiting distributions, in the sense described above. If one estimator has a variance of the limiting distribution at least as small as that for the other estimator, then the first estimator is described as being asymptotically more efficient than the second. Alternatively, one might simply say that a given estimator is asymptotically efficient: this means that the estimator is at least as efficient (asymptotically) as all other estimators in some clearly defined class.

We now appear to have moved some way from the problems of practical model building, but there is a reason for the digression. It is very convenient when the economic model does fit into the standard linear form and all the assumptions are satisfied, but the model should not be forced into this framework, when some of the assumptions are at odds with reality. So we are certainly not losing sight of the modelling objective. On the contrary, we want to be able to build models which are as realistic as possible and, if this can only be achieved at the cost of weaker statistical properties, then this is a cost that must be accepted.

In the next chapter, the format of the model is extended to allow for further explanatory variables and, to start with, the full list of assumptions is restored. Conducting the analysis under strong conditions may now seem to be at odds with the objectives of economic realism, but a further lesson of the asymptotic analysis is that the relaxation of assumptions does not always destroy the estimator properties completely and, although the results may eventually have to be modified, there is still a great deal to be learnt from a discussion of the basic model.

2.11   Exercises (solutions on p. 275)

2.1 The outcomes of a game consisting of two tosses of a coin are represented by two independent random variables V_1 and V_2. Numerical values are assigned to these random variables by the code head = 1, tail = 0. It is assumed that, on each throw, the outcomes 1 and 0 are equiprobable. A new random variable L is then defined as

$$L = 0 \cdot 2 V_1 + 0 \cdot 8 V_2$$

List the possible values of L. Given that each value of L is associated with a probability of $1/4$, show that

$$E(L) = 0 \cdot 2 E(V_1) + 0 \cdot 8 E(V_2)$$

and

$$\text{var}(L) = 0 \cdot 04 \, \text{var}(V_1) + 0 \cdot 64 \, \text{var}(V_2)$$

Explain the significance of these results.

2.2 (*a*) Using the data given in exercise 1.4, find point estimates for the parameters of the model

$$C_t = \alpha + \beta D_t + u_t; t = 1, 2, \ldots, n$$

As a check on your own calculations, you are given the following information:

$$\Sigma C_t = 717 \cdot 44 \qquad \Sigma D_t = 814 \cdot 03$$
$$\Sigma (D_t - \bar{D})^2 = 441 \cdot 136 \qquad \Sigma (D_t - \bar{D})(C_t - \bar{C}) = 280 \cdot 789$$

When you have read Section 2.7, you can continue to part (*b*) below.

(*b*) Calculate the standard error for the slope estimate obtained above: you may wish to note that $\Sigma(C_t - \bar{C})^2 = 181\cdot130$.

2.3 A problem requiring a knowledge of calculus: show that minimizing the sum of squared residuals does lead to the normal equations 2.1.7.

2.4 Demonstrate the equivalence of the following expressions for $\hat{\beta}$, the least squares slope estimator:

$$\hat{\beta} = \Sigma x_t y_t / \Sigma x_t^2$$

$$\hat{\beta} = [\Sigma X_t Y_t - (\Sigma X_t/n)\Sigma Y_t] / [\Sigma X_t^2 - (\Sigma X_t/n)\Sigma X_t]$$

2.5 Prove that $\hat{\beta}$ can be expressed as in equation 2.3.4:

$$\hat{\beta} = \beta + \Sigma x_t u_t / \Sigma x_t^2$$

2.6 As an alternative to the method of proof given in the text, use the definition

$$\text{var}(\hat{\beta}) = E([\hat{\beta} - E(\hat{\beta})]^2)$$

to show that

$$\text{var}(\hat{\beta}) = \sigma^2 / \Sigma x_t^2$$

3 The linear model with further explanatory variables

3.1 Introduction

A dependent variable that represents measurements taken from an economic system is unlikely to be related only to a single explanatory variable, and it is now necessary to consider a more general version of the linear model which allows the list of explanatory variables to be extended. We shall continue to use Y to represent the dependent variable and X as a general representation for the explanatory variables, but now individual explanatory variables have to be distinguished in some way. A single observation on one explanatory variable is therefore written as X_{jt}, where j represents a numbering to identify the variable and t represents the observation number, as before. Using k to denote the total number of explanatory variables, the complete set of observations would be

$$Y_t; t = 1, 2, \ldots, n$$

and

$$X_{jt}; j = 1, 2, \ldots, k; t = 1, 2, \ldots, n$$

It is also necessary to distinguish the parameters associated with the different explanatory variables, and so the parameters become

$$\beta_j; j = 1, 2, \ldots, k$$

Within this framework, one can allow for an intercept by saying that X_1 is a 'variable' which can only assume a single value $X_{1t} = 1$ for all values of t. If this is done, β_1 becomes the intercept and the k *variable linear model* can be written as

$$Y_t = \beta_1 + \beta_2 X_{2t} + \ldots + \beta_j X_{jt} + \ldots + \beta_k X_{kt} + u_t; t = 1, 2, \ldots, n \tag{3.1.1}$$

As defined above, k is the number of explanatory variables, including the artificial variable X_1. However, when one uses the description

'k variable' model, this is usually taken to refer to the fact that the model involves the genuine variables $Y, X_2, X_3, \ldots, X_k$. Having made this point, no confusion need arise. So, for example, the two variable model of the previous chapter can now be written as

$$Y_t = \beta_1 + \beta_2 X_{2t} + u_t; t = 1, 2, \ldots, n$$

where the two genuine variables are Y and X_2, but where the explanatory 'variables' are X_2 and the implicit artificial variable X_1.

Equation 3.1.1 may look rather complicated, but it is simply the natural extension of the two variable case. In order to examine the interpretation of the parameters of the model, we shall temporarily ignore the effect of the disturbance term and also the fact that the observations relate to discrete periods of time or to different units in a cross-section, and we shall consider only the underlying linear relationship between the variables, which is

$$Y = \beta_1 + \beta_2 X_2 + \ldots + \beta_j X_j + \ldots + \beta_k X_k \qquad (3.1.2)$$

Equation 3.1.2 has the same essential characteristics as a linear relationship in the two variable case, namely that a change of one unit in a single explanatory variable X_j would lead to a change, equal to β_j, in the dependent variable, and this would be true over the whole range of possible values of X_j. Each β_j (apart from β_1) represents a slope, and the characteristic of a linear relationship is that the slopes are parameters which are constant and which do not depend on the values taken by the variables. But there is now an important qualification on the interpretation of individual slopes. The parameter β_j measures the effect on Y of a unit change in X_j, with all other explanatory variables held constant. An easy way to see this is to note that if X_j is the only explanatory variable to change, all the terms except $\beta_j X_j$ and Y would be constant and could be thought of as being part of the intercept in an artificially constructed 'two variable' relationship of the form

$$Y = \text{intercept} + \beta_j X_j$$

We know that, in such a relationship, β_j would represent the slope, but this interpretation holds only so long as the other explanatory variables are held constant, and so the qualification on the meaning of β_j is important. In economics, the type of change that is envisaged here would often be described as a change in X_j *ceteris paribus*. With this in mind we now consider the use of the full model, complete with random disturbances.

Throughout this chapter, the explanatory variable observations are considered to be nonrandom and, as before, there are various possible interpretations that could be used. In some contexts, it might be reasonable to assume that the explanatory variables can be fixed by policy decision, in which case the purpose of the model would be to explain the impact of the policy on the dependent variable. One would then want to isolate the influence of each of the possible policy measures, and so it would be effects of a *ceteris paribus* change that one would want to find. It is implicit in the formulation of the model that the dependent variable cannot be exactly determined by policy: if this could be done, there would be no point in having the model and it would be quite inappropriate to suggest that the variable in question has a random component.

An alternative interpretation of nonrandom explanatory variables is that the values are determined by other relationships in the system, and we shall now present an example in which this interpretation would have to be used. The example is based, once again, on a version of the consumption function. Suppose that, in addition to disposable income D, the level of liquid assets L held by households is thought to be an important determinant of consumers' expenditure C. The complete model would then be

$$C_t = \beta_1 + \beta_2 D_t + \beta_3 L_t + u_t; t = 1, 2, \ldots, n \qquad (3.1.3)$$

where, as before, all variables are expressed in real terms. It would be unrealistic to regard disposable income and liquid asset holdings as being fixed by policy decision, and the interpretation that would have to be used is that both quantities are determined by other variables in the system, perhaps including more legitimate instruments of fiscal and monetary control. Ideally these other relationships should be built into the model, but we are not yet ready for the complexities of the multiple equation case and, for the time being, the use of equation 3.1.3 must be considered as a partial analysis, conditional on the income and liquid asset values generated elsewhere. Within the confines of the partial model, it would be possible to treat the explanatory variable observations as nonrandom.

Whichever interpretation we choose to give to nonrandom explana-tory variables, it is clear that we do have a problem of measurement. In equation 3.1.3 the parameter β_2 represents the effect of a unit change in disposable income, with liquid assets held constant. Now it may well be that, in the history of the economic system in question, there has never been a change in disposable income that has not been accom-panied by some change in liquid asset holdings. Despite this complication, the object of the analysis must still be to isolate the 'pure' effect of an income change, without any distortion arising from the effects that simultaneous changes in liquid asset holdings may have on consumption. It is this pure effect of an income change that is represented by the parameter β_2 and, in Section 3.3, we shall describe in some detail how the estimation procedure attempts to measure the effects of changes in each explanatory variable, with all other explanatory variables held constant. As a first step it is necessary to consider the more 'mechanical' aspects of least squares in the context of the k variable model, and it is to this that we now turn.

3.2 Solution of the normal equations

The parameter estimators for the k variable model can be obtained by application of the least squares principle, as before, but now the minimization of the sum of squared residuals leads to k linear equations in k unknowns, rather than two linear equations in two unknowns (see exercise 3.1). The equations look rather complicated, but inspection will reveal a regular pattern to the individual terms and the form of the equations is not really too difficult to understand. The equations are

$$\hat{\beta}_1 n \quad + \hat{\beta}_2 \Sigma X_{2t} \quad + \ldots + \hat{\beta}_j \Sigma X_{jt} \quad + \ldots + \hat{\beta}_k \Sigma X_{kt} \quad = \Sigma Y_t$$
$$\hat{\beta}_1 \Sigma X_{2t} + \hat{\beta}_2 \Sigma X_{2t}^2 \quad + \ldots + \hat{\beta}_j \Sigma X_{2t} X_{jt} + \ldots + \hat{\beta}_k \Sigma X_{2t} X_{kt} = \Sigma X_{2t} Y_t$$
$$\begin{array}{ccccc} \cdot & \cdot & \cdot & & \cdot \\ \cdot & \cdot & \cdot & & \cdot \end{array}$$
$$\hat{\beta}_1 \Sigma X_{jt} + \hat{\beta}_2 \Sigma X_{jt} X_{2t} + \ldots + \hat{\beta}_j \Sigma X_{jt}^2 \quad + \ldots + \hat{\beta}_k \Sigma X_{jt} X_{kt} = \Sigma X_{jt} Y_t$$
$$\begin{array}{ccccc} \cdot & \cdot & \cdot & & \cdot \\ \cdot & \cdot & \cdot & & \cdot \end{array}$$
$$\hat{\beta}_1 \Sigma X_{kt} + \hat{\beta}_2 \Sigma X_{kt} X_{2t} + \ldots + \hat{\beta}_j \Sigma X_{kt} X_{jt} + \ldots + \hat{\beta}_k \Sigma X_{kt}^2 \quad = \Sigma X_{kt} Y_t$$

$$(3.2.1)$$

All the sums, sums of squares and sums of products represent quantities that can be calculated from a particular set of data, consisting of observations on the dependent variable Y and all the genuine explanatory variables from X_2 to X_k. All the summations run from $t = 1$ to

$t = n$. The first equation looks different from the rest, but this is because X_1 is not made explicit. Remember that

$$X_{1t} = 1; t = 1, 2, \ldots, n$$

so

$$\Sigma X_{1t}^2 = n, \Sigma X_{1t} Y_t = \Sigma Y_t$$

and

$$\Sigma X_{1t} X_{jt} = \Sigma X_{jt} X_{1t} = \Sigma X_{jt}; j = 2, 3, \ldots, k$$

If it is necessary to estimate the parameters of a model which does not have an intercept term, one could either delete X_1 entirely, counting the genuine variables from X_2 to X_k, or else one could interpret X_1 as a genuine variable. In the first case, one would delete the first row and column from the equation system 3.2.1: in the second case, X_1 would have to appear explicitly in the first row and column of the equation system, in a pattern corresponding exactly to that of the other explanatory variables.

Before attempting any further interpretation, a numerical example would perhaps be helpful. To make the arithmetic easy, artificial data have been used. Suppose that we wish to obtain estimates for β_1, β_2 and β_3 in the model

$$Y_t = \beta_1 + \beta_2 X_{2t} + \beta_3 X_{3t} + u_t; t = 1, 2, \ldots, n \tag{3.2.2}$$

given the following observations on Y, X_2 and X_3:

t	Y_t	X_{2t}	X_{3t}
1	5	5	6
2	6	4	7
3	8	2	9
4	11	3	16
5	10	1	10
$n = 5$	$\Sigma Y_t = 40$	$\Sigma X_{2t} = 15$	$\Sigma X_{3t} = 48$

By setting up further working columns, we obtain the table opposite. In the case $k = 3$, equations 3.2.1 specialize to

$$\begin{aligned}
\beta_1 n + \beta_2 \Sigma X_{2t} + \beta_3 \Sigma X_{3t} &= \Sigma Y_t \\
\beta_1 \Sigma X_{2t} + \beta_2 \Sigma X_{2t}^2 + \beta_3 \Sigma X_{2t} X_{3t} &= \Sigma X_{2t} Y_t \\
\beta_1 \Sigma X_{3t} + \beta_2 \Sigma X_{3t} X_{2t} + \beta_3 \Sigma X_{3t}^2 &= \Sigma X_{3t} Y_t
\end{aligned} \tag{3.2.3}$$

$X_{2t}Y_t$	$X_{3t}Y_t$	X_{2t}^2	X_{3t}^2	$X_{2t}X_{3t}$
25	30	25	36	30
24	42	16	49	28
16	72	4	81	18
33	176	9	256	48
10	100	1	100	10
$\Sigma X_{2t}Y_t$ = 108	$\Sigma X_{3t}Y_t$ = 420	ΣX_{2t}^2 = 55	ΣX_{3t}^2 = 522	$\Sigma X_{2t}X_{3t}$ = 134

Then, using the values obtained from the data above, the equations to be solved are

$$5\hat{\beta}_1 + 15\hat{\beta}_2 + 48\hat{\beta}_3 = 40$$
$$15\hat{\beta}_1 + 55\hat{\beta}_2 + 134\hat{\beta}_3 = 108$$
$$48\hat{\beta}_1 + 134\hat{\beta}_2 + 522\hat{\beta}_3 = 420 \qquad (3.2.4)$$

The method of solution is simply an extension of that used in the two variable case. By multiplying the first equation by $15/5 = 3$ and subtracting the result from the second equation, it is possible to eliminate $\hat{\beta}_1$ from the second equation:

$$[55 - 3(15)]\hat{\beta}_2 + [134 - 3(48)]\hat{\beta}_3 = [108 - 3(40)]$$

or

$$10\hat{\beta}_2 - 10\hat{\beta}_3 = -12$$

By multiplying the first equation by $48/5 = 9{\cdot}6$ and subtracting the result from the third equation, it is possible to eliminate $\hat{\beta}_1$ from the third equation:

$$[134 - 9{\cdot}6(15)]\hat{\beta}_2 + [522 - 9{\cdot}6(48)]\hat{\beta}_3 = [420 - 9{\cdot}6(40)]$$

or

$$-10\hat{\beta}_2 + 61{\cdot}2\hat{\beta}_3 = 36$$

There are now two equations in the two unknowns, $\hat{\beta}_2$ and $\hat{\beta}_3$:

$$10\hat{\beta}_2 - 10\hat{\beta}_3 = -12$$
$$-10\hat{\beta}_2 + 61{\cdot}2\hat{\beta}_3 = 36 \qquad (3.2.5)$$

Eliminating $\hat{\beta}_2$ gives

$$[61{\cdot}2 - 10]\hat{\beta}_3 = [36 - 12]$$
$$51{\cdot}2\hat{\beta}_3 = 24$$
$$\hat{\beta}_3 = 24/51{\cdot}2 = 0{\cdot}4688 \qquad (3.2.6)$$

Given $\hat{\beta}_3$, the value of $\hat{\beta}_2$ can be obtained by substitution in one of the equations 3.2.5:

$$10\hat{\beta}_2 - 10\hat{\beta}_3 = -12$$
$$\hat{\beta}_2 = [-12 + 10(0\cdot4688)]/10$$
$$= -0\cdot7312$$

Finally, the value of $\hat{\beta}_1$ can be obtained from one of the equations 3.2.4:

$$5\hat{\beta}_1 + 15\hat{\beta}_2 + 48\hat{\beta}_3 = 40$$
$$\hat{\beta}_1 = [40 - 15(-0\cdot7312) - 48(0\cdot4688)]/5$$
$$= 5\cdot6931$$

The estimated equation is thus

$$\hat{Y}_t = 5\cdot6931 - 0\cdot7312X_{2t} + 0\cdot4688X_{3t}; t = 1, 2, \ldots, n$$

If you try to reproduce this solution, note that the answers will vary slightly depending on how many decimal places are carried through the calculation.

As in the two variable case, it is possible to set up a slightly different calculation scheme, involving data expressed in the form of deviations from sample means. If $k = 3$ and $y_t = Y_t - \bar{Y}$, $x_{2t} = X_{2t} - \bar{X}_2$, $x_{3t} = X_{3t} - \bar{X}_3$, the normal equations in deviation form are:

$$\hat{\beta}_2 \Sigma x_{2t}^2 + \hat{\beta}_3 \Sigma x_{2t} x_{3t} = \Sigma x_{2t} y_t$$
$$\hat{\beta}_2 \Sigma x_{3t} x_{2t} + \hat{\beta}_3 \Sigma x_{3t}^2 = \Sigma x_{3t} y_t \qquad (3.2.7)$$

A comparison of equations 3.2.3 and 3.2.7 will show that, to obtain the normal equations in deviation form, the first of the original equations is deleted completely, the terms in $\hat{\beta}_1$ are deleted from the other equations and all terms that remain are rewritten with the variables expressed as deviations from sample means. This is quite general. If all sums of squares and products in a k variable model are expressed as deviations from means, the first equation can be deleted completely and the terms in $\hat{\beta}_1$ can be removed from the remaining equations, leaving $k - 1$ equations in $k - 1$ unknowns. These equations are solved for the slope estimates only. The intercept $\hat{\beta}_1$ is found afterwards as

$$\hat{\beta}_1 = \bar{Y} - \hat{\beta}_2 \bar{X}_2 - \hat{\beta}_3 \bar{X}_3 - \ldots - \hat{\beta}_k \bar{X}_k \qquad (3.2.8)$$

In the case $k = 3$, this reduces to

$$\hat{\beta}_1 = \bar{Y} - \hat{\beta}_2 \bar{X}_2 - \hat{\beta}_3 \bar{X}_3 \qquad (3.2.9)$$

In exercise 3.2 the reader is asked to confirm that, with the artificial data of this section, expressed in deviation form, substitution in

3.2.7 produces exactly the same equations for $\hat{\beta}_2$ and $\hat{\beta}_3$ as those obtained in 3.2.5, during the solution of the original normal equations. If this is so, $\hat{\beta}_2$ and $\hat{\beta}_3$ take the same values as before and inspection will reveal that the calculation of $\hat{\beta}_1$ is effectively the same in both cases, so the value of $\hat{\beta}_1$ is also unchanged.

There is one important qualification to add to the argument above. It is valid to work with data adjusted for means, provided that the model does have an intercept term. If X_1 is a genuine variable, the original form of the normal equations must be used, with X_1 made explicit in the first row and column of the equation system. If X_1 does not exist and the variables are counted from X_2 to X_k, the original form must again be used, with the first row and column deleted.

At this stage it will have become obvious to the reader that, even for quite modest values of k, the assembly and solution of the normal equations does represent a lengthy calculation. Although it is quite instructive to perform hand calculations when k is 2, 3 or possibly 4, it must be recognized that, in practical work, a computer would have to be used to obtain parameter estimates. Given the development of microcomputing, the level of hardware provision need not be very elaborate and, to emphasize this point, all the examples reported in this book have been processed on an Apple II microcomputer, using a set of programs written by the author. It is no longer true that the use of econometric techniques is limited by the need to have access to a large scale computer system.

To conclude this section, there are several further details to note. The calculation outlined above is frequently described as a *multiple regression* of Y on $X_1, X_2, \ldots, X_k$, although some authors would prefer to say that it is a regression of Y on X_2 to X_k, with an intercept. In the terminology of regression, the explanatory variables are known as *regressors* and the values obtained for $\beta_1, \beta_2, \ldots, \beta_k$ are *regression coefficients*. Since we have assumed that there is an underlying probability model for the relationship between Y and $X_1, X_2, \ldots, X_k$, the regression coefficients are also estimates of underlying parameters and are subject to a probabilistic interpretation, but this is not true of all regression calculations. One could perform a regression in which one of the X variables, say X_k, acts as the dependent variable and in which the remaining X variables ($X_1, X_2, \ldots, X_{k-1}$) are explanatory. The notion of a regression between X variables may seem somewhat strange, but it is clearly possible. If one can issue computer commands which cause a variable known as Y to be regressed on variables known as $X_1, X_2, \ldots, X_k$, then one can clearly issue computer commands to cause a variable known as X_k to be regressed on variables known as $X_1, X_2, \ldots, X_{k-1}$. What is different about this so-called *auxiliary* regression is that X variables are at present treated as nonrandom quantities, so there can be no question of an underlying probability model in this case. Perhaps surprisingly, the concept of regression between X variables is actually quite useful in helping to provide an interpretation of the coefficients obtained from the main regression of interest, which is that of Y on $X_1, X_2, \ldots, X_k$.

3.3   An interpretation of multiple regression

The knowledge that parameter estimates can be obtained by solution of the normal equations is sufficient to define the least squares method. However, the reader may wonder why no explicit algebraic formulae have been given expressing the estimators for individual parameters in terms of sums, sums of squares and sums of products of the original data. The answer is that such expressions do become rather complicated as the number of explanatory variables is increased. Instead of trying to remember a formula for each parameter estimator, it is easier to write down the normal equations and to solve numerically. But for theoretical analysis of estimator properties and for the interpretation of estimates obtained by solution of the normal equations, it is worth trying to discover a little more about the nature of the regression calculation. What we shall do is to look at the estimators from some very simple models and use these to suggest a general result, which holds for any value of k. It will be possible to write down an algebraic expression for $\hat{\beta}_j$, the least squares estimator for a typical parameter β_j, but the expression obtained is not intended as a formula for hand calculation. Instead, we shall use the expression to show how the estimation procedure attempts to measure the effects of a change in one explanatory variable, with all other explanatory variables held constant. With this objective in mind, I would ask the reader to spend some time in careful study of the discussion which follows.

In Chapter 2 we made use of the two variable model to explain the nature of the least squares calculation. This is the simplest form of model that is likely to be of practical value, but there is an even simpler case from which we can learn something of importance. If $k = 1$ and the only explanatory 'variable' is the artificial variable X_1, the model would be

$$Y_t = \beta_1 X_{1t} + u_t = \beta_1 + u_t; t = 1, 2, \ldots, n \qquad (3.3.1)$$

Equations 3.2.1 are completely general and they can be used to generate the estimators corresponding to any value of k. If $k = 1$ and $X_{1t} = 1; t = 1, 2, \ldots, n$, there would only be a single equation

$$\hat{\beta}_1 n = \Sigma Y_t$$

So the estimator for β_1, based on the model 3.3.1, would be

$$\hat{\beta}_1 = \Sigma Y_t / n = \bar{Y} \tag{3.3.2}$$

This represents the sample mean calculated from the dependent variable observations. For future reference, notice that if X_1 is made explicit, the estimator would be written as

$$\hat{\beta}_1 = \Sigma X_{1t} Y_t / \Sigma X_{1t}^2 \tag{3.3.3}$$

If the model shown in 3.3.1 is used, the values of the dependent variable predicted by the estimated equation would be

$$\hat{Y}_t = \hat{\beta}_1 X_{1t} = \hat{\beta}_1 = \bar{Y}; t = 1, 2, \ldots, n \tag{3.3.4}$$

and the residuals, measuring the differences between the observed and predicted values of the dependent variable, would be

$$e_t = Y_t - \hat{Y}_t = Y_t - \bar{Y} = y_t; t = 1, 2, \ldots, n \tag{3.3.5}$$

So this model can only account for the behaviour of the dependent variable to the extent that it explains a constant component of the observations $Y_t; t = 1, 2, \ldots, n$, a component estimated as $\bar{Y}$. The remaining part of the observed behaviour of Y is not explained and this component is measured by the residuals defined in equation 3.3.5: these are equivalent to deviations of the dependent variable observations from the sample mean $\bar{Y}$.

Now consider the case in which the model contains a single genuine explanatory variable but no intercept term. This model can be written as

$$Y_t = \beta_2 X_{2t} + u_t; t = 1, 2, \ldots, n \tag{3.3.6}$$

where X_2 is used to indicate a genuine explanatory variable, as distinct from the artificial variable X_1. The only equation in 3.2.1 would now be

$$\hat{\beta}_2 \Sigma X_{2t}^2 = \Sigma X_{2t} Y_t$$

and so the estimator for β_2, based on the model 3.3.6, would be

$$\hat{\beta}_2 = \Sigma X_{2t} Y_t / \Sigma X_{2t}^2 \tag{3.3.7}$$

It should be noted that this has the same general form as equation 3.3.3, the only difference being that X_1 is replaced by X_2.

When the model contains both an intercept term and a genuine explanatory variable, it is the standard two variable model of the previous chapter, albeit expressed here in a slightly different notation:

$$Y_t = \beta_1 + \beta_2 X_{2t} + u_t; t = 1, 2, \ldots, n \qquad (3.3.8)$$

In this case the application of equation 3.2.1 would give two equations

$$\hat{\beta}_1 n \quad + \hat{\beta}_2 \Sigma X_{2t} = \Sigma Y_t$$
$$\hat{\beta}_1 \Sigma X_{2t} + \hat{\beta}_2 \Sigma X_{2t}^2 = \Sigma X_{2t} Y_t$$

We already know that it is possible to eliminate $\hat{\beta}_1$ to give a single equation in the slope estimator $\hat{\beta}_2$, and that this equation can be written as

$$\hat{\beta}_2 \Sigma x_{2t}^2 = \Sigma x_{2t} y_t$$

where

$$y_t = Y_t - \bar{Y} \text{ and } x_{2t} = X_{2t} - \bar{X}_2; t = 1, 2, \ldots, n$$

So the estimator corresponding to X_2 is now given by

$$\hat{\beta}_2 = \Sigma x_{2t} y_t / \Sigma x_{2t}^2 \qquad (3.3.9)$$

Finally, consider a regression of X_2 on X_1. In this case it cannot be assumed that there is an underlying probability model involving a random disturbance. Within our present framework, all the X variables are considered to be nonrandom. But there is no reason why such a regression could not be performed and, by analogy with the regression of Y on X_1, the regression of X_2 on X_1 would give residuals which are the deviations $x_{2t} = X_{2t} - \bar{X}_2; t = 1, 2, \ldots, n$. We shall shortly need to make use of this result.

In these simple examples we have taken steps to avoid an unduly complicated system of notation. Thus coefficients based on regressions between the X variables are not given a specific symbolic representation: all that we are interested in is the nature of the residuals. And, for a regression in which Y is the dependent variable, the symbol $\hat{\beta}_j$ is used for the estimator corresponding to the variable X_j, irrespective of the other explanatory variables in the model. When there is any possibility of confusion, the particular regression on which the estimation is based must be stated.

The examples illustrate a very important point. The estimator corresponding to the variable X_2 does change when X_1 is added to the model. In equation 3.3.7, the observations on the variables are used in original form, whereas in equation 3.3.9, the observations are expressed as deviations from the sample means. A similar result holds in the general case. The estimator corresponding to any variable depends on all the other explanatory variables in the model and, if the definition of the estimator is changed as variables are added to or removed from the model, it naturally follows that the estimates, obtained from a given set of data, would also change. In particular, the estimates obtained from a multiple regression of Y on several explanatory variables are not generally the same as those obtained from several two variable regressions, each relating Y to one of the genuine explanatory variables. The only exceptions are when the data have very special (and highly unlikely) properties. Thus equations 3.3.7 and 3.3.9 would give the same result if it happened to be true that $\bar{X}_2$ was exactly zero. Obviously, such accidents of the data are rare.

Now consider what the difference between equations 3.3.7 and 3.3.9 really amounts to. One could consider both of these estimators to be special cases of the general form

$$\hat{\beta}_2 = \Sigma \widetilde{X}_{2t} \widetilde{Y}_t / \Sigma \widetilde{X}_{2t}^2 \qquad (3.3.10)$$

where $\widetilde{X}_{2t}; t = 1, 2, \ldots, n$ are residuals from a regression of X_2 on any other explanatory variables in the model and $\widetilde{Y}_t; t = 1, 2, \ldots, n$ are residuals from a regression of Y on any explanatory variables other than X_2. In the model from which equation 3.3.7 is obtained, there are no other explanatory variables, so $\widetilde{X}_2 = X_2$ and $\widetilde{Y} = Y$. In the model from which equation 3.3.9 is obtained, the only explanatory 'variable', apart from X_2, is the artificial variable X_1. A regression of X_2 on X_1 produces residuals which are the deviations $x_{2t} = X_{2t} - \bar{X}_2; t = 1, 2, \ldots, n$, and a regression of Y on X_1 produces residuals which are the deviations $y_t = Y_t - \bar{Y}; t = 1, 2, \ldots, n$. Hence, in equation 3.3.9, $\widetilde{X}_2 = x_2$ and $\widetilde{Y} = y$.

Although we have not shown the validity of equation 3.3.10 beyond the case of a standard two variable regression, the result is quite general. Given the definitions of $\widetilde{X}_2$ and $\widetilde{Y}$, the estimator $\hat{\beta}_2$ clearly does change as other explanatory variables are added to the model, and an exactly equivalent form holds for the estimator corresponding to any other parameter β_j. Hence, in a multiple regression of Y on $X_1, X_2, \ldots, X_j, \ldots, X_k$, the coefficient attached to X_j can be expressed as

$$\hat{\beta}_j = \Sigma \widetilde{X}_{jt} \widetilde{Y}_t / \Sigma \widetilde{X}_{jt}^2 \qquad (3.3.11)$$

where $\widetilde{X}_j$ is a variable representing the residuals from a regression of X_j on all other explanatory variables in the model, and $\widetilde{Y}$ is a variable representing the residuals from a regression of Y on all explanatory variables except for X_j.

It must be emphasized that equation 3.3.11 is not intended as a formula for hand calculation, but rather as an aid to understanding what happens in a multiple regression when parameter estimates are obtained by solution of the normal equations 3.2.1. Since $\widetilde{X}_j$ represents a variable defined by the residuals from a regression of X_j on all other explanatory variables, we can interpret $\widetilde{X}_{jt}$; $t = 1, 2, \ldots, n$ as a component of the observations on X_j that cannot be explained in terms of the behaviour of the other X variables. So changes in $\widetilde{X}_j$ are not associated with changes in other explanatory variables and $\widetilde{X}_{jt}$; $t = 1, 2, \ldots, n$ can be thought of as a series in which all observed changes are effectively changes in X_j *ceteris paribus*. It is only this 'pure' component of X_j that is used in establishing an estimate of β_j. The fact that Y is also 'adjusted for' the effects of the other explanatory variables is less crucial to the argument, since one would get exactly the same result if the observations on the dependent variable were used in original form. The reason for this is that there is an algebraic identity between $\Sigma \widetilde{X}_{jt} \widetilde{Y}_t$ and $\Sigma \widetilde{X}_{jt} Y_t$: whichever form one uses, it remains true that only a part of the observed behaviour of Y is used in establishing an estimate of β_j.

We now consider a specific example, in which equation 3.3.11 can be used to interpret the estimates obtained by a multiple regression calculation. The example is based on the three variable consumption function

$$C_t = \beta_1 + \beta_2 D_t + \beta_3 L_t + u_t; t = 1, 2, \ldots, n \qquad (3.3.12)$$

It has been argued that, in this model, the parameter β_2 represents the effect on consumers' expenditure C of a unit change in income D *ceteris paribus*. According to the general form 3.3.11, a regression of C on D and L, with an intercept, would give an estimate $\hat{\beta}_2$ exactly equivalent to that which would be obtained by the following stepwise procedure:

1　Regress C on L (with an intercept term) and take the residuals, denoted as $\widetilde{C}_t$; $t = 1, 2, \ldots, n$.
2　Regress D on L (with an intercept term) and take the residuals, denoted as $\widetilde{D}_t$; $t = 1, 2, \ldots, n$.
3　Use $\widetilde{C}$ and $\widetilde{D}$ in the formula

$$\hat{\beta}_2 = \Sigma \widetilde{D}_t \widetilde{C}_t / \Sigma \widetilde{D}_t^2 \qquad (3.3.13)$$

The residuals from the regression of C on L represent a component of the observations on consumers' expenditure that cannot be explained by the variation in liquid asset holdings, and which therefore has to be explained, if possible, by the behaviour of disposable income. Similarly, the residuals from the regression of D on L represent a component of the observations on disposable income that cannot be explained by the behaviour of liquid asset holdings. This last statement does not depend on any direction of causality, between D and L, that we may subsequently want to consider outside the partial model represented by equation 3.3.12. Indeed, it does not depend on there being any true underlying relationship between D and L. The use of the residuals $\widetilde{D}_t$; $t = 1, 2, \ldots, n$ merely represents an attempt to measure a component of the observations on disposable income which is not associated with corresponding changes in liquid asset holdings. It is by using only this 'pure' component of disposable income that the estimation procedure attempts to isolate the effects of a change in income *ceteris paribus*.

To illustrate the example in a more practical manner, we can estimate the parameters of the model 3.3.12, using the data of exercise 3.3. A direct three variable regression gives the estimated equation

$$\hat{C}_t = 7 \cdot 380 + 0 \cdot 6911 D_t + 0 \cdot 1276 L_t; t = 1, 2, \ldots, n$$

In this equation, the estimate of β_2 is supposed to be the same as that obtained by the following steps.

1 Compute residuals from a regression of C on L, with an intercept. By performing this two variable regression, the equation defining the appropriate residuals is found to be

$$\widetilde{C}_t = C_t + 3 \cdot 37401 - 1 \cdot 28791 L_t; t = 1, 2, \ldots, n$$

2 Compute residuals from a regression of D on L, with an intercept. By performing this two variable regression, the equation defining the appropriate residuals is found to be

$$\widetilde{D}_t = D_t + 15 \cdot 5604 - 1 \cdot 67881 L_t; t = 1, 2, \ldots, n$$

3 Perform a regression of $\widetilde{C}$ on $\widetilde{D}$, with no intercept: this simply means using the residuals $\widetilde{C}$ and $\widetilde{D}$ in the formula

$$\beta_2 = \Sigma \widetilde{D}_t \widetilde{C}_t / \Sigma \widetilde{D}_t^2$$

Although it is somewhat tedious to do so when working by hand, one can use the equations for $\widetilde{C}$ and $\widetilde{D}$ to compute a series of values for $\widetilde{C}_t$ and $\widetilde{D}_t$; $t = 1, 2, \ldots, n$. These values can then be used to evaluate $\Sigma \widetilde{D}_t \widetilde{C}_t$ and $\Sigma \widetilde{D}_t^2$. The results are $\Sigma \widetilde{D}_t \widetilde{C}_t = 650 \cdot 888$ and $\Sigma \widetilde{D}_t^2 = 941 \cdot 753$. Using these in the formula for $\hat{\beta}_2$, we obtain

$$\hat{\beta}_2 = 650 \cdot 888 / 941 \cdot 753 = 0 \cdot 6911$$

This confirms the assertion that the estimate of β_2, obtained from the three variable regression, is equivalent to that obtained by the stepwise procedure outlined above.

We now summarize the results of this section. The problem to hand is that of establishing the effect on a dependent variable Y of a unit change in a single explanatory variable X_j *ceteris paribus*. The method used to obtain an estimate of the parameter β_j is that of multiple regression of Y on all the explanatory variables. In the course of the multiple regression calculation, the observations on X_j are effectively 'adjusted for' the presence of the other explanatory variables, and the outcome is equivalent to that obtained by first taking the residuals from a regression of X_j on the other explanatory variables and then using only this 'pure' component of X_j in a formula like 3.3.11. Hence multiple regression implicitly involves an attempt to isolate a component of each explanatory variable, in which all observed changes would be interpreted as changes in that variable *ceteris paribus*. Since virtually any regression run between the explanatory variables would give coefficients that are not exactly zero, the adjustment of X_j will almost invariably make some difference to the estimate obtained. It is theoretically possible for a two variable regression of Y on X_j (and X_1) to give the same estimate for β_j as that obtained from a multiple regression of Y on $X_1, X_2, \ldots, X_j, \ldots, X_k$, but the type of observations that would give rise to this would usually be generated only under laboratory conditions, and economics is not an experimental science. So, in practice, multiple regression has to be used to obtain the parameter estimates.

One final comment is necessary. We have not yet considered the possibility that there is no unique solution to the equations which define the estimators. Our interpretation of the estimation procedure will explain why this situation might arise. If the behaviour of a single explanatory variable X_j can be predicted exactly by means of a regression of X_j on one or more of the other explanatory variables, the residuals, $\widetilde{X}_{jt}$; $t = 1, 2, \ldots, n$ would all take the value zero. There is then no 'pure' variation in X_j on which to base an estimate of the parameter β_j: trying to solve equations 3.2.1 is then equivalent to trying to base an estimate on data which do not exist, and it is not surprising that the estimate does not exist either. Equation 3.3.11 is equivalent to the calculation that is attempted and, if $\tilde{X}_{jt} = 0; t = 1, 2, \ldots, n$, it follows that

$$\hat{\beta}_j = \Sigma \tilde{X}_{jt} \tilde{Y}_t / \Sigma \tilde{X}_{jt}^2 = 0/0$$

The division of zero by zero is an undefined operation and there is no meaningful numerical result. The precise step at which the computer solution would fail depends on the design of the program used, but the outcome would be that it is not possible to obtain a full set of parameter estimates.

Fortunately, the complete breakdown of the estimation procedure is rare with a properly specified model, but there can be problems when there is very little 'pure' variation in X_j. We shall consider these problems in section 3.10. There is one case in which the estimation procedure will definitely fail. At least two observations on the variables are needed to estimate the parameters of the two variable model and, in the general case, at least k observations are required. If n is less than k, the estimation procedure will fail and, in practice, n should be considerably greater than k if satisfactory estimates are to be obtained.

3.4 Multiple correlation

In Section 2.2 the simple correlation coefficient was used as a measure of the extent to which the behaviour of the dependent variable is explained by the behaviour of a single genuine explanatory variable. This is specific to the two variable case, and we shall now take a slightly different approach in an attempt to find a measure that can be used with any linear model, irrespective of the number of explanatory variables.

A regression calculation effectively splits the set of observations on the dependent variable into two components, the predicted values and the residuals. In the k variable model, the predicted values are

$$\hat{Y}_t = \hat{\beta}_1 + \hat{\beta}_2 X_{2t} + \ldots + \hat{\beta}_j X_{jt} + \ldots + \hat{\beta}_k X_{kt}; t = 1, 2, \ldots, n$$

$$(3.4.1)$$

and the residuals are

$$e_t = Y_t - \hat{\beta}_1 - \hat{\beta}_2 X_{2t} - \ldots - \hat{\beta}_j X_{jt} - \ldots - \hat{\beta}_k X_{kt}; t = 1, 2, \ldots, n$$

$$(3.4.2)$$

The predicted values represent a component of the observations on the dependent variable that can be explained as an exact linear function of the explanatory variable observations. The residuals represent a component of the dependent variable observations that is still unexplained, after taking account of the behaviour of the explanatory variables. A single quantity which can act as a measure of the extent to which the estimated relationship fails to explain the behaviour of the dependent variable is provided by the residual sum of squares, Σe_t^2. A relatively high value of Σe_t^2 would indicate a low degree of explanation and a relatively low value would indicate a good explanation. Unfortunately, without some form of scaling, it is very difficult to judge whether a given value is of Σe_t^2 is high or low. Moreover, Σe_t^2 is a measure of 'badness' of fit: what we require is a measure that will increase in value as the fit is improved.

To find an appropriate scale factor, we need to consider a particularly useful property of the residual sum of squares: whenever an explanatory variable is removed from a given model and the least squares calculation is repeated for the modified relationship, the residual sum of squares increases or, strictly speaking, it does not decrease. Conversely, when an explanatory variable is added to a given model, the residual sum of squares will generally decrease and certainly cannot increase. To see why this should be so, consider the following argument.

In a regression of Y on $X_1, X_2, \ldots, X_k$, the regression coefficients take those values which minimize the sum of squared residuals. It is very unusual, with economic data, to find coefficients which are exactly zero; this means that, apart from special and highly unlikely cases, zero is not a value that should be assigned to any coefficient if one wishes to minimize the sum of squared residuals. The significance of this result is that coefficients are implicitly restricted to zero when explanatory variables are deleted from a particular equation and the modified relationship is re-estimated. By the argument above, this must lead to a value of the residual sum of squares which is greater than (or equal to) that previously attained. In particular, if all the genuine explanatory variables are removed, we are left with a regression of Y on the artificial variable X_1. It was shown in equation 3.3.5 that a regression of Y on X_1 produces residuals which are simply deviations of the dependent variable observations from the sample mean. Hence, in the case of a regression of Y on X_1, the residual sum of squares is Σy_t^2, where $y_t = Y_t - \overline{Y}$; $t = 1, 2, \ldots, n$. In all other cases, we continue to denote the residual sum of squares as Σe_t^2. Since the regression defining Σy_t^2 can be obtained by deleting all the genuine explanatory variables from the regression defining Σe_t^2, we may apply the general result concerning the deletion of variables to tell us that

$$\Sigma e_t^2 \leqslant \Sigma y_t^2 \qquad (3.4.3)$$

The one necessary qualification on this result is that the regression defining Σe_t^2 must include the artificial variable X_1.

Given the inequality 3.4.3, we can now obtain an appropriate scaling for Σe_t^2. Since $\Sigma e_t^2 \leqslant \Sigma y_t^2$ and since both quantities are sums of squares, which are therefore non-negative, we have

$$\Sigma e_t^2 \geqslant 0$$

and

$$\Sigma e_t^2 \leqslant \Sigma y_t^2$$

or

$$0 \leqslant \Sigma e_t^2 \leqslant \Sigma y_t^2 \qquad (3.4.4)$$

Except in the meaningless special case in which Σy_t^2 is zero, the inequalities in 3.4.4 can be rewritten as

$$0 \leqslant \Sigma e_t^2 / \Sigma y_t^2 \leqslant 1 \qquad (3.4.5)$$

Finally, if $\Sigma e_t^2 / \Sigma y_t^2$ lies in the interval 0 to 1, it must follow that $1 - \Sigma e_t^2 / \Sigma y_t^2$ also lies in the interval 0 to 1, and this provides our measure of goodness of fit. The required statistic is

$$R^2 = 1 - \Sigma e_t^2 / \Sigma y_t^2 \qquad (3.4.6)$$

The notation R^2 is conventional and the measure is often described literally as *R squared*. Alternative descriptions are the *squared multiple correlation coefficient* and the somewhat old-fashioned *coefficient of determination*.

The interpretation of R^2 is as follows. The quantity Σy_t^2 summarizes, in a single measure, the extent to which the behaviour of the dependent variable is not explained by the artificial variable X_1. After the addition of the genuine explanatory variables X_2 to X_k, the quantum of unexplained behaviour is reduced to Σe_t^2. One can therefore interpret the difference $\Sigma y_t^2 - \Sigma e_t^2$ as the increment of explanation due to the addition of the genuine explanatory variables. The best possible outcome from the addition of X_2 to X_k would be a perfect fit. In this case the residuals would be zero, the residual sum of squares would be zero and $R^2 = 1$. At the other extreme, if the addition of X_2 to X_k achieves no increment of explanation, then $\Sigma e_t^2 = \Sigma y_t^2$ and $R^2 = 0$. In between the two extremes, R^2 expresses the actual increment of explanation as a proportion of the maximum possible increment, which is Σy_t^2. Hence

$$R^2 = (\Sigma y_t^2 - \Sigma e_t^2)/\Sigma y_t^2 = 1 - \Sigma e_t^2/\Sigma y_t^2$$

This is obviously identical to equation 3.4.6.

Not surprisingly, there is a connection between R^2 and the simple correlation coefficient defined in Section 2.2. If one were to compute a value for R^2 in the two variable case, the value obtained would be the square of the simple (or zero order) correlation coefficient r. In the general case, R^2 is still the square of a correlation coefficient, but the coefficient is no longer of a simple kind. There are actually several distinct types of correlation measure, which differ according to the way in which individual explanatory variables are treated. Thus R^2 is a measure which assumes the presence of an intercept term, but which 'gives no credit' for the explanation achieved by the artificial variable X_1. In order to obtain a value for R^2 which is greater than zero, the genuine explanatory variables X_2 to X_k must explain a part of the behaviour of the dependent variable that is not already explained by X_1. One would usually use R^2 as a measure of goodness of fit precisely because it does have this characteristic. The explanation achieved by X_1 adds nothing to our understanding of the economic forces which help to determine the value of the dependent variable, and R^2 is a

---

Technical note 4

The quantity Σy_t^2 is sometimes described as the *total sum of squares* and the increment $\Sigma y_t^2 - \Sigma e_t^2$ as the *explained sum of squares*. It is then true, by definition, that

$$\text{total SS} = \text{explained SS} + \text{residual SS} \qquad (3.4.7)$$

On the other hand, the explained sum of squares can also be defined as

$$\text{explained SS} = \sum_{j=2}^{j=k} (\hat{\beta}_j \Sigma_t x_{jt} y_t)$$

in which case equation 3.4.7 depends on being able to show that

$$\Sigma y_t^2 - \Sigma e_t^2 = \sum_{j=2}^{j=k} (\hat{\beta}_j \Sigma_t x_{jt} y_t)$$

This last statement is true provided that the model does have an intercept term.

measure which reflects this since it takes a value greater than zero only when the genuine explanatory variables do actually add something to the explanation achieved.

Now consider what is meant by saying that R^2 is used on the assumption that there is an intercept term in the model. If the artificial variable X_1 is not present, the inequality 3.4.3 is no longer valid and the value obtained for R^2 can be negative. This can only happen when there is a poor fit to the observed data, which would be discouraging in itself, but a negative value for R^2 could make one think that something has gone disastrously wrong with the calculation and, perhaps, that the computer program is incorrect. In fact, although R^2 must still be less than (or equal to) 1, a negative value is possible when there is no intercept in the model.

One could obtain a correctly scaled measure, in the absence of an intercept, by using the 'gross' sum of squares ΣY_t^2 in place of the 'deviation' sum of squares Σy_t^2. The argument would be that, if the model excludes X_1, the variables that are present have to explain, where possible, all departures of the dependent variable observations from zero, not just departures from the sample mean. The quantity ΣY_t^2 can be interpreted as the residual sum of squares from a regression in which there are no explanatory variables of any kind. This may seem to be a frivolous point, but it does enable us to use the type of argument employed earlier, to show that Σe_t^2 is always less than (or equal to) ΣY_t^2, whether the model contains an intercept or not. This suggests a statistic which, for want of a better notation, can be written as R_0^2 and which is defined as

$$R_0^2 = 1 - \Sigma e_t^2 / \Sigma Y_t^2 \qquad (3.4.8)$$

In practice this statistic is not widely used, because one cannot compare a value for R_0^2, obtained from a model with no intercept, with a value of R^2, obtained from an otherwise equivalent model which does have an intercept. Thus many authors report values of R^2 for both types of model, a procedure which is acceptable for descriptive purposes but which is definitely not acceptable if the correlation measure is subsequently used for hypothesis testing.

The discussion above provides two examples of correlation measures that can be defined with reference to a given list of variables, but there are many other possibilities. Formally, all squared multiple, partial and 'zero order' coefficients can be expressed as special cases of a general form that can be written as

$$\widetilde{R}^2 = 1 - S_1/S_2 \qquad (3.4.9)$$

The quantities S_1 and S_2 are residual sums of squares from appropriately defined regression equations and are such that $S_1 \leqslant S_2$. We shall not pursue this point, but it should be noted that, from now on, when we talk of correlation, we use the term in a general sense. In particular, we do not always mean correlation of a type that would be adequately measured by a simple correlation coefficient. It should also be noted that the use of correlation measures is not confined to cases which involve the dependent variable. One could also compute coefficients measuring the association between the explanatory variables, and measures of this kind are used in Section 3.10. But there is an important difference between measures that involve the dependent variable and those that do not. Under the assumptions of our underlying model, the observations on the dependent variable have a random component, whereas those on the explanatory variables are considered to be non-random. So a coefficient involving Y is a realization of a random variable: a coefficient involving only the X variables is nonrandom and is a purely numerical measure of association.

To conclude this section, there are some further comments to be made concerning the use of R^2. It is often the case that one is faced with two alternative explanations of the behaviour of the dependent variable. Subject to certain qualifications, it is reasonable to choose the relationship with the highest value of R^2. An important requirement is that both alternatives must be equally acceptable in terms of economic interpretation. Statistical criteria alone cannot identify a valid economic model. Next, it must be remembered that R^2 is a measure based on the dependent variable observations and so it is a random variable: to some extent, the value obtained depends on the particular sample of observations used. Finally, there is a problem caused by the fact that R^2 will always increase (strictly, cannot decrease) as variables are added to the model, and so it is always possible to achieve an apparent improvement by expanding the list of explanatory variables, even when the added variables do not seem to be particularly relevant. The reason for this can be seen by recalling the definition of R^2. As variables are added to the model, Σe_t^2 will almost always decrease and certainly cannot increase, but Σy_t^2 will remain the same. So $\Sigma e_t^2 / \Sigma y_t^2$ is reduced and R^2 is increased. Because R^2 has this property, an alternative measure is sometimes used. This measure, denoted as $\bar{R}^2$, involves a penalty weighting for the number of explanatory variables:

$$\bar{R}^2 = 1 - [(1 - R^2)(n - 1)/(n - k)] \qquad (3.4.10)$$

For given values of R^2 and n, the higher the value of k, the number of explanatory variables, the lower is the value of $\bar{R}^2$. Although $\bar{R}^2$ is less than 1, it is not necessarily greater than zero and, for very poor fits, negative values can be observed.

3.5 Nonlinear relationships

We have described a method of estimation, for linear models, without a detailed consideration of the characteristic of a linear model that enables the method to be used. It is fairly obvious that it must be possible to write the model in the standard form

$$Y_t = \beta_1 + \beta_2 X_{2t} + \ldots + \beta_j X_{jt} + \ldots + \beta_k X_{kt} + u_t; t = 1, 2, \ldots, n$$

$$(3.5.1)$$

but there is no reason whatsoever why Y and $X_j; j = 2, 3, \ldots, k$ should represent economic variables in exactly the form in which they are originally observed. To illustrate this point, consider the following alternative specifications for the consumption function:

$$C_t = \beta_1 + \beta_2 \sqrt{(D_t)} + u_t; t = 1, 2, \ldots, n$$
$$C_t = \beta_1 + \beta_2 D_t + \beta_3 D_t^2 + u_t; t = 1, 2, \ldots, n$$
$$\log C_t = \beta_1 + \beta_2 \log D_t + u_t; t = 1, 2, \ldots, n$$

In each case the underlying relationship between C and D is nonlinear, but it is still possible to estimate the parameters by application of the standard least squares method. Obviously this statement requires some elaboration and, in this section, we consider a number of questions raised by the use of linear least squares, in the context of models which are nonlinear in the original economic variables.

Of the examples considered above, only the logarithmic form is widely used in practice. Despite this, it is convenient to start with an example that does not involve a transformation of the dependent variable and so the first case that we consider is that in which the underlying relationship is

$$C = \beta_1 + \beta_2 D + \beta_3 D^2 \tag{3.5.2}$$

This equation involves only two economic variables, consumption and income, but income enters both as D and as D^2. Obviously, the relationship between C and D is not linear. The graph is drawn in Figure 8 on the assumption that β_1 and β_2 are positive, β_3 is negative and β_2 is considerably greater than $-\beta_3$. From the graph it can be seen that, as

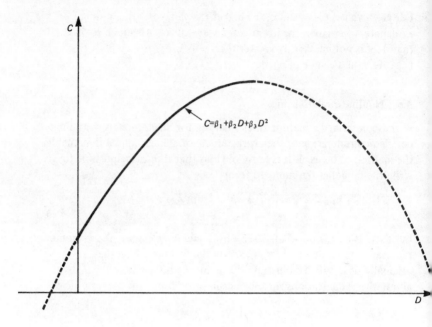

Figure 8

income is increased, the marginal propensity to consume (the slope of the curve) decreases, at least for a range of income values on the left of the curve. Of course, if β_3 is zero, equation 3.5.2 reduces to a linear relationship between C and D and, in principle, one could use a model based on equation 3.5.2 to test whether the marginal propensity to consume does vary with income. If β_3 turned out to be significantly different from zero, this would indeed be the case, at least in so far as one could accept the validity of the underlying model.

Turning now to the question of estimation, the crucial point is that it is possible to express a model, based on equation 3.5.2, in the standard form 3.5.1, even though the underlying relationship is non-linear in the variables C and D. To do this, we would set $Y = C$, $X_2 = D$ and $X_3 = D^2$. The observations used would then be consumption, income and the square of income, and X_3 would not represent an economic variable as originally observed. But since equation 3.5.2 can be written into the standard form, given suitable definitions for the variables, the linear least squares method can be used to generate parameter estimates. The formal requirement is that the normal equations should still be linear in the parameter estimators, $\hat{\beta}_j$; $j = 1, 2, \ldots, k$

and, in the example above, this would certainly be the case.

To illustrate the example in a more practical way, the data of exercise 3.3 have been used to create a set of observations on D^2 from the given observations on D, and the augmented data set has then been used to perform a three variable regression of C on D and D^2, with an intercept. This gives the estimated relationship

$$\hat{C}_t = -19 \cdot 738 + 1 \cdot 651 D_t - 0 \cdot 0067 D_t^2; t = 1, 2, \ldots, n$$

The coefficient on D^2 looks rather small, but it can be shown that β_3 is significantly different from zero, using a t test procedure which is very similar to that used in the two variable case. This procedure is discussed further in Section 3.6. For the moment, we simply note that $\hat{\beta}_3$ is negative and that $\hat{\beta}_2$ is considerably greater than $-\hat{\beta}_3$. However, the intercept is also negative and, in this respect, the estimated equation differs from the function sketched in Figure 8. Whereas it seemed reasonable, a priori, to draw the graph in such a way that, at zero income, the implied consumption level would be positive, the estimated equation does not support this assumption. It is worth considering briefly whether this is an important limitation on the results obtained.

In Figure 8 some portions of the curve are shown by dotted lines. This is intended to signify that there are ranges of the variables for which the relationship is defined in mathematical terms, but for which there is no real economic meaning (negative values for consumption or income) or for which the approximation to economic behaviour is no longer appropriate (the downward sloping part of the curve). It is perfectly reasonable to use a portion of the curve, corresponding to points that can actually be observed, as the basis of a model, so long as one does not attempt to draw conclusions by extrapolating well away from the observed points. Similar reasoning applies to the use of a linear relationship. A linear approximation may be reasonable for values of the variables close to those observed in practice, but it can be dangerous to extrapolate too far from this part of the estimated line. This is one reason why the intercept estimate is often of limited interest. It can be misleading to attach any real significance to the mathematical interpretation of the intercept as the value of the dependent variable that would hold when all the explanatory variables are zero: this point is usually well away from available observations on the variables. Hence we should not be unduly concerned about the fact that our example produces a negative intercept when, in drawing the graph, it did seem reasonable to assume that the intercept would be positive. By imposing a particular curvature in the region of the observed data, we have produced an estimated relationship which does not intersect the consumption axis at a positive consumption level. But this point of intersection is well away from the values observed in practice.

One method of transformation that is frequently used is to express the data in terms of logarithms of the original variables. The type of logarithms most frequently used for performing calculations are to base 10, but in economic modelling one would usually employ natural logarithms, which use the mathematical constant e as the base. Logarithms have the following properties:

1 log a is not defined when a is negative.
2 For any positive number a and any number b,

$$\log (a^b) = b \log a$$

3 For any two positive numbers a and c,

$$\log (ac) = \log a + \log c$$

These properties hold for all logarithms, irrespective of the base used, but in all our applications it is to be understood that log signifies a logarithm to base e.

Before proceeding any further, there is one characteristic of a logarithmic relationship that we should mention. Consider the example

$$\log Y = \alpha + \beta \log X$$

In this equation, the parameter β measures the effect on log Y of a unit change in log X. This corresponds to the elasticity of Y with respect to changes in X and, in the case of a relationship that is linear in logarithms, the elasticity is a constant which does not vary with changes in X. In an equation which is linear in original variables, such as

$$Y = a + bX$$

the elasticity is $b(X/Y)$, and this does vary with X. A similar interpretation holds for k variable relationships, the only difference being that, if the relationship is linear in logarithms, the parameters now represent partial elasticities.

Instead of using yet another version of the consumption function, we now change the example by considering the relationship between the demand for real money balances M and the rate of interest r. To simplify, other relevant variables are ignored. In one version of the

IS–LM model, a shape similar to that in Figure 9 is assumed for this relationship. The change in M associated with a given change in r is not thought of as constant over the range of r and, in particular, it is argued that as the interest rate falls to a given low level, the demand for money rises sharply and becomes very large. To capture this behaviour, the equation of the curve shown in Figure 9 is

$$M = a(r - 2)^b \tag{3.5.3}$$

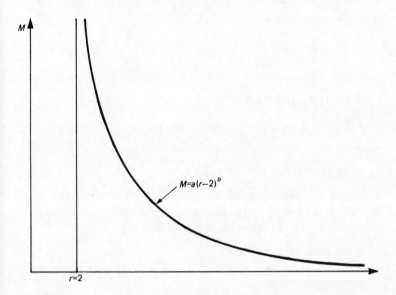

Figure 9

Technical note 5

If $Y = \mathrm{fn}(X)$, the elasticity of Y with respect to X is

$$\epsilon = (\mathrm{d}Y/\mathrm{d}X)(X/Y)$$

An alternative but equivalent expression is

$$\epsilon = \mathrm{d} \log Y / \mathrm{d} \log X$$

A similar definition holds for partial elasticities, the only difference being that $\mathrm{d}Y/\mathrm{d}X$ would be replaced by an appropriate partial derivative.

where a is positive and b is negative. It is implicit in this equation that r cannot fall below 2 per cent and that, as r approaches 2, M would become very large. The equation is certainly nonlinear in the variables, but now we also have nonlinearity in the way in which the parameters enter the relationship and it is not possible to use equation 3.5.3, as it stands, as the basis for a model in which the parameters are to be estimated by the linear least squares method. However, by applying the log transformation to both sides of the equation and adding a disturbance term, it is possible to obtain a model in the standard linear form. The steps are as follows:

$$\log M = \log [a(r-2)^b]$$
$$= \log a + \log [(r-2)^b]$$

or

$$\log M = \log a + b \log (r-2) \qquad (3.5.4)$$

If $Y = \log M$, $X_2 = \log (r-2)$, $\beta_1 = \log a$ and $\beta_2 = b$, the transformed model can be written, with a disturbance term, as

$$Y_t = \beta_1 + \beta_2 X_{2t} + u_t; t = 1, 2, \ldots, n$$

The linear estimation method, applied to the transformed model, will produce estimators for β_1 and β_2, which can then be used to produce estimators for a and b, using the relationships

$$\log \hat{a} = \hat{\beta}_1, \text{ so that } \hat{a} = \exp (\hat{\beta}_1)$$

and

$$\hat{b} = \hat{\beta}_2$$

There is one important qualification that should be mentioned here. In the example above, the linear form was obtained by transformation of both variables and parameters and any properties that may be obtained for the estimators from a linear model would apply to the transformed parameters, but not necessarily to the original parameters. The parameter b in equation 3.5.3 is a special case, because the transformation of the original relationship does not alter b in any way. The parameter a is transformed and any properties of linear estimators apply to $\log \hat{a}$ but not necessarily to $\hat{a}$ itself. It should also be noted that the disturbance has been attached to the transformed relationship, and it is this disturbance that would have to satisfy the usual assumptions.

Since equation 3.5.3 represents a somewhat naïve hypothesis, it would be interesting to see whether any sensible result can be obtained using 'real' data. In exercise 3.4 the reader is asked to estimate the parameters of a model which is based on equation 3.3.5 but which contains a number of additional variables. Although some material from the next section is needed to evaluate the results properly, the exercise does provide an opportunity to experiment with data transformations, prior to using the linear least squares method.

In specifying the relationship between M and r, a specific pattern of behaviour has been imposed on the model, based on a prior assumption about the rate of interest at which the demand for money would theoretically be infinite. This level was assumed to be 2 per cent, which explains the use of the term $r - 2$ in equation 3.5.3. If, instead of assuming a level of 2 per cent, we had decided to estimate the appropriate value from given data, the equation would become

$$M = a(r - c)^b \qquad (3.5.5)$$

where a, b and c are parameters. The complete model based on the transformed relationship would now be

$$\log M_t = \log a + b \log (r_t - c) + u_t; t = 1, 2, \ldots, n \qquad (3.5.6)$$

and it would no longer be possible to define $\log (r - c)$ as an observable variable, to be denoted by X_2, because this term depends on the unknown quantity c. There is now no way in which the transformed relationship can be written so as to correspond to the standard form for a linear model and, although one could still try to find the estimates which minimize the sum of squared residuals, this criterion would no longer lead to a set of equations which are linear in the parameter estimates. There are methods for searching for solutions in the truly nonlinear case, but such methods are beyond the scope of this book. The only way in which we could proceed, within our present framework, is to perform a whole series of regressions for different values of the parameter c, finally choosing the set of estimates for a, b and c which correspond to the regression having the smallest residual sum of squares. For various reasons, including the fact that there ought to be some additional explanatory variables, it would not be sensible to attempt this exercise on the model as it stands. Moreover, one would need to be a little cautious about the interpretation to be attached to an estimate of c, bearing in mind our earlier comments concerning estimates which refer to values of variables outside the range for which observations are made. But, to show that it is possible to use a simple search over possible values of c, we have used the data of exercise 3.4 to produce the relationship

$$\log M = -1\cdot57 - 0\cdot19 \log(r - 3\cdot73) + 1\cdot10 \log Y - 0\cdot28 \log P$$

where Y is total final expenditure and P is the price level. The implied value of c is $3\cdot73$: this corresponds to the lowest observed value of the residual sum of squares in a series of experiments, each involving a different value of c.

From the discussion in this section, it is apparent that the basic least squares method is rather more powerful than it might appear, at first sight, to be. Some nonlinear relationships can be transformed to give an equation for estimation which is in standard linear form, although in other cases the problem is intrinsically nonlinear and requires an iterative solution method. Since it is often necessary to transform the observed economic variables, it is very useful if the computer program used for estimation has the facility for performing simple transformations. But it must be remembered that, when the calculation is performed on a transformed relationship, it is this relationship that is treated as though it were a linear model. Thus, in the example of the demand for money function, the computed value of R^2 would measure the proportion of variation in $\log M$ that is explained by a relationship in which the explanatory variables are also in logarithmic form. This is not the same as the proportion of variation in M explained by using the implied parameter estimates in the original equation. It is very important to remember this when comparing the fit between two versions of a model in which the dependent variable enters in different forms. If, in one case, the dependent variable is in logarithmic form and, in a different version, the dependent variable is in original form, the R^2 values are not comparable. Although the method of transformation is very convenient, one does have to pay attention to the implications of using the transformed relationship as the basis for estimation.

3.6　Properties of the estimators

We now consider the statistical properties of the parameter estimators in the context of the k variable linear model. The disturbances are assumed to behave exactly as in the two variable case, the explanatory variable observations are still treated as nonrandom quantities, and the only additional assumption required is that it must actually be possible to solve the equations which define the estimators. Given these assumptions, it can be shown that each parameter estimator $\hat{\beta}_j; j = 1, 2, \ldots, k$ is best linear unbiased and normal. We did not prove all the corresponding properties in the two variable case, but it was possible to obtain the expectation, variance and distribution of the least squares slope estimator by appealing to some results on linear functions of random variables. It does seem reasonable to suppose that similar properties will hold in the general case, because any single estimator derived on the basis of the k variable model has the same general form as the slope estimator used in the two variable case. The general form is

$$\hat{\beta}_j = \Sigma \widetilde{X}_{jt} \widetilde{Y}_t / \Sigma \widetilde{X}_{jt}^2 \qquad (3.6.1)$$

where $\widetilde{X}_j$ and $\widetilde{Y}$ represent variables defined as residuals from the regressions of X_j and Y, respectively, on the other explanatory variables. The statistical properties can be derived by using equation 3.6.1 to express $\hat{\beta}_j$ in terms of the disturbances. The general form for this expression is

$$\hat{\beta}_j = \beta_j + \Sigma \widetilde{X}_{jt} u_t / \Sigma \widetilde{X}_{jt}^2 \qquad (3.6.2)$$

Since this is obviously a linear function of random disturbances, one can use the methods of Sections 2.3–2.5 to show that, for each $\hat{\beta}_j$; $j = 1, 2, \ldots, k$

$$E(\hat{\beta}_j) = \beta_j \qquad (3.6.3)$$

$$\text{var}\,(\hat{\beta}_j) = \sigma^2 / \Sigma \widetilde{X}_{jt}^2 \qquad (3.6.4)$$

$$\hat{\beta}_j \sim N(\beta_j, \sigma^2 / \Sigma \widetilde{X}_{jt}^2) \qquad (3.6.5)$$

These results suggest that the arguments used in Chapter 2 are based on a special case of the general form and, if this is so, it is not surprising to find that equivalent properties hold in the general case.

Now remember how the properties are applied when the two variable model is used. The slope estimator, which would now be written as $\hat{\beta}_2$, has a normal distribution and a standard error which, when based on an estimated disturbance variance, is given by

$$\text{se}\,(\hat{\beta}_2) = \hat{\sigma} / \sqrt{\Sigma x_{2t}^2}$$

where

$$\hat{\sigma}^2 = \Sigma e_t^2 / (n - 2)$$

An approximate 95 per cent confidence interval for the true parameter is then given by

$$\hat{\beta}_2 \pm 2\,\text{se}\,(\hat{\beta}_2)$$

When the number of observations is relatively small, this interval will contain the true parameter with a probability of rather less than 0·95 and, to obtain an exact 95 per cent confidence interval, one should use a critical value taken from the t distribution with $n - 2$ degrees of freedom. In the k variable model the parameter estimator $\hat{\beta}_j$ still has a normal distribution, and one can still obtain an approximate confidence interval as

$$\hat{\beta}_j \pm 2 \; \text{se} \; (\hat{\beta}_j) \tag{3.6.6}$$

The difference is that the standard error is now defined as

$$\text{se} \; (\hat{\beta}_j) = \hat{\sigma}/\sqrt{\Sigma \widetilde{X}_{jt}^2} \tag{3.6.7}$$

where

$$\hat{\sigma}^2 = \Sigma e_t^2/(n - k) \tag{3.6.8}$$

Although the forms for the standard error, the disturbance variance estimator and the confidence interval are similar to those used in the two variable case, the denominator in the standard error is modified and there are now k parameters to be estimated before the residuals can be obtained. This indicates that the residual sum of squares is now associated with $n - k$ degrees of freedom. In all other respects, the argument for the use of the t distribution parallels that given in Sections 2.7 and 2.8, but the resulting t distribution now has $n - k$ degrees of freedom rather than $n - 2$. An exact 95 per cent confidence interval for β_j is thus given by

$$\hat{\beta}_j \pm t_{n-k}^{0.025} \; \text{se} \; (\hat{\beta}_j) \tag{3.6.9}$$

From now on, we shall generally assume that the coefficients and standard errors would be obtained as part of the computer output, but there is one case (apart from $k = 2$) in which hand calculations are sometimes used for illustrative purposes. If $k = 3$ and $X_{1t} = 1; t = 1, 2, \ldots, n$, one can analyse the behaviour of the slope estimators by adjusting the data for sample means and then using the two equations 3.2.7 to find values for $\hat{\beta}_2$ and $\hat{\beta}_3$. In this special case, the standard errors for the slope estimators are

$$\text{se} \; (\hat{\beta}_2) = \hat{\sigma}/\sqrt{\Sigma \widetilde{X}_{2t}^2}$$

and

$$\text{se} \; (\hat{\beta}_3) = \hat{\sigma}/\sqrt{\Sigma \widetilde{X}_{3t}^2}$$

where

$$\Sigma \widetilde{X}_{2t}^2 = \Sigma x_{2t}^2 - [(\Sigma x_{2t} x_{3t})^2/\Sigma x_{3t}^2] \tag{3.6.10}$$

$$\Sigma \widetilde{X}_{3t}^2 = \Sigma x_{3t}^2 - [(\Sigma x_{2t} x_{3t})^2/\Sigma x_{2t}^2] \tag{3.6.11}$$

$$\hat{\sigma}^2 = \Sigma e_t^2/(n - 3)$$

and

$$\Sigma e_t^2 = \Sigma y_t^2 - \hat{\beta}_2 \Sigma x_{2t} y_t - \hat{\beta}_3 \Sigma x_{3t} y_t \qquad (3.6.12)$$

It should be easy for the reader to verify equations 3.6.10 and 3.6.11, bearing in mind that $\Sigma \widetilde{X}_{2t}^2$ and $\Sigma \widetilde{X}_{3t}^2$ can each be defined as the residual sum of squares from a two variable regression.

We now consider the way in which the results of an econometric estimation exercise are reported. The first point to note is that one seldom sees explicit confidence intervals, although the information necessary to compute such intervals is available. The estimated equation is written with the standard errors given in brackets underneath each coefficient, although some authors give t test statistics instead. As we shall see below, either format will provide the information needed. One would also expect to find the value of R^2, or $\bar{R}^2$ and either the residual sum of squares or the disturbance variance estimate, together with at least one other test statistic that we shall discuss in due course. For reporting purposes, we shall use the abbreviations RSS for the residual sum of squares and VAR for the disturbance variance estimate. We shall also give standard errors, rather than t statistics, in the brackets underneath each coefficient.

To illustrate the reporting conventions, we now provide further details concerning the estimation of parameters in the model

$$C_t = \beta_1 + \beta_2 D_t + \beta_3 L_t + u_t; t = 1, 2, \ldots, n \qquad (3.6.13)$$

where C is real consumers' expenditure, D is real personal disposable income and L is real liquid asset holdings in the personal sector. Using the data of exercise 3.3, which relates to the UK economy for the years 1963–80, we obtain the estimated equation

$$\hat{C} = 7 \cdot 38 + 0 \cdot 691D + 0 \cdot 128L; \quad 1963{-}80$$
$$\quad (2 \cdot 20) \ (0 \cdot 021) \quad (0 \cdot 056)$$
$$\text{RSS} = 6 \cdot 398 \quad \text{VAR} = 0 \cdot 427 \quad R^2 = 0 \cdot 992$$

Since there are 18 observations, there are $18 - 3 = 15$ degrees of freedom and, from Table B (p. 269), the critical value $t_{15}^{0 \cdot 025}$ is found to be $2 \cdot 13$. Hence an exact 95 per cent confidence interval for the income parameter is $0 \cdot 691 \pm 2 \cdot 13(0 \cdot 021)$, or $0 \cdot 646$ to $0 \cdot 736$. If all the usual assumptions are satisfied, one would be '95 per cent sure' that this interval does contain the true value of the unknown parameter β_2. So, from the information provided, one can obtain a confidence interval. It is also possible to test hypotheses concerning the individual parameters, and we now consider how this is done.

The problem to hand is that of deciding whether an individual parameter β_j is really zero, given that the corresponding estimate is unlikely to reflect this condition exactly. By analogy with the two variable case, one would set up the null hypothesis that β_j is zero and the alternative that β_j is not zero. Then, using the reported parameter estimate and the standard error, one can calculate a value for the t test statistic as

$$t_j = \hat{\beta}_j/\text{se}\,(\hat{\beta}_j) \tag{3.6.14}$$

Obviously, if t statistics are given in place of the standard errors, one can extract the standard errors for use in the calculation of confidence intervals, but one does not need to use equation 3.6.14 to obtain a value for t_j. Assuming a significance level of 0·05, the decision rule would state that a value of t_j outside the interval $-t_{n-k}^{0·025}$ to $+t_{n-k}^{0·025}$ would lead to rejection of the null hypothesis and the conclusion that β_j is different from zero. Alternatively, one might use the approximate critical values -2 and $+2$, recognizing that the significance level is then higher than 0·05, when the sample size is small.

To illustrate the test procedure, consider the null hypothesis that the liquid assets parameter in equation 3.6.13 is really zero, that is, $H_0: \beta_3 = 0$, against $H_a: \beta_3 \neq 0$. Assuming a significance level of 0·05, the critical value is again $t_{15}^{0·025} = 2·13$ and the calculated value of the test statistic is

$$t_3 = \hat{\beta}_3/\text{se}\,(\hat{\beta}_3) = 0·128/0·056 = 2·286$$

Since the value of the test statistic is actually greater than the critical value 2·13, the formal conclusion is that we are able to reject the null hypothesis $\beta_3 = 0$ at the chosen level of significance. However, the calculated value of the test statistic is very close to the critical value and, given that the data set does not contain all that many observations, it might be sensible to conclude that further experimentation is needed. To illustrate the fact that changing the model can produce rather different results, we now consider the following alternative specification:

$$C_t = \beta_1 + \beta_2 D_t + \beta_3 L_t + \beta_4 \Delta P_t + \beta_5 t + u_t; t = 1, 2, \ldots, n \tag{3.6.15}$$

In equation 3.6.15, ΔP is the year-on-year change in the price level and t is time, measured as $t = 1, t = 2, \ldots, t = n$. For this model, the estimated equation is

$$\hat{C} = 16\cdot33 + 0\cdot510D + 0\cdot123L - 0\cdot083\Delta P + 0\cdot448t; \qquad 1963\text{–}80$$
$$(2\cdot00)\ (0\cdot049)\quad (0\cdot044)\quad (0\cdot032)\quad (0\cdot076)$$
$$\text{RSS} = 1\cdot678 \quad \text{VAR} = 0\cdot129 \quad R^2 = 0\cdot998$$

If the t test discussed above is repeated, using the new equation, $t_3 = 2\cdot80$, $t_{13}^{0\cdot025} = 2\cdot16$ and H_0: $\beta_3 = 0$ is now rejected rather more strongly in favour of the alternative $\beta_3 \neq 0$.

In the example shown here, the model has apparently been 'improved' by adding some new variables. In a different case, it may happen that one or more of the t test statistics is well inside the interval $-t_{n-k}^{0\cdot025}$ to $+t_{n-k}^{0\cdot025}$ and, in such a case, it is tempting to delete all the variables for which this is true. In fact, such a procedure would not be correct. Quite apart from the danger of treating a failure to reject as automatically implying acceptance of a given null hypothesis, particularly when there is reason to suspect data deficiency, it has to be recognized that, when a variable is deleted, it is implicitly accepted that the original model is not correct. So, before any further analysis can be performed, it is necessary to re-estimate the parameters associated with the remaining variables and the corresponding standard errors. It is quite possible that this will alter the conclusions to be drawn from the t tests relating to the remaining variables. So, after the estimation of a given relationship, one should never delete more than a single variable on the basis of the associated t statistic.

Suppose now that one variable has been removed, that the new relationship has been estimated and that one of the newly computed t statistics still lies between $-t_{n-k}^{0\cdot025}$ and $+t_{n-k}^{0\cdot025}$. The fact that the model has been re-estimated would seem to answer the objection raised in the previous paragraph, but there is still a problem. The deletion of the first variable could, with a nonzero probability, have been the wrong thing to do. As a result of this, the probabilities of drawing the wrong conclusion in a two step procedure are not exactly those suggested by treating the second step in isolation. There is an alternative way of testing hypotheses concerning two or more parameters, and it is to this that we now turn.

3.7   Tests involving several parameters

Instead of testing a sequence of hypotheses, each concerning one parameter, it is possible to set up a single null hypothesis under which several parameters are simultaneously set to zero. Suppose that we had a model of the form

$$Y_t = \beta_1 + \beta_2 X_{2t} + \beta_3 X_{3t} + \beta_4 X_{4t} + u_t; t = 1, 2, \ldots, n \qquad (3.7.1)$$

and that we wished to test the null hypothesis

$$H_0: \beta_2 = 0 \text{ and } \beta_4 = 0 \qquad (3.7.2)$$

against the alternative that at least one of β_2, β_4 is not zero. Before an appropriate test statistic can be constructed, it is necessary to compute two sets of estimates, the first based on the model 3.7.1 and the second based on the model as it would appear under the conditions of the null hypothesis:

$$Y_t = \beta_1 + 0X_{2t} + \beta_3 X_{3t} + 0X_{4t} + u_t; t = 1, 2, \ldots, n$$

or

$$Y_t = \beta_1 + \beta_3 X_{3t} + u_t; t = 1, 2, \ldots, n \qquad (3.7.3)$$

Even when the null hypothesis is true, the estimates obtained from the two versions of the model will tend to be different, and we now need a notation for the estimators which reflects this fact. Since the second set of estimates is obtained subject to the restrictions that $\beta_2 = 0$ and $\beta_4 = 0$, the estimators obtained from equation 3.7.3 are described as *restricted* estimators, which are denoted generally as $\hat{\beta}_{Rj}; j = 1, 2, \ldots, k$. The usual notation, $\hat{\beta}_j; j = 1, 2, \ldots, k$, is now reserved for the estimators obtained without explicit restrictions. By running a regression which corresponds to equation 3.7.3 one can generate values for $\hat{\beta}_{R1}$ and $\hat{\beta}_{R3}$, and these will almost certainly be different from the values taken by $\hat{\beta}_1$ and $\hat{\beta}_3$, the estimators based on equation 3.7.1. At the risk of being somewhat pedantic, it could also be said that the restricted estimators corresponding to β_2 and β_4 are given implicitly as $\hat{\beta}_{R2} = 0$ and $\hat{\beta}_{R4} = 0$. The unrestricted estimators $\hat{\beta}_2$ and $\hat{\beta}_4$ will generally take nonzero values.

The required test statistic can now be constructed from the sums of squares of the residuals associated with the two sets of estimators. In the unrestricted case, the relevant quantity would be

$$\Sigma e_t^2 = \Sigma (Y_t - \hat{\beta}_1 - \hat{\beta}_2 X_{2t} - \hat{\beta}_3 X_{3t} - \hat{\beta}_4 X_{4t})^2 \qquad (3.7.4)$$

Since we shall make considerable use of residual sums of squares, the notation is simplified by means of the definition

$$S = \Sigma e_t^2 \qquad (3.7.5)$$

The corresponding quantity for the restricted case is written as S_R, which in this example would be defined by

$$S_R = \Sigma(Y_t - \hat{\beta}_{R1} - \hat{\beta}_{R3}X_{3t})^2 \qquad (3.7.6)$$

To complete the definition of the test statistic, it is necessary to know the number of parameters to which the value zero is assigned under the null hypothesis. This is the number of restrictions, denoted generally as g. In the example, the null hypothesis states that β_2 and β_4 are zero and, as this involves two restrictions, $g = 2$. Finally, we need to know the number of degrees of freedom associated with the residual sum of squares in the unrestricted estimation, given generally by $n - k$. In the example, $k = 4$, and so $n - k = n - 4$. Given all this information, the test statistic for a particular null hypothesis can be found by application of the formula

$$F = \frac{(S_R - S)/g}{S/(n - k)} \qquad (3.7.7)$$

The notation F reflects the fact that, if the null hypothesis is true, the statistic has a distribution known as the *F distribution*.

Before we show how to conduct the formal test, we shall try to interpret the information that is used in constructing the test statistic. Equation 3.7.7 is based primarily on two residual sums of squares, and we already know that the residual sum of squares acts as a measure of the extent to which the behaviour of the dependent variable is not explained by a particular set of explanatory variables. We also know, from the discussion in Section 3.4, that removing explanatory variables from an existing relationship will increase, or at least cannot decrease, the residual sum of squares. It follows that the residual sum of squares subject to the restrictions imposed by the null hypothesis must be greater than (or equal to) the residual sum of squares of the original fit without the restrictions. Hence $S_R \geqslant S$ and $S_R - S$ will be positive or zero.

Now, in the example above, if β_2 and β_4 are zero, the variables X_2 and X_4 should have very little measured effect on the explanation of the dependent variable. Consequently, there should be very little difference between the residual sum of squares without X_2 and X_4, given by S_R, and the residual sum of squares with X_2 and X_4, given by S. Even when β_2 and β_4 do have true values equal to zero, the estimates corresponding to $\hat{\beta}_2$ and $\hat{\beta}_4$ are unlikely to be exactly zero, and this is why there is usually some difference between S_R and S. However, the difference will tend to be 'small' when β_2 and β_4 are zero and relatively 'large' when at least one of β_2, β_4 is different from zero, so that X_2 and X_4 do add something to the explanation of the behaviour of the dependent variable. In the F test statistic, $S_R - S$ is divided by S: this gives a quantity that does not depend on the units of measurement and, since S is a sum of squares, $(S_R - S)/S$ is still positive (or zero). The statistic is also adjusted for the values of g and $n - k$: once again these are positive, so F is always greater than or equal to zero. This is as far as we can get with an intuitive interpretation of the information used in constructing the F test statistic, and we now consider how the formal test procedure is carried out.

Since large values of the test statistic would suggest that the null hypothesis is not true, it is not surprising to find that there is a critical value above which the null hypothesis is rejected and below which the null hypothesis is not rejected. Table C (p. 270) gives critical values for the F distribution. As in the case of the t distribution, the critical values depend on the number of degrees of freedom, but there are now two distinct quantities involved. In the unrestricted case there are k parameters to be estimated before the residuals can be obtained, and S is associated with $n - k$ degrees of freedom. In the restricted case, g parameters are not estimated: instead the values of these parameters are specified by the restrictions. So S_R is associated with $n - (k - g) = n - k + g$ degrees of freedom, and the difference $S_R - S$ is associated with g degrees of freedom. In Table C the two sets of degrees of freedom associated with the F distribution are represented by df_1 and df_2: in this particular application, $\mathrm{df}_1 = g$ and $\mathrm{df}_2 = n - k$. Because there are two sets of degrees of freedom, an entire table is used to provide critical values for a single upper tail probability. In Table C this probability is 0·05.

The most obvious difference between the F distribution and the t distribution is that the former depends on two sets of degrees of freedom. There is, however, another difference to note. When we use the t distribution to test H_0: $\beta_j = 0$ against H_a: $\beta_j \neq 0$, at a 5 per cent significance level, the rejection region consists of values which are either less than $-t_{n-k}^{0·025}$ or greater than $+t_{n-k}^{0·025}$. As we shall see below, one could use the F distribution to test this same hypothesis, at the same level of significance, but whereas a 5 per cent significance level in the t test implies an upper tail probability of 0·025, the same significance level in the F test implies an upper tail probability of 0·05. By analogy with the notation used for critical values from the t distribution, we can write a critical value from the F distribution in the form $F_{g, n-k}^{0·05}$, where 0·05 is the upper tail probability, g is the value taken by

df_1 and $n - k$ is the value taken by df_2.

The initial discussion of the F test procedure has been somewhat lengthy, but the test is in fact remarkably easy to apply. The calculation of the test statistic consists basically of finding the two sums of squares S_R and S, and to do this one has only to run two regressions and take the residual sum of squares from each. A readymade example is provided by the two versions of the consumption function reported at the end of the previous section. One version of the model is

$$C_t = \beta_1 + \beta_2 D_2 + \beta_3 L_t + \beta_4 \Delta P_t + \beta_5 t + u_t; t = 1, 2, \ldots, n$$

(3.7.8)

but under the null hypothesis $\beta_4 = 0$ and $\beta_5 = 0$, the model becomes

$$C_t = \beta_1 + \beta_2 D_t + \beta_3 L_t + u_t; t = 1, 2, \ldots, n \qquad (3.7.9)$$

For convenience, the estimates corresponding to both versions are re-reproduced here:

$$\hat{C} = 16 \cdot 33 + 0 \cdot 510 D + 0 \cdot 123 L - 0 \cdot 083 \Delta P - 0 \cdot 448 t; \qquad 1963 - 80$$
$$(2 \cdot 00) \ (0 \cdot 049) \quad (0 \cdot 044) \quad (0 \cdot 032) \quad (0 \cdot 076)$$
$$\text{RSS} = 1 \cdot 678 \quad \text{VAR} = 0 \cdot 129 \quad R^2 = 0 \cdot 998$$

$$\hat{C} = 7 \cdot 38 + 0 \cdot 691 D + 0 \cdot 128 L; \qquad 1963 - 80$$
$$(2 \cdot 20) \ (0 \cdot 021) \quad (0 \cdot 056)$$
$$\text{RSS} = 6 \cdot 398 \quad \text{VAR} = 0 \cdot 427 \quad R^2 = 0 \cdot 992$$

To test the null hypothesis $\beta_4 = 0$ and $\beta_5 = 0$, against the alternative that at least one of β_4, β_5 is nonzero, one would take S to be the residual sum of squares from the regression corresponding to equation 3.7.8 and S_R to be the residual sum of squares from the regression corresponding to equation 3.7.9. Hence $S = 1 \cdot 678$ and $S_R = 6 \cdot 398$. The null hypothesis involves 2 restrictions, so $g = 2$, and there are 18 observations and 5 parameters to be estimated in the unrestricted version of the model, so $n - k = 13$. The F test statistic is therefore

$$F = [(S_R - S)/g] / [S/(n - k)]$$
$$= [(6 \cdot 398 - 1 \cdot 678)/2] / [1 \cdot 678/(18 - 5)]$$
$$= 18 \cdot 28$$

Note that the denominator in the F test statistic is simply the unrestricted disturbance variance estimate, which could be taken directly from the results above. From Table C the critical value $F_{2,13}^{0 \cdot 05}$ is found (by interpolation) to be $3 \cdot 81$. Since the calculated value of the test statistic is considerably greater than the critical value, the null hypothesis is rejected and we conclude that at least one of the parameters β_4, β_5 is different from zero. On the basis of this particular test, it would seem that the model involving ΔP and t as explanatory variables is to be preferred to the model which excludes these variables.

There are two special cases of the F test that should be noted. It was suggested above that the procedure could be used to test a hypothesis concerning a single parameter. Thus if S is taken from a full k variable regression and S_R from a regression excluding X_j, then equation 3.7.7 would provide a test of the null hypothesis that $\beta_j = 0$. In this case $g = 1$, but we already know that a t test can be used here, and it turns out that the F test statistic is the square of the t test statistic. The critical value $F_{1,\,n-k}^{0\cdot 05}$ is also the square of the critical value $t_{n-k}^{0\cdot 025}$. So, when $g = 1$, the tests are equivalent.

The second case concerns a test of the null hypothesis that all the slope parameters are zero, against the alternative that at least one slope parameter is not zero. Under the null hypothesis the genuine variables X_2 to X_k do not appear in the model, and so the model offers no 'economic' explanation for the behaviour of the dependent variable. In this case, S_R would be the residual sum of squares from a regression involving only the artificial variable X_1, and the null hypothesis would involve $g = k - 1$ restrictions. From the discussion in Sections 3.3 and 3.4 we know that S_R would be given by Σy_t^2, the sum of squares about the mean of the dependent variable. So, for the null hypothesis $\beta_2 = \beta_3 = \ldots = \beta_k = 0$, the test statistic can be expressed as

$$F = [(\Sigma y_t^2 - \Sigma e_t^2)/(k-1)]/[\Sigma e_t^2/(n-k)] \qquad (3.7.10)$$

where Σe_t^2 is the residual sum of squares from the regression of Y on $X_1, X_2, \ldots, X_k$. There are two alternative forms for 3.7.10. One follows from the fact that $\Sigma y_t^2 - \Sigma e_t^2$ is the explained sum of squares from the regression of Y on $X_1, X_2, \ldots, X_k$. Hence we can write

$$F \ [\text{explained SS}/(k-1)]/[\text{residual SS}/(n-k)] \qquad (3.7.11)$$

The other form follows from the fact that R^2 is defined as

$$R^2 = 1 - (\Sigma e_t^2/\Sigma y_t^2)$$

This enables us to write 3.7.10 as

$$F = [R^2/(k-1)]/[(1-R^2)/(n-k)] \qquad (3.7.12)$$

Even when the null hypothesis is true, the estimates corresponding to $\beta_j; j = 2, 3, \ldots, k$ would tend to be somewhat different from zero and R^2 will take a small positive value. But in such a case any apparent explanation is due entirely to random variation, and the small positive value of R^2 does not signify any true explanation of the behaviour of the dependent variable. In this sense, 3.7.12 provides a test to see whether the value of R^2 is significantly different from zero. Rejection of the null hypothesis would indicate that a nonzero value for R^2 has some meaning and that some real explanation has been achieved by the chosen model.

3.8 The use of restrictions

The type of null hypothesis used in the previous section involves the imposition of several restrictions on the parameters of a given model. These are of a very simple type, known as *exclusion restrictions*, under which certain parameter estimates are constrained to take the value zero, thereby removing the corresponding variables from the model. As a result of changing the list of explanatory variables in this way, the estimates of the remaining parameters are altered. Both the way in which the restricted estimates are obtained and the way in which the restrictions themselves are tested will continue to work for any set of linear restrictions. A given restriction is linear if it can be written so as to fit the standard form

$$r_1\beta_1 + r_2\beta_2 + \ldots + r_j\beta_j + \ldots + r_k\beta_k = r_0 \tag{3.8.1}$$

where $r_j; j = 0, 1, \ldots, k$ are known constants. To illustrate the use of the standard form, consider two examples. If we have a restriction which states that $\beta_3 = \beta_4$, one could set $r_3 = 1, r_4 = -1$ and all other r_j values, including r_0, to zero. This would give

$$0\beta_1 + 0\beta_2 + 1\beta_3 - 1\beta_4 + \ldots + 0\beta_k = \beta_3 - \beta_4 = 0$$

or

$$\beta_3 = \beta_4 \tag{3.8.2}$$

Similarly, for a restriction which states that $\beta_2 = 1$, we would have $r_2 = 1$ and $r_0 = 1$, with all other r_j values equal to zero:

$$0\beta_1 + 1\beta_2 + \ldots + 0\beta_k = 1$$

or

$$\beta_2 = 1 \tag{3.8.3}$$

Suppose now that we wished to impose the restrictions 3.8.2 and 3.8.3 on the model

$$Y_t = \beta_1 + \beta_2 X_{2t} + \beta_3 X_{3t} + \beta_4 X_{4t} + u_t; t = 1, 2, \ldots, n \tag{3.8.4}$$

The first step would be to write the restrictions into the model

$$Y_t = \beta_1 + 1 X_{2t} + \beta_3 X_{3t} + \beta_3 X_{4t} + u_t; t = 1, 2, \ldots, n$$

The restriction $\beta_3 = \beta_4$ is imposed by actually writing the same parameter on X_3 and X_4 and the restriction $\beta_2 = 1$ is written in directly. Any terms involving the same parameter should be taken together

$$Y_t = \beta_1 + 1 X_{2t} + \beta_3 (X_{3t} + X_{4t}) + u_t; t = 1, 2, \ldots, n$$

and any terms involving a known parameter should be removed to the left hand side of the relationship and subtracted from the dependent variable

$$(Y_t - X_{2t}) = \beta_1 + \beta_3 (X_{3t} + X_{4t}) + u_t; t = 1, 2, \ldots, n \tag{3.8.5}$$

If $(Y - X_2)$ is treated as the dependent variable and $(X_3 + X_4)$ as a single genuine explanatory variable, the resulting regression would give estimates corresponding to the restricted estimators $\hat{\beta}_{R1}$ and $\hat{\beta}_{R3}$. The remaining restricted estimators are given implicitly as $\hat{\beta}_{R2} = 1$ and $\hat{\beta}_{R4} = \hat{\beta}_{R3}$.

What we have done here is to impose the restrictions by substitution. It is then possible to write the restricted model into a form in which the parameters can be estimated by the standard least squares method. In doing this, some simple transformations of the original variables are used, and it is a considerable advantage if the computer program used for estimation enables such transformations to be carried out. The substitution technique can be used for any set of linear restrictions, and the estimates obtained are exactly the same as those from a formalized version of the method, described in more advanced texts as *restricted least squares*.

The restrictions can also be tested in exactly the same way as exclusion restrictions. A regression based on equation 3.8.4 would give an unrestricted residual sum of squares S, and a regression based on equation 3.8.5 would give a restricted residual sum of squares S_R. It is again true that S_R is greater than or equal to S. The null hypothesis would be that the restrictions are valid, that is, $\beta_2 = 1$ and

$\beta_3 = \beta_4$. The alternative would be that at least one restriction is not valid. Under the null hypothesis, the test statistic

$$F = \frac{(S_R - S)/g}{S/(n - k)} \tag{3.8.6}$$

would have an F distribution with g and $n - k$ degrees of freedom, where g is the number of restrictions and $n - k$ is the number of degrees of freedom in the unrestricted estimation. In the example, $k = 4$ and $g = 2$. The calculation of the test statistic again requires only that two regressions are run, to give values for S and S_R. So the value of the test statistic is easily found. If this value is greater than $F_{g,\,n-k}^{0.05}$, the null hypothesis is rejected at the 5 per cent significance level and the restrictions are not supported by the data. Otherwise, the null hypothesis is not rejected and the restrictions are consistent with the observations on the real system.

When a model contains several explanatory variables there are many sets of restrictions that could be tested, and one must obviously concentrate on those restrictions which have an economic interpretation of particular interest. An example is provided by the *Cobb-Douglas production function*, which is a simple form of relationship between output Q and labour and capital inputs L and K:

$$Q = aL^b K^c \tag{3.8.7}$$

As it stands, this cannot form the basis of a model in which the parameters are to be estimated by linear least squares, but taking logarithms on both sides of the equation gives

$$\log Q = \log (aL^b K^c)$$
$$= \log a + b \log L + c \log K \tag{3.8.8}$$

On adding a disturbance, the transformed model can be written as

$$Y_t = \beta_1 + \beta_2 X_{2t} + \beta_3 X_{3t} + u_t; t = 1, 2, \ldots, n \tag{3.8.9}$$

where $Y = \log Q$, $X_2 = \log L$, $X_3 = \log K$, $\beta_1 = \log a$, $\beta_2 = b$ and $\beta_3 = c$. Now it happens to be true that if $b + c = 1$, equation 3.8.7 exhibits constant returns to scale. This means that if labour and capital inputs are increased by the same proportion, output also increases by that proportion. This is a condition of some interest and, if equation 3.8.9 is used as the basis for estimation, it is worth testing the equivalent hypothesis that $\beta_2 + \beta_3 = 1$. The estimator subject to this restriction

can be obtained by writing the restriction into the model as
follows:

$$Y_t = \beta_1 + \beta_2 X_{2t} + (1 - \beta_2)X_{3t} + u_t; t = 1, 2, \ldots, n$$

or

$$(Y_t - X_{3t}) = \beta_1 + \beta_2(X_{2t} - X_{3t}) + u_t; t = 1, 2, \ldots, n \qquad (3.8.10)$$

The regression of $(Y - X_3)$ on $(X_2 - X_3)$ would give the estimator $\hat{\beta}_{R2}$,
and $\hat{\beta}_{R3}$ can be found as

$$\hat{\beta}_{R3} = 1 - \hat{\beta}_{R2} \qquad (3.8.11)$$

One can then use the F statistic 3.8.6 to test for constant returns to
scale. The restricted residual sum of squares S_R would be obtained
from a regression based on equation 3.8.10, and the unrestricted
quantity S from a regression based on equation 3.8.9. If the restriction is supported by the data, one might want to make use of the
restricted estimates. There can be certain advantages to this, discussed
in the next section. If the restriction is rejected, one could simply
conclude that it is not true that there are constant returns to scale in
the economic system under investigation, and the unrestricted estimates would then be used. Alternatively, one might argue that
constant returns to scale is an essential feature of the proposed model.
In this case one would simply impose the restriction without testing or,
if a test is performed and the null hypothesis is rejected, the entire
model may be discarded as unsatisfactory.

The balance between prior belief and empirical observation is a matter
of considerable debate between economists, and this is perhaps a question
on which the individual must reach his or her own conclusions. There
are methods which formalize the process of using the two types of
information together, based on a rather different scheme of statistical
inference to that which we have used. These methods, based on the
Bayesian approach, are outside the scope of this book, but we can
make some progress within the existing framework. It may be wrong
to rely entirely on observed data but, on the other hand, economic
theory is usually developed in the context of an ideal system and it
may be equally wrong to expect the restrictions suggested by the
theory to be exactly realized in practice. Instead, one might want to
use stochastic restrictions, in which disturbance terms are added, to
allow the restrictions to hold in an approximate rather than an exact
sense.

A stochastic linear restriction can be written as

$$r_0 = \beta_1 r_1 + \beta_2 r_2 + \ldots + \beta_j r_j + \ldots + \beta_k r_k + v \qquad (3.8.12)$$

where v is a random disturbance. The reason for writing the restriction in this way is that there is a striking parallel between equation 3.8.12 and the statement of the model for a single time period:

$$Y_t = \beta_1 + \beta_2 X_{2t} + \ldots + \beta_j X_{jt} + \ldots + \beta_k X_{kt} + u_t \qquad (3.8.13)$$

The terms Y_t and r_0 are both known as 'left hand sides', and each $X_{jt}; j = 1, 2, \ldots, k$ is a known quantity, similar to the corresponding $r_j; j = 1, 2, \ldots, k$. The term $X_{1t} = 1$ is implicit in equation 3.8.13, but it is there nonetheless. Finally, u_t and v are both random disturbances. The apparent similarity between equations 3.8.12 and 3.8.13 is very real, since the model specification actually does consist of n stochastic restrictions on the parameters $\beta_j; j = 1, 2, \ldots, k$.

The analogy that has been drawn suggests a way in which any stochastic linear restriction can be imposed on the parameter estimates. If r_0 is added to the observations on Y and each $r_j; j = 1, 2, \ldots, k$ is added to the observations on the corresponding X_j, a regression run on this augmented data would actually impose the constraint upon the estimates. Moreover, several such restrictions can be handled the same way. But there are some practical difficulties: there is no reason why the disturbance v should have the same properties as the disturbances $u_t; t = 1, 2, \ldots, n$ and, in particular, the variance attached to v is usually specified, by the investigator, as a measure of the confidence attached to the prior information contained in the restriction. Since this is unlikely to be the same as the unknown variance associated with each u_t, it is not true that the disturbances in the augmented model are all identically distributed. It is possible to overcome this problem, using methods developed in the next chapter, but the realization that the restrictions are so similar to the statement of the model is the most important single step towards understanding the use of stochastic restrictions and, even though the practical difficulties remain, an important principle has been established.

There is one case which can be dealt with here. In Section 2.9 we introduced an *ex post* test for the predictive performance of the two variable model. If the model parameters are estimated on the basis of data for the periods $t = 1, 2, \ldots, n$, the question is whether the same model holds in period $n + 1$. The null hypothesis is that the model does hold:

$$Y_{n+1} = \alpha + \beta X_{n+1} + u_{n+1}; \text{ where } E(u_{n+1}) = 0 \qquad (3.8.14)$$

with α and β representing the same parameter values as those which apply in the data period. But this is simply a stochastic restriction on α and β and, moreover, it is assumed that the disturbance u_{n+1} has exactly the same properties as u_t; $t = 1, 2, \ldots, n$. If we wished to impose the restriction 3.8.14 on the parameter estimates, as well as the restrictions imposed by the statement of the model for the data period, it would seem natural to re-estimate the parameters on the basis of observations for $t = 1, 2, \ldots, n$ and $n + 1$. This is precisely what we have suggested for the imposition of any stochastic restriction.

The t test given in equation 2.9.9 is specific to the two variable model, but the test can be generalized and, at the same time, expressed in a form which is convenient for computer calculation. Once again an F statistic replaces the t statistic, and the generalization allows both for the extension to the k variable model and also for the test to be applied to several additional time periods. A regression run only on the original data is an unrestricted regression, giving a residual sum of squares denoted as S. A regression run on the original data and the additional observations is a restricted regression, in which the estimates satisfy extra stochastic constraints and the residual sum of squares is denoted as S_R. Obviously the additional observations have to be available, and this is why predictive power is tested only in an *ex post* sense. The test statistic is given by

$$F = \frac{(S_R - S)/g}{S/(n - k)} \tag{3.8.15}$$

where g is now the number of stochastic restrictions and n refers to the original number of observations. The number of stochastic restrictions is obviously equivalent to the number of additional periods for which the model structure is to be tested. The critical value for the test is found from an F table entry corresponding to g and $n - k$ degrees of freedom, and a calculated value of the test statistic which is greater than the critical value leads to rejection of the null hypothesis. The interpretation of the conclusions to be drawn from the test is exactly parallel to that given for the t test in Section 2.9. In the special case of a two variable model and only one additional observation ($k = 2$ and $g = 1$), the F statistic is the square of the t statistic and the tests are identical.

3.9 Specification error

The statistical properties of the least squares estimators have been obtained on the basis of an assumed 'true' model, but since this represents an ideal situation, which may or may not be attained in practice, it is as well to be aware of the effects of making a specification error by inadvertently choosing a version of the model that will imply a violation of the assumptions. To conduct the analysis it is still necessary to assume that there is a version of the model that is true, and it is also necessary to assume that some specific type of error is made. In any practical application we would not know with certainty that such an error had occurred, but from the analysis in this section it will be possible to obtain some idea of what is likely to happen as a result of certain decisions that can be made in a practical context.

For the moment we shall confine our attention to the situation in which the list of explanatory variables is incorrect, and two special cases are considered. The first is where some of the variables that should be included are omitted, and the second is where some variables that should be omitted are incorrectly included. The discussion is based on the comparison between a three variable model and a two variable model, and in the first case the three variable model

$$Y_t = \beta_1 + \beta_2 X_{2t} + \beta_3 X_{3t} + u_t; t = 1, 2, \ldots, n \qquad (3.9.1)$$

is assumed to be correct. The two variable model is then written as

$$Y_t = \beta_1 + \beta_2 X_{2t} + v_t; t = 1, 2, \ldots, n \qquad (3.9.2)$$

where $v_t; t = 1, 2, \ldots, n$ is used to distinguish the disturbances to the incorrect model 3.9.2 from those to the true model 3.9.1. This distinction is necessary because, if equation 3.9.1 is correct, the implied disturbances to equation 3.9.2 are

$$v_t = \beta_3 X_{3t} + u_t; t = 1, 2, \ldots, n \qquad (3.9.3)$$

It is also convenient to have a system of notation to distinguish between the estimators based on the two alternative versions of the model. It is relatively easy to find such a system, because equation 3.9.2 can be obtained from equation 3.9.1 by imposing the (incorrect) restriction $\beta_3 = 0$. Hence the estimators obtained from a regression of Y on X_1 and X_2 are treated as restricted estimators and are denoted as $\hat{\beta}_{R1}$ and $\hat{\beta}_{R2}$ ($\hat{\beta}_{R3}$ is implicitly set to zero). The usual notation, $\hat{\beta}_1, \hat{\beta}_2$ and $\hat{\beta}_3$, is reserved for the unrestricted estimators, obtained from a regression of Y on X_1, X_2 and X_3.

Since equation 3.9.2 represents a two variable model, the slope estimator $\hat{\beta}_{R2}$ is given by

$$\hat{\beta}_{R2} = \Sigma x_{2t} y_t / \Sigma x_{2t}^2 \qquad (3.9.4)$$

We know from Section 2.3 that the estimator can also be written in terms of the disturbances which, in equation 3.9.2, are denoted by $v_t; t = 1, 2, \ldots, n$ rather than $u_t; t = 1, 2, \ldots, n$. The appropriate expression is therefore given by

$$\hat{\beta}_{R2} = \beta_2 + \Sigma x_{2t} v_t / \Sigma x_{2t}^2$$

or

$$\hat{\beta}_{R2} = \beta_2 + \Sigma w_t v_t \qquad (3.9.5)$$

where

$$w_t = x_{2t} / \Sigma x_{2t}^2; t = 1, 2, \ldots, n$$

The argument leading to the unbiasedness of estimators which are based on a true model requires that the random disturbances in an expression like 3.9.5 should have a zero expectation. But v_t does not represent a disturbance from the true model: if equation 3.9.1 is true, it follows that

$$v_t = \beta_3 X_{3t} + u_t; t = 1, 2, \ldots, n$$

The expectation of a single disturbance v_t would then be $\beta_3 X_{3t}$ and, in general, the expectation of $\Sigma w_t v_t$ will be nonzero, so that $\hat{\beta}_{R2}$ would be a biased estimator. There are two special cases in which this conclusion does not hold. The first is where β_3 is really zero, in which case there is no specification error. The second is where it so happens that $\Sigma w_t X_{3t}$ is exactly zero, for then $\Sigma w_t v_t$ would reduce to $\Sigma w_t u_t$, which does have a zero expectation. This last case corresponds to the situation in which the addition of X_3 to the model makes absolutely no difference to the estimator corresponding to X_2, which in turn requires that the zero order correlation coefficient between X_2 and X_3 is exactly zero. We know that, when economic data are used, such cases are extremely rare, and so we can say that, in general, the incorrect omission of one or more variables will cause a bias in the estimation of the remaining parameters. It should be obvious that there is also a bias in the estimation of the parameters of the omitted variables: the estimates are implicitly set to zero but, if the variables are wrongly excluded, the true values are nonzero.

It has already been suggested that the omission of X_3 from equation

3.9.1 corresponds to the incorrect imposition of an exclusion restriction. The restriction states that $\beta_3 = 0$ when, in fact, this is not true. The conclusion that this will generally cause a bias in the estimation of the remaining parameters generalizes to any linear restriction which is incorrectly imposed.

Now consider the opposite situation which, in terms of our example, is that the two variable model is true. We should now rewrite equation 3.9.2 as

$$Y_t = \beta_1 + \beta_2 X_{2t} + u_t; t = 1, 2, \ldots, n \qquad (3.9.6)$$

where u_t is used in place of v_t, to signify that the disturbances in the two variable model are now 'true' disturbances, which can be assumed to satisfy the usual conditions. The question to be asked in this case is what will happen if the three variable model is used as the basis for estimation when, in fact, β_3 is really zero. It is not necessary to alter equation 3.9.1, rewritten here as

$$Y_t = \beta_1 + \beta_2 X_{2t} + \beta_3 X_{3t} + u_t; t = 1, 2, \ldots, n \qquad (3.9.7)$$

since, if β_3 is zero, equations 3.9.6 and 3.9.7 are actually identical models with identical disturbances. So there is no reason why the estimators from a regression of Y on X_1, X_2 and X_3 should be biased. Since it is still true that equation 3.9.6 is a restricted version of equation 3.9.7, we may still denote estimators based on the two variable model as restricted estimators, whereas those based on the three variable model are unrestricted. The difference between this case and that considered earlier is that the restriction $\beta_3 = 0$ is now supposed to be valid, whereas previously this restriction was false. Given that $\beta_3 = 0$ is a valid restriction, both sets of estimators are unbiased and it remains to be seen what the penalty for the incorrect inclusion of a variable actually is.

To answer this question it is necessary to recall, from Section 3.6, that the variance of a single parameter estimator can be expressed in the general form

$$\text{var} (\hat{\beta}_j) = \sigma^2 / \Sigma \widetilde{X}_{jt}^2 \qquad (3.9.8)$$

where $\widetilde{X}_j$ represents the variable formed by the residuals from the regression of X_j on all the other explanatory variables currently included in a given model. This general form holds for both restricted and unrestricted versions of the model, so long as the 'true' disturbances satisfy the assumptions of constant variance and independence (or at least zero covariance). In particular, the general form can be applied to the estimator corresponding to β_2, regardless of whether this is obtained on the basis of the two variable model or the three variable model. But the specific interpretation of the general form does differ in the two cases. If the three variable model is used, $\widetilde{X}_2$ would represent the residuals from a regression of X_2 on X_1 and X_3. If the two variable model is used, $\widetilde{X}_2$ would represent the residuals from a regression of X_2 on X_1 alone. We know that the addition of variables to a given regression decreases (or, at least, cannot increase) the residual sum of squares, and this applies equally to the auxiliary regression of X_2 on other explanatory variables. Hence $\Sigma\widetilde{X}_{2t}^2$ would take a smaller value when equation 3.9.7 is used (that is, when X_3 is included in the model) than would be the case when equation 3.9.6 is used (that is, when X_3 is excluded from the model). The only exception would be when X_2 and X_3 are completely uncorrelated: if this happens, the addition of X_3 would have no effect on $\Sigma\widetilde{X}_{2t}^2$. Since this special case is rather unlikely, we can conclude that the addition of X_3 will generally reduce $\Sigma\widetilde{X}_{2t}^2$. Given the form of equation 3.9.8, this means that the addition of X_3 will increase the variance of the estimator for β_2. Generalizing this conclusion, we can say that the variance of a parameter estimator cannot decrease, and will generally increase, as variables are added to a given model.

A word of warning is in order here. The result established above concerns the theoretical variances of the parameter estimators, all of which involve σ^2, the variance of the disturbance process. The result does not necessarily apply to standard errors, which are based on an estimate of the disturbance variance. Thus it is possible to observe a decrease in (estimated) standard errors, as variables are added to a model, even though the theoretical variances must increase or, exceptionally, remain unchanged.

In the example above, the addition of X_3 corresponds to a failure to impose the restriction that $\beta_3 = 0$ and, as we have seen, there is a cost in terms of increased variance of all the parameter estimators. Conversely, the imposition of the restriction reduces the estimator variance (or at least leaves it unchanged) and, as this conclusion is true of all exact linear restrictions, we can see why it is advantageous to use any restrictions that are available, so long as those restrictions are valid. The use of invalid restrictions leads to bias in the estimation procedure. Since the variance measures the spread of individual estimates about the expected value of the estimator, it is of little use when there is a relatively small spread about an expected value which is some distance from the true parameter. This is what happens when there is a small variance but a relatively large bias. On the other hand, there is little point in having an unbiased estimator if there is also a very high variance, since the probability of finding a single estimate well away from the true value would be relatively high. A best linear unbiased estimator is one for which the variance is as small as possible, given that there is to be no bias at all. But there are situations in which the lack of bias can only be achieved at the cost of some very high variances. In such a case it may be preferable to impose some restrictions that are not exactly true, thereby inducing some bias, if at the same time one can achieve a significant reduction in the variances associated with the parameter estimators. Despite the fact that this would amount to the deliberate use of an incorrect model, it is possible for the estimators attached to the remaining variables to be 'better' estimators of some of the parameters of the true model, as judged by a combination of bias and variance.

Although the analysis in this section is based on a theoretical comparison between a model which is known to be 'true' and a model which is known to be 'false', there are some useful practical implications. One can decrease the chance of bias in the estimation procedure by adding more explanatory variables that may conceivably be relevant. But this involves a cost, possibly an unacceptable cost, in terms of higher variances of the estimators. In the next section we shall see why the variances can sometimes be very large and why there is usually a limit to the number of variables that can be added in this way.

3.10 Multicollinearity

Observations on economic variables are not generated under controlled conditions, such as those that may be used in experimental science. As a result, there is always some general intercorrelation between the explanatory variables. This does not refer only to correlations of a kind that could be adequately represented by a simple correlation coefficient. From the discussion in Section 3.4, we know that there are many different types of correlation measure and, in general, virtually any such measure applied to relationships between the explanatory variables will take a value which is somewhat different from zero. The name given to this phenomenon is *multicollinearity*, and it is precisely because of this property of economic data that multiple regression is used to estimate the parameters of a k variable model. As long as none of the correlations between explanatory variables is particularly high, there is no difficulty associated with multicollinearity. The phenomenon exists and our estimation method is designed accordingly. What is usually referred to as the problem of multicollinearity arises from the effects on the estimators of very high correlations between the explanatory variables. We now consider what these effects are.

The first step is to state precisely what we mean by 'very high' correlations between explanatory variables. Although there are many different types of correlation measure, one can always detect a high level of multicollinearity between the genuine explanatory variables by considering squared multiple correlation coefficients of the form

$$R_j^2 = 1 - \Sigma \widetilde{X}_{jt}^2 / \Sigma x_{jt}^2 \qquad (3.10.1)$$

To understand what R_j^2 represents, recall that $\widetilde{X}_{jt}$; $t = 1, 2, \ldots, n$ are residuals from the auxiliary regression of X_j on all other explanatory variables in the model. In contrast, $x_{jt} = X_{jt} - \overline{X}_j$; $t = 1, 2, \ldots, n$ can be interpreted as residuals from a regression of X_j on the artificial variable X_1. Taking $\Sigma \widetilde{X}_{jt}^2$ as the analogue of Σe_t^2 and Σx_{jt}^2 as the analogue of Σy_t^2, it becomes obvious that R_j^2 is very similar to the squared multiple correlation coefficient R^2, defined in Section 3.4. Moreover, if there is an intercept in the model, we have the inequalities

$$0 \leqslant \Sigma \widetilde{X}_{jt}^2 \leqslant \Sigma x_{jt}^2 \qquad (3.10.2)$$

and

$$0 \leqslant R_j^2 \leqslant 1 \qquad (3.10.3)$$

The difference between R^2 and the statistics R_j^2; $j = 2, 3, \ldots, k$ is that the former relates to a regression of Y on $X_1, X_2, \ldots, X_k$, whereas each of the latter relates to an auxiliary regression of one X_j on all other explanatory variables, including X_1.

It is possible to show that the highest R_j^2 from a given data set is greater than or equal to all other squared correlation coefficients which 'assume the presence of an intercept' but which do not 'give credit for' explanation achieved by X_1. Since this group includes all the conventional types of coefficient, including zero order, partial and multiple correlations, it follows that any 'high' coefficients of this type will imply at least one 'high' R_j^2. The one case that will not be revealed in this way is where X_j is highly 'correlated' with the artificial variable X_1. What this means is that X_j exhibits very little variation, so that Σx_{jt}^2 will be 'small'. It is convenient to treat lack of variation separately from serious multicollinearity, although both have essentially the same effect on parameter estimation. We therefore define serious multicollinearity to be the case in which at least one R_j^2; $j = 2, 3, \ldots, k$ is close to 1, whereas lack of variation is the case in which Σx_{jt}^2 is close to 0. This last condition is somewhat imprecise, and one could construct an appropriately scaled measure, but lack of variation is easy to detect by inspection of the data. If one suspects the presence of serious multicollinearity, one can check to see whether this is actually the case by calculating values for each $R_j^2; j = 2, 3, \ldots, k$. Assuming that a computer is used, the simplest way to do this is by running the auxiliary regressions: when X_j is regressed on all other explanatory variables, R_j^2 is the value identified as 'R squared' on the computer output.

Having defined serious multicollinearity to be the situation in which at least one R_j^2 is close to 1, it is now possible to consider the implications for parameter estimation. We already know how the estimation procedure attempts to deal with the lack of control in the generation of economic data. A single parameter β_j is estimated by using only that part of the variation in X_j that is not associated with the other explanatory variables in the model. This 'pure' component of X_j is represented by the residuals $\widetilde{X}_{jt}; t = 1, 2, \ldots, n$. The estimator $\hat{\beta}_j$ can then be written as

$$\hat{\beta}_j = \Sigma \widetilde{X}_{jt} Y_t / \Sigma \widetilde{X}_{jt}^2$$

or as

$$\hat{\beta}_j = \Sigma \widetilde{X}_{jt} \widetilde{Y}_t / \Sigma \widetilde{X}_{jt}^2 \tag{3.10.4}$$

where $\widetilde{Y}_t; t = 1, 2, \ldots, n$ are residuals from the regression of Y on all the explanatory variables except X_j. The variance of $\hat{\beta}_j$ is given by

$$\text{var}(\hat{\beta}_j) = \sigma^2 / \Sigma \widetilde{X}_{jt}^2 \tag{3.10.5}$$

If R_j^2 were equal to 0, there would be no measured correlation between X_j and the other explanatory variables and $\Sigma \widetilde{X}_{jt}^2$ would be equal to Σx_{jt}^2. In any other case, the presence of the other genuine explanatory variables reduces the 'effective' variation in the observations X_{jt}; $t = 1, 2, \ldots, n$. Instead of using the total observed variation, as measured by Σx_{jt}^2, the estimation procedure uses only the 'pure' variation as measured by $\Sigma \widetilde{X}_{jt}^2$. This leads directly to an increase in var $(\hat{\beta}_j)$ relative to the value that would hold if R_j^2 were equal to 0. The extent to which this occurs obviously depends on the value of R_j^2: the closer this is to 1, the greater is the increase in var $(\hat{\beta}_j)$ that is attributable to the effects of multicollinearity. In the extreme case in which X_j is perfectly correlated with one or more of the other genuine explanatory variables, R_j^2 will be equal to 1, $\Sigma \widetilde{X}_{jt}^2$ will be equal to 0, there will be no 'pure' variation and the estimation procedure will fail. This is the situation described at the end of Section 3.3 and from now on we will refer to the extreme case as perfect or complete multicollinearity. The only other case in which there is no unique solution to the normal equations is when the model contains an intercept and, at the same time, one of the values $\Sigma x_{jt}^2; j = 2, 3, \ldots, k$ is actually zero. This is the extreme case of lack of variation, in which X_j is 'perfectly correlated' with the artificial variable X_1: the estimation procedure will fail, because there cannot be any 'pure' variation in a situation in which there is no variation to start with.

Fortunately, with a properly specified model, perfect multicollinearity is rare, and we now concentrate on the case in which multicollinearity is serious but not complete. We shall also assume that none of the values $\Sigma x_{jt}^2; j = 2, 3, \ldots, k$ is equal to 0. There is then no reason why any of the original assumptions should be violated, and the various results obtained earlier should still apply. In particular, the standard error of $\hat{\beta}_j$ is still given by the formula

$$\text{se}(\hat{\beta}_j) = \hat{\sigma}/\sqrt{\Sigma \widetilde{X}_{jt}^2} \tag{3.10.6}$$

and an exact 95 per cent confidence interval for β_j is still

$$\hat{\beta}_j \pm t_{n-k}^{0.025} \, \text{se}(\hat{\beta}_j) \tag{3.10.7}$$

The effect of serious multicollinearity on these measures may seem obvious, but there is one important point to be made. The standard errors depend on the disturbance variance estimator $\hat{\sigma}^2$, and this means that the standard errors are random variables. As it happens, the distribution of $\hat{\sigma}^2$ does not depend on the level of multicollinearity, provided that the model is properly specified. So the only way in which multicollinearity affects a given standard error is through the value of $\Sigma \widetilde{X}_{jt}^2$ and, since this affects all possible realizations in the same way, we can conclude that the presence of multicollinearity will lead to a systematic and marked increase in those standard errors for which R_j^2 is 'high'. It then follows that the associated confidence intervals are wider than would otherwise be the case.

Turning now to a test of the null hypothesis $\beta_j = 0$, against the alternative $\beta_j \neq 0$, the test statistic is

$$t_j = \hat{\beta}_j/\text{se}(\hat{\beta}_j) \tag{3.10.8}$$

Given that there is no particular reason for violation of the original assumptions, this statistic will still have a t distribution, with $n - k$ degrees of freedom, provided that the null hypothesis is true. The increased standard error merely reflects the fact that the distribution of $\hat{\beta}_j$ is more widely dispersed and, under the null hypothesis, the presence of multicollinearity has no effect on the probability of finding t_j in the interval $-t_{n-k}^{0.025}$ to $+t_{n-k}^{0.025}$, or in any other symmetric interval around zero. If β_j is not zero, t_j no longer has a simple t distribution, but it is possible to show that the exact form of distribution under the alternative hypothesis depends on a parameter which is obtained in the following way. The first step is to square the t statistic, to remove the distinction between positive and negative values of t_j. Hence

$$
\begin{aligned}
t_j^2 &= \hat{\beta}_j^2/(\hat{\sigma}^2/\Sigma \widetilde{X}_{jt}^2) \\
&= \hat{\beta}_j^2 \Sigma \widetilde{X}_{jt}^2/\hat{\sigma}^2
\end{aligned}
\tag{3.10.9}
$$

Next, the estimators $\hat{\beta}_j$ and $\hat{\sigma}^2$ are replaced by the corresponding parameters β_j and σ^2. Using λ to denote the resulting composite parameter, we have

$$
\begin{aligned}
\lambda &= \beta_j^2/(\sigma^2/\Sigma \widetilde{X}_{jt}^2) \\
&= \beta_j^2/\text{var}(\hat{\beta}_j) \\
&= \beta_j^2 \Sigma \widetilde{X}_{jt}^2/\sigma^2
\end{aligned}
\tag{3.10.10}
$$

Although it is not easy to see directly what effect multicollinearity will have on the random variable t_j, the effect on the parameter λ is fairly obvious. As R_j^2 is increased, $\Sigma \widetilde{X}_{jt}^2$ is decreased and so λ is decreased, for given values of β_j and σ^2. The one case in which there is no effect is when β_j is zero, that is, when the null hypothesis is true. Since t_j^2 is the sample analogue of λ, one would expect a reduction in the value of λ to increase the probability of finding 'small' values of t_j^2 and hence also to increase the probability of finding 'small' values of t_j. This is exactly what happens. The probability of finding t_j within any given distance of zero is a decreasing function of λ and hence an increasing function of var $(\hat{\beta}_j)$, except in the case in which $\beta_j = 0$. In particular, the probability of finding t_j in the interval

$$
-t_{n-k}^{0.025} \text{ to } +t_{n-k}^{0.025}
\tag{3.10.11}
$$

is an increasing function of var $(\hat{\beta}_j)$, when β_j is not zero. Since a value of t_j in this interval would correspond to a failure to reject the null hypothesis, and since the null hypothesis is false if β_j is not zero, we may say that the presence of multicollinearity increases the probability of type II error. This holds for all significance levels and for all nonzero values of β_j.

What we have said above has rather serious implications for the use of the model as an experimental device, to see which regressors are really important in explaining the dependent variable. If one obtains a value for t_j which lies between $-t_{n-k}^{0.025}$ and $+t_{n-k}^{0.025}$, this might mean that β_j is really zero, but it could simply be that the data do not contain enough information to show convincingly that β_j is different from zero. This problem does not occur only under conditions of serious multicollinearity, but the existence of multicollinearity does exacerbate the situation because of the increased probability of type II error. Unfortunately, the decision as to whether β_j is really zero is sometimes of crucial importance and, for this reason, a slightly different approach to the t test is frequently adopted in practical model building. Instead of using the critical value for a particular significance level as a definite boundary between 'acceptance' and 'rejection' of the null hypothesis, the t statistic is treated as an indicator of the performance of a particular explanatory variable. Thus, although one might decide to delete a variable for which t_j is say 0·5, one might be reluctant to delete a variable for which t_j is 1·5, particularly when one suspects the presence of serious multicollinearity or a lack of variation in the original data series. In taking such decisions, one should give some weight to any prior beliefs concerning the role of the variable in question and also to the likely costs of misspecification that would result from taking the wrong decision. If one had reason to believe that X_j was relevant to the explanation of the behaviour of the dependent variable, one might treat a small value of t_j as indicative of the need to experiment further rather than as definite evidence that β_j is zero. This would be especially true of a variable that could be subject to very large changes: in such a case, treating even a small nonzero value of β_j as though it were zero could lead to rather serious errors when the model is used for forecasting or policy simulation.

So far, we have shown that the presence of multicollinearity leads to increased uncertainty as to the location of at least some parameters in a given model. This is reflected in higher standard errors and wider confidence intervals. It is also reflected in the fact that if a given parameter β_j is nonzero, it is relatively more difficult to show this on the basis of the available data. Since each of these consequences concerns individual parameters, it is tempting to conclude that it is in the estimation of individual parameters that the effects of multicollinearity are most marked, but this is not so. It is quite frequently the case that the most difficult quantity to estimate is the difference between two parameters, and we now explain briefly why this is so. The obvious way to estimate a difference of the form $\beta_i - \beta_j$ is to take the difference between the estimators, $\hat{\beta}_i - \hat{\beta}_j$. The precision with which this can be done is determined by var $(\hat{\beta}_i - \hat{\beta}_j)$, which is given by the expression

$$\text{var } (\hat{\beta}_i - \hat{\beta}_j) = \text{var } (\hat{\beta}_i) + \text{var } (\hat{\beta}_j) - 2 \text{ cov } (\hat{\beta}_i, \hat{\beta}_j) \qquad (3.10.12)$$

We have not previously mentioned, in the context of the k variable model, that covariances of the form cov $(\hat{\beta}_i, \hat{\beta}_j)$ are generally nonzero. If this is so, the distributions of $\hat{\beta}_i$ and $\hat{\beta}_j$ are certainly not independent. Equation 3.10.12 shows that if cov $(\hat{\beta}_i, \hat{\beta}_j)$ is negative, the variance of the difference is at least as great as the sum of the individual variances. The significance of this result is that certain types of positive correlation between two variables, X_i and X_j, will lead directly to a relatively large negative covariance between $\hat{\beta}_i$ and $\hat{\beta}_j$. Hence serious multicollinearity will often lead to very considerable uncertainty as to the true value of the difference between two parameters. Not surprisingly, this would be reflected in relatively high probabilities of type II error in an F test of null hypothesis $\beta_i = \beta_j$, against the alternative $\beta_i \neq \beta_j$. If one has a highly collinear data set, one should be especially careful about interpreting a failure to reject H_0: $\beta_i = \beta_j$ as definite evidence to the effect that the restriction is true.

In complete contrast, there are some types of F test that are not affected by the presence of multicollinearity. It is quite possible that one could obtain a relationship in which no t statistic takes a value outside the range $-t_{n-k}^{0 \cdot 025}$ to $+t_{n-k}^{0 \cdot 025}$, but in which the explanation of the behaviour of the dependent variable is good, as judged by the value of R^2. In such a case, one would almost certainly reject the null hypothesis $\beta_2 = \beta_3 = \ldots = \beta_k = 0$, in favour of the alternative that at least one β_j; $j = 2, 3, \ldots, k$ is not zero. It would then be quite clear that the explanatory variables do jointly determine a significant part of the behaviour of the dependent variable. The problem would be in isolating the individual effects. It is for this reason that it is sometimes asserted that multicollinearity does not affect the use of a given relationship for forecasting. If one can assume that the pattern of intercorrelation between the individual explanatory variables will remain unchanged, the estimated relationship could be used for forecasting, and it need not matter that it is difficult to isolate the effects of individual variables. But, in such a case, the forecasts are conditional on assumptions about the future behaviour of explanatory variables to an even greater extent than usual, and the estimated relationship would certainly not be useful for predicting the effects of a policy decision that would break the pattern of intercorrelation, by changing only one of the explanatory variables. Moreover, one could have a disastrous forecasting performance if the presence of multicollinearity, or lack of variation, led to the incorrect deletion of an explanatory variable which was subsequently subject to changes much greater than those experienced in the estimation period.

There is one other effect of serious multicollinearity that we should mention, if only because it can alert the investigator to the fact that a problem exists. It can happen that the parameter estimates exhibit considerable instability in the face of small changes to the data, such as the correction of data entry errors, or the use of some revisions to an official data series, or the use of a different year as the price base, for expressing data in real as opposed to current price terms. A closely related problem is loss of accuracy in the computer calculation, whereby changes which ought not to affect the solution, such as reordering variables, do produce changes in the answer obtained. One might also observe this in trying to reproduce solutions on a different machine, or using a different program. If one does notice marked parameter instability, or apparently excessive rounding error, the chances are that this is due to serious multicollinearity or to almost total lack of variation in the original data series, and one should take steps to discover the nature of the problem before making any further use of the data set in question.

Having examined the consequences of serious multicollinearity in some detail, we now consider whether anything can be done to mitigate the effects on parameter estimation. In theory one can reduce estimator variances, without cost, by imposing valid restrictions. One can also reduce the variances, at the cost of some bias, by imposing false restrictions. Intuitively, if the restrictions are 'almost valid', the resulting bias should be relatively small, and there are various techniques of variance reduction that attempt to exploit this fact. Some examples are given in Section 5.2, in the context of distributed lag models, but otherwise such methods have not been widely used in econometrics, at least not in single equation studies, despite the existence of a fairly extensive theoretical literature. An alternative approach is to try to increase the information content of the data by obtaining additional observations. Extending a time series that is dominated by multicollinearity would not help much if the new observations are subject to the same problem, but data deficiency can also be caused by lack of variation, or by having insufficient observations. Because of this, there are cases in which extending a time series can be quite effective. One can also combine cross-section and time series data, provided that the information obtained from the two sources is basically compatible. If, for example, the time series data relate to an economy-wide aggregate, whereas the cross-section relates to individual households or firms, the parameters obtained from fitting an equation to a cross-section at a single point in time may not be directly applicable to an equation designed to represent the generation of the aggregate variable over a number of time periods. Apart from the different level of aggregation, there is a tendency for equations based on a cross-section to pick up long run responses, whereas the estimates obtained from fitting the same equation to a time series may well represent essentially short run effects. However, if one is careful, the combination of cross-section and time series data can represent a significant addition to the information available and can help to overcome deficiencies in the original data set.

Unless one can find suitable restrictions, or add to the available data, there is really very little that one can do to improve estimates which are subject to the effects of serious multicollinearity. It is simply a fact that the available data do not contain enough information to enable one to obtain satisfactory estimates of all the parameters in the proposed model. If this is so, we should perhaps ask why it has been necessary to discuss the effects in such detail. The reason is that one does need to be aware of the consequences of serious multicollinearity and, indeed, of other forms of data deficiency, to avoid drawing conclusions which are not really justified on the basis of the information available. Thus, if one is faced with 'small' t statistics, one should ask whether there are enough observations, whether the data series exhibit a reasonable amount of variation, and whether there exist any very high correlations between the explanatory variables. If these possibilities can be eliminated, it may then seem more reasonable to suppose that a 'small' t statistic does indicate that a particular explanatory variable has no influence on the dependent variable, but there is still one further problem. Throughout this section we have assumed that the model is correctly specified, except possibly for the inclusion of a single variable for which β_j is zero. Unfortunately, one can also obtain 'small' t statistics because of omitted variables bias. If some variables are incorrectly excluded, the estimator $\hat{\beta}_j$ will be biased. This bias may be positive or negative. However, in this situation the disturbance variance estimator $\hat{\sigma}^2$ will also be biased and, in this case, the bias is always positive, which means that $\hat{\sigma}^2$ will systematically overestimate the true disturbance variance. The effect on the t statistic cannot be determined with any great precision, but broadly the bias in $\hat{\beta}_j$ will either tend to cancel out the bias in $\hat{\sigma}^2$ or will reinforce the tendency for the bias in $\hat{\sigma}^2$ to move the t statistic towards zero. If this occurs, one can observe an apparently perverse effect whereby the t

ios are 'improved' (moved away from zero) as variables are added to the model, despite the fact that this will increase (cannot decrease) the theoretical variances. Given this additional problem, the lesson of this section must be that one should be very careful when claiming that a particular explanatory variable has 'no effect'. At the very least one should perform a certain amount of experimentation and some careful diagnostic checking before attempting to draw this particular conclusion.

3.11 Dummy variables

The final section of this chapter is concerned with the problems that arise when a given set of data divides naturally into two or more subsets, according to the categories of some qualitative variable. Thus one might have data for two or more regions, or a long series containing prewar and postwar observations, or data relating to periods with and without an incomes policy, or quarterly data relating to different seasons of the year, and so on. We shall use region as a convenient example, but what is said would apply equally to any other qualitative influence. For simplicity, we base the discussion on the two variable model, in the original notation:

$$Y_t = \alpha + \beta X_t + u_t; t = 1, 2, \ldots, n \tag{3.11.1}$$

Now suppose that there are just two regions, labelled regions 1 and 2. It may well be that the appropriate true parameters are different in the two regions and, if this is so, the model should be based on two distinct relationships between Y and X:

$$Y_t = \alpha_1 + \beta_1 X_t + u_t; \text{ in region 1}$$
$$Y_t = \alpha_2 + \beta_2 X_t + u_t; \text{ in region 2} \tag{3.11.2}$$

There are also some other possible specifications. If the intercept differs between regions but the slope does not, the model would be

$$Y_t = \alpha_1 + \beta_1 X_t + u_t; \text{ in region 1}$$
$$Y_t = \alpha_2 + \beta_1 X_t + u_t; \text{ in region 2} \tag{3.11.3}$$

where the subscript on β is now redundant. In this version of the model, a unit change in X has the same effect on Y irrespective of region, but the observations on Y have an additional constant component that is present in one region but not in the other. It is also possible that the intercepts are the same but the slopes are different:

$$Y_t = \alpha_1 + \beta_1 X_t + u_t; \text{ in region 1}$$
$$Y_t = \alpha_1 + \beta_2 X_t + u_t; \text{ in region 2} \tag{3.11.4}$$

Unless the intercept does have some specific meaning, this is unlikely to be a version of the model that is of interest. The final possibility is that both parameters are the same in both regions, which would give

$$Y_t = \alpha_1 + \beta_1 X_t + u_t; \text{ in region 1}$$
$$Y_t = \alpha_1 + \beta_1 X_t + u_t; \text{ in region 2} \tag{3.11.5}$$

where the subscripts on α and β are now redundant. In this version of the model, the underlying relationship is the same in both regions and there is no point in writing two separate equations. So equations 3.11.5 can be written as

$$Y_t = \alpha + \beta X_t + u_t; \text{ in regions 1 and 2} \tag{3.11.6}$$

where the subscripts on α and β have now been removed.

The various versions of the model are illustrated in Figure 10. It is obvious that the number of possibilities increases with the number of explanatory variables, and also with the number of categories of the qualitative variable. With several explanatory variables and several regions, there would be many alternative specifications, only one of which could correspond to a 'true' model.

The introduction of models based on a number of different equations obviously raises some problems of estimation and testing that we have not encountered previously. But there is a very simple 'trick' which enables us to convert any of the models 3.11.2–3.11.5 into the form of a single relationship and, if this can be done, then our existing methods can still be used.

Suppose that we create two *dummy variables* denoted D_1 and D_2 and defined so that

$$D_{1t} = 1; \text{ in region 1}$$
$$\qquad = 0; \text{ in region 2}$$
$$D_{2t} = 0; \text{ in region 1}$$
$$\qquad = 1; \text{ in region 2}$$

We can now write the version of the model given in 3.11.2 as

$$Y_t = \alpha_1 D_{1t} + \alpha_2 D_{2t} + \beta_1 (D_1 X)_t + \beta_2 (D_2 X)_t + u_t;$$
$$\text{in regions 1 and 2} \tag{3.11.7}$$

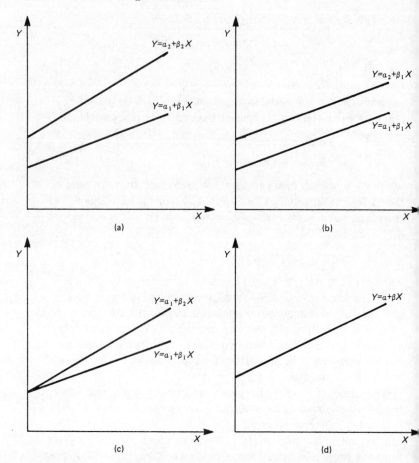

Figure 10

where D_1X and D_2X are variables formed as the products of the observations on X with the corresponding values of each of the dummy variables. So, for example,

$$(D_1X)_t = X_t; \text{ in region 1}$$
$$= 0; \text{ in region 2}$$

Equation 3.11.7 is equivalent to the equations 3.11.2 since, in region 1, $D_{1t} = 1$ and $D_{2t} = 0$, so equation 3.11.7 becomes

$$Y_t = \alpha_1 + \beta_1X_t + u_t; \text{ in region 1}$$

In region 2, $D_{1t} = 0$ and $D_{2t} = 1$, so equation 3.11.7 becomes

$$Y_t = \alpha_2 + \beta_2 X_t + u_t; \text{ in region 2}$$

Once the basic model is written in the form of a single equation, it is easy to see how the alternative versions can also be written in this way. For example, in equations 3.11.3, $\beta_1 = \beta_2$ and, starting from equations 3.11.7, we can derive a form equivalent to equations 3.11.3 by actually setting $\beta_1 = \beta_2$:

$$\begin{aligned}
Y_t &= \alpha_1 D_{1t} + \alpha_2 D_{2t} + \beta_1 [(D_1 X)_t + (D_2 X)_t] + u_t \\
&= \alpha_1 D_{1t} + \alpha_2 D_{2t} + \beta_1 X_t + u_t; \text{ in regions 1 and 2} \quad (3.11.8)
\end{aligned}$$

since

$$(D_1 X)_t + (D_2 X)_t = X_t, \text{ for all values of } t.$$

Again, the subscript on β_1 is now redundant and could be dropped. It is clear that equation 3.11.8 is derived from equation 3.11.7 by imposing the restriction that $\beta_1 = \beta_2$. In the original formulation this would be a cross-equation restriction, but in the dummy variable formulation the restriction is a simple 'within equation' equality, which can be imposed and tested by our existing methods.

Before we proceed further, it should be noted that equation 3.11.7 can be expressed in a slightly more convenient form. Since $D_{1t} + D_{2t} = 1$ for all values of t, it is not necessary to make explicit use of both dummy variables. Instead one can eliminate D_1, giving

$$\begin{aligned}
Y_t &= \alpha_1(1 - D_{2t}) + \alpha_2 D_{2t} + \beta_1 [(1 - D_2)X]_t + \beta_2(D_2 X)_t + u_t \\
&= \alpha_1 + (\alpha_2 - \alpha_1)D_{2t} + \beta_1 X_t + (\beta_2 - \beta_1)(D_2 X)_t + u_t
\end{aligned}$$

or

$$Y_t = \alpha_1 + \delta_2 D_{2t} + \beta_1 X_t + \gamma_2(D_2 X)_t + u_t; \text{ in regions 1 and 2}$$
$$(3.11.9)$$

where

$$\delta_2 = \alpha_2 - \alpha_1$$
$$\gamma_2 = \beta_2 - \beta_1$$

In equation 3.11.9, δ_2 represents the difference between the intercepts in the two regions and γ_2 represents the difference between the slopes. This is more convenient than equation 3.11.7 for two reasons. First, the restrictions are now simple exclusions: if the intercepts are equal, $\delta_2 = 0$, and if the slopes are equal, $\gamma_2 = 0$. Exclusion restrictions can be imposed by simply omitting the corresponding variables. The omission of D_2X gives a specification equivalent to equation 3.11.3, the omission of D_2 gives a specification equivalent to equation 3.11.4 and the omission of both D_2 and D_2X gives a specification equivalent to equations 3.11.5 or 3.11.6. In all these versions of the model there is a 'proper' intercept term, since the parameter α_1 is attached to a 'variable' which takes the value 1 in both regions. Specifications based on equation 3.11.7 do not have a proper intercept term. Many computer programs automatically insert an intercept unless the user takes specific steps to avoid this and, if both dummy variables are used in addition to a 'variable' which is always equal to 1, we would have complete multicollinearity, caused by the fact that $D_{1t} + D_{2t} = 1$, for all values of t. These problems are avoided by using equation 3.11.9, rather than 3.11.7, as the starting point for the imposition of restrictions.

Suppose now that we wished to test the null hypothesis of no difference between regions. Under the null hypothesis, region has no influence on the relationship between Y and X and $\alpha_1 = \alpha_2, \beta_1 = \beta_2$. The equivalent null hypothesis, in terms of δ_2 and γ_2, is that $\delta_2 = 0$ and $\gamma_2 = 0$. The general form for the test statistic for exact restrictions is

$$F = \frac{(S_R - S)/g}{S/(n-k)} \tag{3.11.10}$$

where S_R is the residual sum of squares with restrictions imposed, S is the residual sum of squares without restrictions, g is the number of restrictions under test and k refers to the number of parameters to be estimated in the unrestricted form. A regression corresponding to equation 3.11.9 would give estimates corresponding to $\hat{\alpha}_1, \hat{\delta}_2, \hat{\beta}_1$ and $\hat{\gamma}_2$ and, implicitly, $\hat{\alpha}_2 = \hat{\alpha}_1 + \hat{\delta}_2$ and $\hat{\beta}_2 = \hat{\beta}_1 + \hat{\gamma}_2$. It would also give a value for S and, since four parameters are estimated, $k = 4$. It should be noted that n refers to the total number of observations from both regions. To find the restricted sum of squares, the restrictions $\delta_2 = 0$ and $\gamma_2 = 0$ are imposed by deleting D_2 and D_2X, and a regression based on

$$Y_t = \alpha_1 + \beta_1 X_t + u_t; \text{ in regions 1 and 2} \tag{3.11.11}$$

would give restricted estimators $\hat{\alpha}_{R1}$ and $\hat{\beta}_{R1}$ and the restricted residual sum of squares S_R. Note that the subscripts on α and β are again redundant and that, since there are two restrictions, $g = 2$. Assembling this information into equation 3.11.10 will give a value for the F test statistic and, as usual, the null hypothesis would be rejected if the value obtained is greater than the critical value for g and $n - k$ degrees of freedom. Rejection means that at least one of the parameters α, β is different as between regions, so that region does have some effect on the relationship between Y and X.

In the special case described above, in which the objective is to discriminate between the totally restricted and totally unrestricted versions of the model, it is not actually necessary to make use of the dummy variable formulation, except in so far as that formulation is used to suggest an appropriate test procedure. The reason is that the parameters of the unrestricted version of the model can be estimated by fitting two separate regressions, and this will give exactly the same estimates of $\alpha_1, \beta_1, \alpha_2$ and β_2 as those derived from a single regression based on equation 3.11.9. The unrestricted residual sum of squares S can be obtained by adding the residual sums of squares from the individual regressions. Thus if S_1 is the residual sum of squares from a regression on the data from the first region only and S_2 is the corresponding quantity from the second region, then $S = S_1 + S_2$. The restricted residual sum of squares, S_R, refers to equation 3.11.11, which implies a single regression fitted to the data from both regions. So, in this special case, the dummy variable formulation suggests the test statistic and shows how one should assign values to n, k and g, but it is not necessary to introduce dummy variables explicitly. The special case is sometimes described as a *Chow test*, particularly in the context of testing for the stability of parameters between two time periods, each of which involves sufficient observations to enable separate regressions to be estimated.

In any situation in which one wants to estimate a version of the model which lies between the extremes of total restriction and total lack of restriction, the dummy variable method is used explicitly. Thus, to estimate the parameters in a specification in which the intercepts are different in each of three regions, but in which the slopes are the same, one would estimate a single relationship

$$Y_t = \alpha_1 + \delta_2 D_{2t} + \delta_3 D_{3t} + \beta X_t + u_t; t = 1, 2, \ldots, n \qquad (3.11.12)$$

where

$\quad D_{2t} = 1$; in region 2

$\qquad = 0$; elsewhere

$\quad D_{3t} = 1$; in region 3

$\qquad = 0$; elsewhere

and

$$\delta_2 = \alpha_2 - \alpha_1; \quad \delta_3 = \alpha_3 - \alpha_1$$

Obviously, as the number of explanatory variables is increased, one could form specifications which allow some slope parameters to differ between regions while others do not. It is also possible to allow for differences between some regions and no difference between others. And one could introduce further dummy variables to allow for additional qualitative effects. The only limitation to the process of expansion of the model is that there must be enough observations to allow all the parameters to be estimated, and it is possible to encounter problems of data inadequacy if the process of expansion is taken too far. Despite this, it is obvious that the dummy variable formulation does offer great flexibility in the specification of models which incorporate the effects of qualitative variables.

The method of testing is also quite general and can be used in an attempt to choose between any two versions of a given model, so long as one structure is a restricted version of the other. It must be understood, in this context, that 'unrestricted' and 'restricted' are relative descriptions. For the purpose of a particular test, the least restricted version of the model becomes the 'unrestricted' model, giving a residual sum of squares S and degrees of freedom $n - k$, where n refers to the total number of observations in all categories of the qualitative variable, and k refers to the total number of parameters to be estimated in the (relatively) unrestricted version of the model. Similarly, S_R refers to the residual sum of squares in the more restricted version and g refers to the number of restrictions under test.

Before leaving this topic, we should note an important assumption that underlies our treatment so far. When a model is written in terms of a single relationship, it is assumed that the disturbances behave as in any single equation model and, throughout the discussion, we have assumed that the disturbances are independent, or at least uncorrelated, with common variance σ^2. In the next chapter we shall see how this assumption can be modified, but for the moment our assumptions imply that the disturbances for each category of the qualitative variable are independent of the disturbances in all other categories and that the disturbances for all categories have a common variance.

When the methods of this section are used to allow for the effects of a qualitative variable, one is seldom interested in how well the qualitative variable explains the behaviour of the dependent variable. What we are really interested in is the way in which the qualitative variable

affects the relationship between the economic variables in the underlying model. For this reason, the qualitative variables are often referred
to as 'nuisance' variables, which have to be allowed for in order to
avoid distortion in the estimates of the parameters of the underlying
economic relationship. The dummy variable formulation shows exactly
what such distortion would imply. If the parameters of a given model
do vary between regions, but the relevant dummy variables are omitted,
there will be bias in the estimation of the parameters of the 'economic'
variables.

A final comment on the use of qualitative variables relates to the
problem of *seasonality* in quarterly data. Season is a somewhat special
case, because it is possible to obtain data which have already been
adjusted for any known effects which are specific to particular quarters
of the year. In some cases, two sets of data are available, one seasonally
adjusted and one set which is not adjusted. There is then a problem of
choice as to which set of data should be used. The answer to this
question depends heavily on the particular situation under investigation,
but we can perhaps give some indication as to how the choice should be
made and as to what difference this is likely to make.

Consider a specific example, in which the sales of a particular commodity Y are related to disposable income X and in which sales reach a
seasonal peak in the fourth quarter of the year. Suppose, for convenience only, that there are no other relevant 'economic' variables.
If the seasonal peak is explained entirely by the behaviour of income in
the fourth quarter, the model would be

$$Y_t = \alpha + \beta X_t + u_t; \text{ in all quarters}$$

In this case, it would be inappropriate to use seasonally adjusted sales
data, since this would remove part of the phenomenon to be explained
by the behaviour of income. In contrast, if the sales peak has nothing
to do with the level of income, the seasonal effect is a distortion to the
underlying relationship and, if unadjusted data are used, an appropriate
specification would be

$$Y_t = \alpha + \beta X_t + \delta_4 D_{4t} + u_t; \text{ in all quarters} \tag{3.11.13}$$

where $D_4 = 1$ in quarter 4 and zero otherwise. Alternatively, one could
use

$$Y_t^a = \alpha + \beta X_t + u_t; \text{ in all quarters} \tag{3.11.14}$$

where Y^a represents the sales variable, in seasonally adjusted form. In
the rather unlikely event that Y^a is obtained as a residual from the

regression of Y on D_4, estimates of α and β, based on equation 3.11.13, would be exactly the same as estimates based on equation 3.11.14. With any other method of seasonal adjustment there would be some difference between the estimates, despite the fact that both models represent attempts to remove a seasonal effect which is seen as a distortion.

There are several other specifications that might be applicable to the example above. Thus we might argue that the seasonal peak is not explained by the level of income in the fourth quarter, but rather by a fourth quarter shift in the marginal propensity to consume for the commodity in question. In this case, one could set up a model which includes a 'slope' dummy, that is

$$Y_t = \alpha + \beta X_t + \gamma_4 (D_4 X)_t + u_t \text{; in all quarters} \qquad (3.11.15)$$

Alternatively, one could combine 3.11.13 and 3.11.15, allowing both slope and intercept to shift in the fourth quarter. This does illustrate an important point: if unadjusted data are used, together with appropriately specified dummy variables, the investigator does have considerable freedom of choice as to the way in which seasonality is to be handled. So we can reach the tentative conclusion that, where possible, unadjusted data should be used, providing of course that the necessary dummy variables are added to allow for seasonal effects that are not an integral part of the underlying relationship.

3.12 Exercises (solutions on⏐p. 279)

3.1 This exercise requires a knowledge of calculus. Show, for the k variable model, that minimizing the sum of squared residuals leads to the normal equations 3.2.1.

3.2 Use the artificial data of Section 3.2 to demonstrate that the slope estimates can be obtained by expressing the data in the form of deviations from sample means and then solving equations equivalent to 3.2.7.

3.3 The following data consist of observations on real consumers' expenditure C, real personal disposable income D, real liquid asset holdings of the personal sector L and the year-on-year change in the consumer expenditure deflator ΔP, for the UK economy 1963–80. C, D and L are in £ thousand million at 1975 prices. Experiment with the data set and, in particular, attempt to reproduce the results reported in Section 3.6.

Year	C	D	L	ΔP
1963	49·725	53·767	42·946	0·8
1964	51·274	55·781	44·635	1·4
1965	52·131	57·205	45·720	2·1
1966	53·184	58·498	46·980	1·7
1967	54·385	59·385	48·196	1·2
1968	56·026	60·613	49·965	2·2
1969	56·313	61·244	49·954	2·8
1970	57·814	63·745	49·691	3·1
1971	59·724	64·544	50·626	4·6
1972	63·270	70·214	54·165	3·9
1973	66·332	75·059	57·149	5·5
1974	65·049	74·049	55·426	11·9
1975	64·652	74·005	50·301	19·1
1976	64·707	73·437	48·627	15·6
1977	64·517	72·288	46·819	17·6
1978	68·227	78·259	49·610	11·8
1979	71·599	83·666	51·073	18·4
1980	71·550	84·771	51·976	26·1

Sources: C, D and ΔP from *Economic Trends*, annual supplement, 1983 edition. *L* constructed from *Financial Statistics*, various issues.

3.4 The data on page 148 consist of observations on the end period money stock M1, the rate of interest on long dated government securities r, total final expenditure Y and the price deflator for total final expenditure P, for the UK economy 1964–80. M1 and Y are measured in £ million. Experiment with this data set and, in particular, estimate the parameters of the model

$$\log M1_t = \beta_1 + \beta_2 \log (r_t - 2) + \beta_3 \log Y_t + \beta_4 \log P_t + u_t;$$
$$t = 1, 2, \ldots, n$$

3.5 Suppose that the specification

$$Y_t = \alpha + \beta X_t + u_t; t = 1, 2, \ldots, n$$
$$E(u_t) = 0; t = 1, 2, \ldots, n$$

is correct. An investigator attempts to estimate β by running a regression of Y on X, without an intercept term. What can one say about the resulting estimator for β? Can you state your argument algebraically?

Year	M1	r	Y	P
1964	7673	5·98	39954	39·73
1965	7838	6·56	42591	41·48
1966	7828	6·94	45269	43·16
1967	8497	6·80	48006	44·30
1968	8975	7·55	52899	46·62
1969	8996	9·05	56537	48·97
1970	9785	9·25	62254	52·46
1971	10710	8·90	69532	56·79
1972	12260	8·97	77233	60·85
1973	12900	10·78	92058	66·95
1974	14330	14·77	110512	80·83
1975	17080	14·39	133918	100·00
1976	18980	14·43	161572	116·27
1977	23180	12·73	186513	132·59
1978	27020	12·47	210437	144·61
1979	29470	12·99	246931	163·88
1980	30570	13·79	283392	191·56

Source: Economic Trends, annual supplement, 1982 edition: M1 adjusted for changes in coverage

3.6 (a) A consumption function similar to equation 3.6.15 is estimated by the least squares method, using quarterly data for the UK economy 1963–80. The function has five explanatory variables (including an intercept), plus three seasonal dummies of the form Q_2D, Q_3D and Q_4D. D is disposable income. $Q_2 = 1$ in quarter 2 and 0 elsewhere, $Q_3 = 1$ in quarter 3 and 0 elsewhere, and $Q_4 = 1$ in quarter 4 and 0 elsewhere. With the dummy variables included, RSS = 2·581. With the dummy variables excluded, RSS = 13·485. Test for the effect of seasonality, explaining carefully the form taken by the seasonal effect under the alternative hypothesis.
(b) When the sample is split between 1963–69 and 1970–80, using the function including Q_2D, Q_3D and Q_4D, an OLS regression for 1963–69 gives RSS = 0·485 and a regression for 1970–80 gives RSS = 1·575. What use can you make of this information?
(c) The function including Q_2D, Q_3D and Q_4D is then estimated for 1963–76 and RSS = 1·793. Test the null hypothesis that the model is unchanged for 1977–80, using the forecast test given as equation 3.8.15.

Interlude

With the introduction of the k variable model, we have at our disposal a method of considerable practical value. It is now possible to explain the behaviour of a dependent variable in terms of several explanatory variables and, subject only to the limitations imposed by multi-collinearity, to isolate the individual factors influencing the dependent variable. It is also possible to test a variety of hypotheses, to impose linear restrictions and to examine the effects of various qualitative influences on the model. Moreover, the model need not be based on a linear relationship between the original economic variables: certain types of nonlinear relationship can be used.

We also know that the least squares estimators have certain desirable properties; however, these properties depend on a particular set of assumptions, and this is a limitation on the applicability of the methods described so far. There are cases in which a particular assumption cannot be satisfied because of some specific feature of the chosen economic model, and there are other situations in which it is unlikely that an assumption will be satisfied, in which case it is safer to relax that assumption. Whenever this is done, there are two basic questions to be answered. The first concerns the implications of the new situation for existing methods of estimation, and the second is concerned with the possibility that an alternative estimator may be a better choice for the new situation. It is important to be able to answer both questions. It is necessary to be able to say why existing methods are deficient before we can look for an alternative which is, in some sense, better. We also need to be able to state the likely consequences of using existing methods, perhaps because of ignorance as to the true situation, or because one has chosen to ignore the fact that a particular assumption has been violated.

The remaining chapters of the book deal with the relaxation of assumptions under three headings. Chapter 4 is concerned with the use of different specifications for the behaviour of the disturbances in the model. Chapter 5 examines some of the implications of making the main part of the model dynamic, and Chapter 6 extends the analysis to models containing several interrelated equations. We shall find that the methods introduced are not fundamentally different from those used so far. Indeed, many of the alternative estimators considered are extensions of the basic least squares method and, because of this, the detailed and rather lengthy analysis of the basic k variable model does provide a useful foundation for estimation and testing with more realistic representations of economic behaviour.

To enable the appropriate distinctions to be drawn we shall, in future, refer to the basic least squares estimators as *ordinary least squares* (OLS) estimators. Alternative estimators are then given different names, but it is important to note that these names refer to a complete estimation procedure. We shall often find that, at one stage of such a procedure, it is necessary to perform a regression calculation of the kind that we have already described. With reference to that one stage, such a calculation is an OLS regression, and it can be carried out by using a computer program designed for OLS. This is very convenient: it may enable us to describe an estimation procedure in terms of one or more OLS regression calculations, together with any additional transformations of the original model, and it may not always be necessary to write down explicit formulae for the modified estimators. Moreover, it may not be essential to have additional computer programs for all the new methods that are introduced.

4 Alternative disturbance specifications

4.1 Introduction

So far, it has been assumed that a satisfactory form of model is one in which the disturbances are independent, or at least uncorrelated random variables, with zero mean and constant variance. For some purposes, notably for the construction of test statistics, it has also been assumed that the disturbance distributions are normal. We already know that certain errors of specification in the main part of the model might imply disturbances which do not have zero mean, but with a properly specified model there are relatively few cases in which it would not be reasonable to assume that the means of the disturbance distributions are all zero. A nonzero mean implies a systematic component of the disturbances, which should really be included in the main part of the model. So, for example, in the case in which each disturbance has the same nonzero mean μ, one could simply add μ to the intercept. The model

$$Y_t = \alpha + \beta X_t + u_t; t = 1, 2, \ldots, n \qquad (4.1.1)$$
$$E(u_t) = \mu; t = 1, 2, \ldots, n$$

could therefore be transformed as

$$Y_t = (\alpha + \mu) + \beta X_t + (u_t - \mu); t = 1, 2, \ldots, n \qquad (4.1.2)$$

The new disturbances $u_t - \mu$ would have a zero mean for all values of t, and $\alpha + \mu$ and β could be estimated under standard assumptions. Admittedly it would not be possible to estimate α and μ separately, but the intercept is not always a meaningful economic parameter and this would seldom be a real problem. Similarly, the normality assumption is not unduly restrictive: although one can sometimes argue that it is not appropriate to assume normality of the disturbance distributions, there is no obvious alternative that is widely applicable and, in any case, the results which hold exactly when the disturbances are normal will often hold approximately, in large samples, when the disturbances are not restricted to normality. This leaves the assumptions of constant variance and independence (or zero covariance), and there certainly are occasions on which one might object to the limitations imposed by these conditions. In this chapter, we consider the removal of each of these assumptions in turn. To concentrate attention on the problem to hand, very simple forms of model are used to illustrate the discussion and it is implicit that, where possible, when a particular assumption is removed, all other assumptions continue to hold. It should also be noted that, although we might refer to the removal of the independence assumption, this might equally be taken to refer to the removal of the weaker assumption of lack of correlation (zero covariance). It is certainly not intended that independence is simply replaced by zero covariance: the case to be considered is that in which there is some specific pattern of association between disturbances, so that at least some cov (u_t, u_s) are nonzero, for $s \neq t$.

The properties of the OLS estimators which depend on the disturbances being at least uncorrelated and having constant variance are

1 The fact that the form of var $(\hat{\beta}_j)$ is

$$\text{var}(\hat{\beta}_j) = \sigma^2/\Sigma \widetilde{X}_{jt}^2 \qquad (4.1.3)$$

2 The minimum variance property that makes OLS a best linear unbiased estimator.

Now it may or may not be true that the removal of the assumptions invalidates these properties, but it is certainly likely that this would happen, for it seems pointless to make assumptions unless they are needed. In fact, the consequences of removing the assumptions are precisely what we would expect. The variance of a single OLS estimator would now be different from that shown in equation 4.1.3 and, although the OLS estimators are still linear unbiased, they no longer have the minimum variance property that makes them best linear unbiased. This essentially disposes of one of the questions that should be asked on introducing new conditions for the disturbances. It is also suggestive as to the answer to the other question, concerning alternative methods of estimation. If the OLS estimators are no longer best linear unbiased, then we should look for an alternative estimator that does have this property. To see how best linear unbiased estimators can be obtained, we consider the first special case, that in which the disturbances do not have equal variance. The section which follows is rather long, but there is a reason for this. The first special case is used to establish general principles for dealing with disturbance 'problems' and, having dealt with one case in some detail, we will find it relatively easy to apply similar principles to alternative patterns of disturbance behaviour.

4.2 Heteroscedasticity

When the disturbances do not have constant variance, the model is said to be subject to *heteroscedasticity*: alternatively, we may say that the disturbances are heteroscedastic. To illustrate the nature of the problem, consider a simple model with a single 'genuine' explanatory variable but no intercept term:

$$Y_t = \beta X_t + u_t; t = 1, 2, \ldots, n \tag{4.2.1}$$

The variances of the disturbance terms are now written as

$$\text{var}(u_t) = \sigma_t^2; t = 1, 2, \ldots, n \tag{4.2.2}$$

where the subscript t signifies the fact that the individual variances may all be different. We shall, in due course, give examples to show why heteroscedasticity may occur, but first we shall concentrate on the implications for the estimation of the parameter β.

A simple regression run on equation 4.2.1 would provide an estimate of β, but this estimate would be a particular value taken by the OLS estimator. From the discussion in the previous section, we know that the OLS estimator is still linear unbiased, but is no longer best linear unbiased. We should therefore try to find an alternative estimator which is a minimum variance estimator, and there is a very useful trick which enables us to do this directly.

The model shown in equation 4.2.1 violates the original list of assumptions because the disturbance variances are not equal. If we can find a way to transform the model, so that the variances in the transformed model are equal, then, as long as all the other assumptions continue to be satisfied, the use of OLS on the transformed model would provide a best linear unbiased estimator.

Before we can show how the transformation works, it is necessary to recall that, if a random variable V is multiplied by a constant c, the variance of the new random variable is given by

$$\text{var}(cV) = c^2 \text{var}(V) \tag{4.2.3}$$

This is a special case of the result given in Section 2.4 concerning the variance of a linear function of random variables.

We can now apply equation 4.2.3 to the individual disturbance terms in equation 4.2.1, using a different nonrandom quantity with each u_t; $t = 1, 2, \ldots, n$. If a single disturbance u_t is multiplied by the corresponding value of $1/\sigma_t$, the transformed disturbance would have a variance given by

$$\text{var}(u_t/\sigma_t) = \text{var}(u_t)/\sigma_t^2 = \sigma_t^2/\sigma_t^2 = 1 \qquad (4.2.4)$$

An equivalent result holds for all values of t. To preserve the identity of the model, the same transformation must be applied to each term and so the transformed model would be

$$(Y_t/\sigma_t) = \beta(X_t/\sigma_t) + (u_t/\sigma_t); t = 1, 2, \ldots, n \qquad (4.2.5)$$

The transformation does not violate any of the other assumptions of the original model, and equation 4.2.4 shows that the variances of the transformed disturbances are constant (in fact a known constant, equal to 1). The application of OLS to equation 4.2.5, treating Y_t/σ_t as the dependent variable and X_t/σ_t as the explanatory variable, would therefore produce a best linear unbiased estimator for β. There is, however, a problem. To carry out the transformation shown in equation 4.2.5 it is necessary to know the value of each disturbance variance $\sigma_t^2; t = 1, 2, \ldots, n$. There are some cases in which it is reasonable to suppose that the relative size of individual variances would be known, but it is difficult to think of any case in which the absolute size of each variance would be known. The specification of the variances is therefore modified to

$$\text{var}(u_t) = \sigma_t^2 = \sigma^2\lambda_t^2; t = 1, 2, \ldots, n \qquad (4.2.6)$$

where σ^2 is an unknown constant and λ_t^2 is a value specific to the disturbance u_t. Initially, the values $\lambda_t^2; t = 1, 2, \ldots, n$ are assumed to be known. From equation 4.2.6 we can find a transformation that will produce a constant disturbance variance in the transformed model. This constant variance is unknown, but that is no different from the situation prevailing in the models considered earlier. All that we need to do is to use the positive square roots of the known components of each disturbance variance in the original model. Then

$$\text{var}(u_t/\lambda_t) = \text{var}(u_t)/\lambda_t^2 = \sigma^2\lambda_t^2/\lambda_t^2 = \sigma^2; t = 1, 2, \ldots, n \qquad (4.2.7)$$

and the appropriate transformed model is

$$(Y_t/\lambda_t) = \beta(X_t/\lambda_t) + (u_t/\lambda_t); t = 1, 2, \ldots, n \tag{4.2.8}$$

or

$$Y_t^* = \beta X_t^* + u_t^*; t = 1, 2, \ldots, n \tag{4.2.9}$$

where

$$Y_t^* = Y_t/\lambda_t;\ X_t^* = X_t/\lambda_t;\ u_t^* = u_t/\lambda_t; t = 1, 2, \ldots, n$$

It is now clear why we chose σ^2 as a representation for the unknown component in equation 4.2.6: this emerges as the unknown disturbance variance in the transformed model. It is also clear why we used squared values for the specific components: the transformation uses the positive square roots $\lambda_t; t = 1, 2, \ldots, n$.

Equation 4.2.9 is in the standard form for a linear model in the variables Y^* and X^*, and equation 4.2.7 shows that the variances of the transformed disturbances are constant. The other assumptions of the original model remain valid, so a regression run on equation 4.2.9 would define a best linear unbiased estimator. The one remaining problem is what we should call the estimator that is obtained in this way. In terms of Y^* and X^*, the variables of the transformed model, we have an OLS estimator, but in terms of Y and X, the variables of the original model, we do not have an OLS estimator. Instead, we use the description *generalized least squares* (GLS) and the distinguishing notation $\hat{\beta}_G$

$$\begin{aligned}
\hat{\beta}_G &= \Sigma X_t^* Y_t^* / \Sigma X_t^{*2} \\
&= \Sigma\left[(X_t/\lambda_t)(Y_t/\lambda_t)\right] / \Sigma\left[(X_t/\lambda_t)^2\right]
\end{aligned} \tag{4.2.10}$$

Before we go any further, we should ask whether this is the estimator that we would have obtained by using the original transformation shown in equation 4.2.5. We shall anticipate the answer to this question by using the same notation for an estimator based on equation 4.2.5:

$$\hat{\beta}_G = \Sigma\left[(X_t/\sigma_t)(Y_t/\sigma_t)\right] / \Sigma\left[(X_t/\sigma_t)^2\right] \tag{4.2.11}$$

If we now replace σ_t by $\sigma\lambda_t$, the unknown constant σ will cancel from the numerator and denominator of equation 4.2.11, leaving an expression exactly equal to 4.2.10.

Although the modified transformation 4.2.8 leaves the disturbance variance in the transformed model unknown, the transformed model can be treated exactly like any other model which satisfies all the basic assumptions. So it is possible to estimate σ^2 as

$$\hat{\sigma}^2 = \Sigma e_t^{*2}/(n-1) \qquad (4.2.12)$$

where

$$e_t^* = Y_t^* - \hat{\beta}_G X_t^*; t = 1, 2, \ldots, n \qquad (4.2.13)$$

Note that these residuals are taken from the transformed model and not from the original model. Note also that, in this example, there are $n - 1$ degrees of freedom, because the model has only a single genuine explanatory variable, with no intercept term.

Heteroscedasticity is only one of the disturbance 'problems' that we shall consider in this chapter, but in each case a similar method of estimation is used. The procedure is

1 To transform the model, so as to create disturbances which are independent (or at least uncorrelated) and which have constant variance
2 To apply OLS to the transformed model.

Again, in each case, the estimator is described as a *GLS estimator*, with reference to the variables in the original model. The transformation required does vary from problem to problem and the GLS estimator does not always take the form shown in equation 4.2.10: apart from anything else, this expression applies only to a model with single explanatory variable and no intercept term. Even for this special case, the form of the estimator changes under different disturbance specifications. But we do not really need explicit expressions for the estimators. As well as showing what GLS estimation actually does, the method of transformation is a very convenient practical procedure. Once we know the appropriate transformation for a particular disturbance problem, all that we need to do is to run a standard regression calculation on the transformed model. It is worth pursuing the implications of this a little further.

First, it should be noted that one can use exactly the same procedure when there are several explanatory variables. The appropriate transformation follows from a property of the disturbances and the number of variables in the original model is irrelevant. All that we do is to apply the transformation to all the variables that are used. Then, by treating a regression on the transformed model exactly like any

other regression calculation, one can produce standard errors and test
statistics as well as the parameter estimates. What we actually want are
measures appropriate to GLS estimation, rather than those for OLS
estimation. In fact, because the regression is run on the transformed
model, almost all the statistics produced are correct. We have already
seen that one can obtain an estimate of σ^2, the unknown component of
the original disturbance variance, and it can be shown that this corresponds to the correct unbiased estimator. The standard errors and t
statistics would also be correct, but there is a potential problem with
the appropriate definition of R^2. The statistic that would be calculated
'automatically' from a regression on the transformed model relates
to the transformed dependent variable observations. The usual practice
in GLS estimation is to employ the conventional R^2, defined in
Section 3.4, which relates to the original dependent variable observations. Note that, in this case, if the degree of explanation is very low,
it is technically possible for R^2 to be negative.

There is also one further point that we should mention here. The
original model, shown in equation 4.2.1, does not contain an intercept
term, and the same is true of the transformed model shown in equation
4.2.8. Even when the original model does have an intercept, the transformed model may not. Consider the example

$$Y_t = \alpha + \beta X_t + u_t\,; t = 1, 2, \ldots, n \qquad (4.2.14)$$
$$\text{var}\,(u_t) = \sigma^2 \lambda_t^2; t = 1, 2, \ldots, n$$

After transformation, this becomes

$$(Y_t/\lambda_t) = \alpha(1/\lambda_t) + \beta(X_t/\lambda_t) + (u_t/\lambda_t); t = 1, 2, \ldots, n \qquad (4.2.15)$$

The variable attached to the parameter α is now a genuine variable,
which would, by definition, take different values for different observations if heteroscedasticity is present in the original model. So, in
estimating the parameters of equation 4.2.14, from a regression run on
equation 4.2.15, the input variables would be Y/λ, X/λ and $1/\lambda$, but
there would be no additional intercept term. This does have implica-
tions for hand calculation since, in this case, it is no longer correct to
work with data expressed as deviations from the sample means.

Before moving on to some examples of economic models which are
likely to involve heteroscedastic disturbances, it might be useful to
consider the GLS estimator, shown in equation 4.2.10, in a slightly
different way. The implication of unequal disturbance variances is that
individual observations on the dependent variable are no longer of
equal reliability. If the variance of one particular disturbance is

relatively high, there is a correspondingly greater probability of finding
a value of that disturbance which is well away from zero. This means
that the corresponding value of the dependent variable is more likely
to contain a relatively large random error. In this sense, an observation
associated with a relatively high disturbance variance contains less
information about the underlying relationship between Y and X.

This argument would suggest that a suitable method of estimation
would be one in which individual observations are not given equal weight
in the choice of the estimated line. Those observations corresponding to
a relatively high disturbance variance should be given a relatively low
weight, since a high variance implies low reliability: observations
corresponding to relatively low disturbance variances should be given
a high weighting. This is precisely what the estimator shown in equation
4.2.10 does. The estimator is

$$\hat{\beta}_G = \Sigma\,[(X_t/\lambda_t)(Y_t/\lambda_t)]\,/\,\Sigma\,[(X_t/\lambda_t)^2]$$
$$= \Sigma\,[(1/\lambda_t^2)X_tY_t]\,/\,\Sigma\,[(1/\lambda_t^2)X_t^2]$$

or

$$\hat{\beta}_G = \Sigma(w_tX_tY_t)\,/\,\Sigma(w_tX_t^2) \tag{4.2.16}$$

where

$$w_t = 1/\lambda_t^2;\, t = 1, 2, \ldots, n$$

When the variance of a particular disturbance is high, the weight w_t is
low, and vice versa. An estimator in the form of equation 4.2.16 is
sometimes called a *weighted least squares estimator*, and this description holds for any set of nonrandom weights $w_t; t = 1, 2, \ldots, n$. But
it is only when the weights are those that make the estimator best
linear unbiased that the weighted least squares estimator is also a GLS
estimator.

We now consider whether it is reasonable to assume that the values
$\lambda_t^2; t = 1, 2, \ldots, n$ would be known. If one has some specific reason to
suspect the presence of heteroscedasticity, it might well be possible to
proceed in this way. Suppose that we have observations relating to
household expenditure on food F and household disposable income D,
for a cross-section of individual households during a single time period.
To keep the illustration simple, suppose that we are satisfied with a
linear relationship between F and D and that we ignore any other
complications, such as household size. The model might then be

$$F_t = \beta D_t + u_t;\, t = 1, 2, \ldots, n \tag{4.2.17}$$

where the subscript t identifies individual households. According to the model, household expenditure on food is a constant proportion β of household disposable income, and the only departures from this rule are assumed to consist of effects that can be adequately represented by random disturbance terms.

The main part of this model is really too simple to justify the assumption that the disturbances are purely random, but even with a more elaborate specification it is possible that we would still be faced with the following problem. Although, in some average sense, food expenditure may be related to disposable income, high income households are not constrained to follow this rule as closely as those with lower levels of income. In giving reasons for this, we must be careful. One might cite differential holdings of liquid assets or different opportunities for bulk purchase as examples of the sort of influence that would allow high income households greater freedom in varying their pattern of food purchase from that suggested by disposable income in a given period. It is certainly true that both of these factors would tend to increase the apparent disturbance variance of high income households, given the specification of the model shown in equation 4.2.17. On the other hand, it might be argued that influences of this kind, which can be identified, ought properly to belong to the main part of the model and that it is the many small unidentified influences on the purchasing behaviour of households that make up the 'natural' disturbances to the expenditure—income relationship. One should certainly be careful to include all major influences in the main part of the model, to avoid specification bias, but even when one does this it is still possible that the disturbances to a cross-section expenditure—income relationship will exhibit the symptoms of heteroscedasticity.

There is some further information implicit in the statement of the problem above. It was argued that high income households would tend to be associated with relatively high disturbance variances and, if we assume that the disturbance variances are actually proportional to disposable income, we would have

$$\text{var}\,(u_t) = \delta D_t\,; t = 1, 2, \ldots, n \tag{4.2.18}$$

where δ is an unknown parameter. Once we have this additional hypothesis, the disturbance variances follow a specification equivalent to equation 4.2.6. The values $D_t\,; t = 1, 2, \ldots, n$, represent a set of known values which are equivalent to $\lambda_t^2\,; t = 1, 2, \ldots, n$, and δ is an unknown constant, equivalent to σ^2 in equation 4.2.6. The application

of the transformation shown in equation 4.2.8 to this particular case
would therefore give a transformed model

$$(F_t/\sqrt{D_t}) = \beta(D_t/\sqrt{D_t}) + (u_t/\sqrt{D_t});$$
$$= \beta(\sqrt{D_t}) + (u_t/\sqrt{D_t}); t = 1, 2, \ldots, n \qquad (4.2.19)$$

A regression run on equation 4.2.19 would provide a best linear unbiased estimator for β, provided of course that the underlying model is
correctly specified. In the particular example given, that assumption is
somewhat optimistic.

The relationship between food expenditure and disposable income
can be used to provide a second example of a model with heteroscedastic disturbances, and the main purpose of this example is to show that
heteroscedasticity may arise simply because of a data problem. Suppose
that the only data available consist of average food expenditure and
average disposable income for groups of households. The results of
official expenditure surveys are often published in precisely this form,
with households grouped according to the level of income. Suppose
that there are m income groups, indexed as $i = 1, 2, \ldots, m$ and that, in
group i, there are $n(i)$. Then suppose that we have exactly the same hypothesis as before, except that individual observations are now indexed by
group and number within the group. The model can be written as

$$F_{it} = \beta D_{it} + u_{it}; t = 1, 2, \ldots, n(i); \; i = 1, 2, \ldots, m \qquad (4.2.20)$$

Ideally, we should use equation 4.2.20 as the basis for estimation but,
because of the lack of suitable data, this is impossible. Instead we have
to derive a form of model which relates to the averages for each income
group. The averaging process consists of adding over all observations in
a given group and then dividing by the number of households in that
group. To preserve the identity of the model, the averaging operation
has to be applied to both sides of equation 4.2.20. This gives

$$\sum_{t=1}^{t=n(i)} F_{it}/n(i) = \sum_{t=1}^{t=n(i)} (\beta D_{it} + u_{it})/n(i)$$

$$= \beta \left[\sum_{t=1}^{t=n(i)} D_{it}/n(i) \right] + \left[\sum_{t=1}^{t=n(i)} u_{it}/n(i) \right]$$

or
$$\bar{F}_i = \beta \bar{D}_i + \bar{u}_i$$

where $\bar{F}_i, \bar{D}_i$ and $\bar{u}_i$ are all group averages. Hence the derived model is

$$\bar{F}_i = \beta \bar{D}_i + \bar{u}_i; i = 1, 2, \ldots, m \qquad (4.2.21)$$

Because equation 4.2.21 does not represent the original model, the properties of the disturbances $\bar{u}_i; i = 1, 2, \ldots, m$ should really be derived from assumptions concerning the original disturbances u_{it}; $t = 1, 2, \ldots, n(i); i = 1, 2, \ldots, m$. To bring out the main point of the example, we shall assume that the original variances are constant. This is not a serious constraint: if there is heteroscedasticity associated with the disturbances to the original model, one would require only a small modification to the method presented below. We therefore assume that

$$\text{var}\,(u_{it}) = \sigma^2; t = 1, 2, \ldots, n(i);\ i = 1, 2, \ldots, m \qquad (4.2.22)$$

It then follows that the variances in the derived model would be

$$\text{var}\,(\bar{u}_i) = \sigma^2/n(i); i = 1, 2, \ldots, m \qquad (4.2.23)$$

This last statement can be verified by applying the rule for the variance of a linear function to the expression

$$\bar{u}_i = \sum_{t=1}^{t=n(i)} [1/n(i)]\,u_{it}$$

Given that the disturbances are at least uncorrelated, the result is

$$\text{var}\,(\bar{u}_i) = \sum_{t=1}^{t=n(i)} [1/n(i)]^2\,\text{var}\,(u_{it}) = n(i)\sigma^2/[n(i)]^2 = \sigma^2/n(i)$$

An exactly equivalent result holds for each $\bar{u}_i; i = 1, 2, \ldots, m$.

The implication of equation 4.2.23 is that there will be a problem of heteroscedasticity inherent in using the derived model as the basis for estimation, unless it so happens that all the income groups are of the same size. However, the pattern of heteroscedasticity again corresponds to the general specification shown in equation 4.2.6, with σ^2 as an unknown constant and $1/n(i); i = 1, 2, \ldots, m$ as a set of known specific components. The application of the transformation shown in equation 4.2.8 would therefore give

$$\sqrt{[n(i)]}\,\bar{F}_i = \beta\sqrt{[n(i)]}\,\bar{D}_i + \sqrt{[n(i)]}\,\bar{u}_i; i = 1, 2, \ldots, m \qquad (4.2.24)$$

and a regression run on equation 4.2.24 would provide a best linear unbiased estimator for β, provided again that the underlying model is correctly specified.

The examples presented above show that one can proceed by assuming a pattern of heteroscedasticity similar to equation 4.2.6, treating the specific weights as known values. In practice it may be more sensible to use these ideas to suggest a possible pattern of heteroscedasticity, but to conduct an appropriate test to see whether some form of GLS estimation is actually needed. Before discussing this alternative approach, there is one further example to consider.

In Section 3.8 it was argued that a stochastic restriction of the form

$$r_0 = \beta_1 r_1 + \beta_2 r_2 + \ldots + \beta_j r_j + \ldots + \beta_k r_k + v \qquad (4.2.25)$$

could be imposed on the parameters of the general model

$$Y_t = \beta_1 + \beta_2 X_{2t} + \ldots + \beta_j X_{jt} + \ldots + \beta_k X_{kt} + u_t; t = 1, 2, \ldots, n \qquad (4.2.26)$$

by treating r_0 as an additional observation on the dependent variable and $r_j; j = 1, 2, \ldots, k$ as additional observations on each of the explanatory variables. There is no particular reason to suppose that the disturbances $u_t; t = 1, 2, \ldots, n$ would be heteroscedastic, but the variance of v would be specified by the investigator as a measure of the precision of the stochastic constraint, and it is highly unlikely that this would be the same as the disturbance variances in equation 4.2.26. So there will be a problem in the estimation of the parameters of the complete model, consisting of equations 4.2.25 and 4.2.26. Taking both types of disturbance together, we have

$$\text{var}(u_t) = \sigma^2; t = 1, 2, \ldots, n \text{ and } \text{var}(v) = \delta^2 \qquad (4.2.27)$$

where δ^2 is a known constant. What is needed is a transformation that will equalize the variances in the transformed model. If σ^2 were known, all that we would do is to transform the restriction as

$$(r_0 \sigma/\delta) = \beta_1(r_1 \sigma/\delta) + \beta_2(r_2 \sigma/\delta) + \ldots + \beta_k(r_k \sigma/\delta) + (v\sigma/\delta) \quad (4.2.28)$$

for then

$$\text{var}(v\sigma/\delta) = \text{var}(v)\sigma^2/\delta^2 = \sigma^2$$

Unfortunately σ^2 is not likely to be known, and so the following strategy might be used. A regression run on equation 4.2.26, without the restriction, will provide a set of unrestricted estimates $\hat{\beta}_j; j = 1, 2, \ldots, k$ and a set of residuals $e_t; t = 1, 2, \ldots, n$. From these residuals, it is possible to estimate σ^2 as

$$\hat{\sigma}^2 = \Sigma e_t^2/(n-k)$$

We could then use the transformation shown in equation 4.2.28, with $\hat{\sigma}^2$ in place of the unknown true value σ^2 and, having transformed the restriction in this way, a second regression could be run on equation 4.2.26, together with the transformed restriction. In later sections of this chapter, we shall find that there are many cases in which one has to adopt this type of two step approach; however, we shall also find that there are some implications for estimator properties, which are considered in Section 4.6.

4.3   Testing for heteroscedasticity

In each of the examples mentioned in the previous section there was some reason to expect heteroscedasticity to occur, but it is clearly possible to find cases in which one would not anticipate the problem, or in which there is some uncertainty as to whether or not the disturbances are heteroscedastic. It is therefore necessary to consider methods for testing the null hypothesis of no heteroscedasticity, against some alternative which does allow the disturbance variance to change between observations. Ideally, any such test would be based on the disturbances u_t; $t = 1, 2, \ldots, n$, but these cannot be observed, so residuals must be used instead. One could consider using GLS residuals, but it would be very awkward to have to pick an appropriate GLS estimator in advance of a test designed to see whether GLS is actually needed. It is clearly more convenient to use OLS residuals, which in the general case are given by

$$e_t = Y_t - \hat{\beta}_1 - \hat{\beta}_2 X_{2t} - \ldots - \hat{\beta}_k X_{kt}; t = 1, 2, \ldots, n \qquad (4.3.1)$$

Unfortunately, OLS residuals do not reproduce the behaviour of the disturbances exactly. Because the residuals are linked by the estimators $\hat{\beta}_1, \hat{\beta}_2, \ldots, \hat{\beta}_k$, one can show that e_t; $t = 1, 2, \ldots, n$ are neither independent nor uncorrelated, even when the disturbances are 'well behaved'. This means that the distributions of test statistics based on OLS residuals are rather more complicated than those of the corresponding (but unobservable) quantities based on the disturbances. One could simply accept this complexity and proceed to derive the small sample distribution for a test statistic based on OLS residuals, but there are alternative approaches. One possibility, which forms the basis for a number of suggested tests, is to obtain a set of residuals which are uncorrelated. In this connection, the reader may find references in the literature to BLUS residuals, to recursive residuals and to tests based on partitioning a given set of data into two or more regimes. Another possibility is to use OLS residuals, but to employ a large sample approximation to the distribution of the chosen test statistic. Although such an approach does have certain disadvantages, in that there are approximations involved, it does allow us to produce a test procedure which is relatively simple to implement and which does have a fairly strong intuitive appeal.

Before proceeding any further, it is useful to note a slightly different way of expressing a conventional regression model. Suppose that we have

$$Y_t = \beta_1 + \beta_2 X_{2t} + \ldots + \beta_k X_{kt} + u_t;$$
$$E(u_t) = 0; t = 1, 2, \ldots, n \tag{4.3.2}$$

Provided that the explanatory variable observations are nonrandom, equation 4.3.2 implies that

$$E(Y_t) = \beta_1 + \beta_2 X_{2t} + \ldots + \beta_k X_{kt}; t = 1, 2, \ldots, n \tag{4.3.3}$$

Although one cannot observe $E(Y_t)$ directly, a regression of Y on $X_1, X_2, \ldots, X_k$ provides a means of estimating the parameters $\beta_1, \beta_2, \ldots, \beta_k$. Now suppose that we believe that the disturbance variance could be expressed as a linear function of some nonrandom variable Z. In many cases, Z would be one of the explanatory variables in the original model, but it could also be a time trend, a dummy variable, or some other variable which does not appear in the original model. The suggested relationship can be written as

$$\text{var}(u_t) = \sigma_t^2 = \delta_1 + \delta_2 Z_t; t = 1, 2, \ldots, n \tag{4.3.4}$$

or, since $\text{var}(u_t) = E([u_t - E(u_t)]^2)$ and $E(u_t) = 0; t = 1, 2, \ldots, n$, we could also write

$$\text{var}(u_t) = E(u_t^2) = \delta_1 + \delta_2 Z_t; t = 1, 2, \ldots, n \tag{4.3.5}$$

There is an obvious analogy between equations 4.3.3 and 4.3.5: if one can use the observations $Y_t; t = 1, 2, \ldots, n$ to estimate the parameters of 4.3.3, one could in theory use the observations $u_t^2; t = 1, 2, \ldots, n$ to estimate the parameters of 4.3.5. Specifically, if one could run a regression of u^2 on Z, with an intercept, then one would obtain estimates of the parameters δ_1 and δ_2. In practice one would have to use residuals in place of the disturbances, and so what we are suggesting is a regression of e^2 on any variable that is thought to determine the behaviour of the disturbance variance. This clearly gives a way of estimating the parameters associated with a particular pattern of heteroscedasticity: as we shall see below, it also gives a basis for testing to see whether heteroscedasticity is actually present.

In equation 4.3.5 the condition $\delta_2 = 0$ would imply a constant variance, equal to δ_1. The null hypothesis of no heteroscedasticity can therefore be specified by writing equation 4.3.5 with the additional restriction $\delta_2 = 0$. The alternative would be $\delta_2 \neq 0$, implying a pattern of heteroscedasticity in which the disturbance variance is a linear function of Z. This is a slightly more general alternative than the type of strict proportionality discussed in the previous section, and we shall have more to say about this below. For the moment, consider the suggestion of a regression of e^2 on Z, with an intercept. The result of such a regression would be an estimated equation of the form

$$\hat{e}_t^2 = \hat{\delta}_1 + \hat{\delta}_2 Z_t; t = 1, 2, \ldots, n \qquad (4.3.6)$$

It is tempting to conclude that one could apply a conventional t test to equation 4.3.6, to see whether it is possible to reject H_0: $\delta_2 = 0$. In fact, although this is close to the procedure adopted, the t test could only be justified asymptotically, and it is possible to improve on this approach by exploiting the fact that the 'dependent' variable in the proposed regression actually consists of squared residuals from a previous regression. One can also generalize by allowing the disturbance variance to depend on several variables, $Z_1, Z_2, \ldots, Z_p$, where $Z_{1t} = 1$; $t = 1, 2, \ldots, n$.

The complete test procedure is therefore as follows. One would first select those variables Z_2 to Z_p which are thought to have a possible influence on the disturbance variance σ_t^2. As suggested earlier, these variables may actually be a selection from the list X_2 to X_k, but they could also be variables which do not appear in the original model. The next step is to obtain squared residuals from an OLS regression on the original model and to use these to estimate a second regression equation, of the form

$$\hat{e}_t^2 = \hat{\delta}_1 + \hat{\delta}_2 Z_{2t} + \ldots + \hat{\delta}_p Z_p; t = 1, 2, \ldots, n \qquad (4.3.7)$$

In this context, the null hypothesis of no heteroscedasticity in the original model would be equivalent to H_0: $\delta_2 = \delta_3 = \ldots = \delta_p = 0$. The alternative would be that at least one of δ_2 to δ_p is nonzero. If all the necessary assumptions were satisfied, one could use an F test of the type described in Section 3.7. As it is, the use of an F test is not really justified and the statistic actually used is

$$\chi^2 = (S_R - S)/2(\Sigma e_t^2/n)^2 \qquad (4.3.8)$$

Technical note 6

In practice, it may be convenient to use either Σe_t^2 or $\Sigma e_t^2/n$ as a scale factor in the regression 4.3.7. For example, if $\Sigma e_t^2/n$ is used, the 'dependent variable' observations would become $g_t = e_t^2/(\Sigma e_t^2/n) = n e_t^2/\Sigma e_t^2; t = 1, 2, \ldots, n$ and equation 4.3.8 would become

$$\chi^2 = (S_R - S)/2$$

where S_R and S now refer to the modified regression.

In equation 4.3.8, Σe_t^2 is the residual sum of squares from the OLS regression on the original model, S is the residual sum of squares from the regression of e^2 on $Z_1, Z_2, \ldots, Z_p$, and S_R is the residual sum of squares from a regression of e^2 on Z_1, where $Z_{1t} = 1; t = 1, 2, \ldots, n$. Alternatively, the computer output may provide a value for the 'explained' sum of squares: if so, $S_R - S$ is the explained sum of squares from the regression of e^2 on $Z_1, Z_2, \ldots, Z_p$.

Under the null hypothesis of no heteroscedasticity, the test statistic 4.3.8 has approximately a χ^2 (*chi-square*) distribution, with $p - 1$ degrees of freedom. We have not previously used a chi-square test, but the methodology is in most respects similar to that for an F test. Table D (p. 271) gives critical values for upper tail probabilities of 0·10, 0·05 and 0·01. As with an F test, the null hypothesis is rejected if the calculated value of the test statistic is greater than a chosen critical value. However, unlike the F distribution, the chi-square distribution depends only on one set of degrees of freedom. Thus, for a significance level of 0·05, the condition for rejection of the null hypothesis would be $\chi^2 > \chi_{p-1}^{2(0 \cdot 05)}$, where $\chi_{p-1}^{2(0 \cdot 05)}$ is the critical value which gives an upper tail probability of 0·05, for a variable which has a χ^2 distribution, with $p - 1$ degrees of freedom.

The procedure described above is known as the *Breusch-Pagan test*, and it has been shown that exactly the same procedure can be used for detecting patterns of heteroscedasticity such as

$$\sigma_t^2 = (\delta_1 + \delta_2 Z_{2t} + \ldots + \delta_p Z_{pt})^2; t = 1, 2, \ldots, n \qquad (4.3.9)$$

or

$$\sigma_t^2 = \exp(\delta_1 + \delta_2 Z_{2t} + \ldots + \delta_p Z_{pt}); t = 1, 2, \ldots, n \qquad (4.3.10)$$

as well as the purely linear form

$$\sigma_t^2 = \delta_1 + \delta_2 Z_{2t} + \ldots + \delta_p Z_{pt}; t = 1, 2, \ldots, n \qquad (4.3.11)$$

The significance of this result is that, whichever alternative one chooses, a test of the null hypothesis of no heteroscedasticity is still based on the linear regression

$$\hat{e}_t^2 = \hat{\delta}_1 + \hat{\delta}_2 Z_{2t} + \ldots + \hat{\delta}_p Z_{pt}; t = 1, 2, \ldots, n \qquad (4.3.12)$$

If the null hypothesis is rejected, one should use GLS to estimate the parameters of the original model. Unfortunately, this would involve the values $\sigma_t^2; t = 1, 2, \ldots, n$, which depend on the unknown parameters $\delta_1, \delta_2, \ldots, \delta_p$, so the best that one can do is to approximate GLS estimation by first finding an estimating equation for $\sigma_t^2; t = 1, 2, \ldots, n$

and then using the resulting estimates to transform the original model. If the alternative is in the form of equation 4.3.11, the obvious procedure is to use equation 4.3.12 as a sample analogue. This leads to the estimating equation

$$\hat{\sigma}_t^2 = \delta_1 + \delta_2 Z_{2t} + \ldots + \delta_p Z_{pt}; t = 1, 2, \ldots, n$$

For this alternative only, the regression used to produce the estimates $\hat{\sigma}_t^2; t = 1, 2, \ldots, n$ is the same as that used for the Breusch-Pagan test and the estimates are simply predicted values from a regression of e^2 on Z_1 to Z_p. In any other case, one would have to transform the alternative hypothesis in such a way as to suggest an appropriate estimating equation, and this equation will be different to that used in the test. For example, from equation 4.3.10 we have

$$\log (\sigma_t^2) = \delta_1 + \delta_2 Z_{2t} + \ldots + \delta_p Z_{pt}; t = 1, 2, \ldots, n \qquad (4.3.13)$$

Remember that, throughout this book, log is taken to indicate that natural logarithms are used. The sample analogue of 4.3.13 would be a regression of $\log (e^2)$ on Z_1 to Z_p. Setting $q_t = \log (e_t^2)$ and using $\hat{q}_t; t = 1, 2, \ldots, n$ to denote the predicted values from this regression, the disturbance variance estimates would be obtained as

$$\hat{\sigma}_t^2 = \exp (\hat{q}_t); t = 1, 2, \ldots, n$$

Once the disturbance variance estimates have been found, we can transform the original model in the following way

$$(Y_t/\hat{\sigma}_t) = \beta_1(1/\hat{\sigma}_t) + \beta_2(X_{2t}/\hat{\sigma}_t) + \ldots + \beta_k(X_{kt}/\hat{\sigma}_t) + (u_t/\hat{\sigma}_t)$$
$$t = 1, 2, \ldots, n \qquad (4.3.14)$$

Although a regression run on equation 4.3.14 does not produce exact GLS estimates of the parameters $\beta_1, \beta_2, \ldots, \beta_k$, the procedure described does at least produce an approximation to the GLS estimates. As mentioned earlier, there are many cases in which such 'two step' methods are used, and the properties of the resulting estimators are discussed in Section 4.6.

It is perhaps slightly misleading to have concentrated attention on a single test for heteroscedasticity. In practice, many different methods are used. The suggested test does, however, have certain merits. First, it is based on an additional regression calculation and is therefore easy to implement. Next, it is capable of detecting a fairly wide variety of different patterns of heteroscedasticity and so has a generality which is not shared by tests designed for more specific alternatives. Finally, for our purposes, it is helpful to have an example of a χ^2 test, given that we have not previously made use of the χ^2 distribution.

The one remaining problem is that the test suggested above does not appear to cover examples of the kind used in the previous section, in which the disturbance variance is strictly proportional to observations on a single variable. In a sense, this is a special case of equation 4.3.11, in which $\delta_1 = 0$. Unfortunately, the test assumes that δ_1 is not zero. If we had the form

$$\sigma_t^2 = \delta_1 + \delta_2 Z_t; t = 1, 2, \ldots, n \qquad (4.3.15)$$

with $\delta_1 = 0$ by assumption and $\delta_2 = 0$ under the null hypothesis, the implication would be a null hypothesis of zero disturbance variance rather than a constant nonzero disturbance variance. In fact, this difficulty is more apparent than real. One approach would be to modify the proportionality hypothesis, admitting the slightly more general linear form 4.3.15. Another would be to maintain proportionality, but to argue that a test based on the linear form should be capable of detecting this. Finally, we could exploit the fact that the test is capable of detecting a pattern such as equation 4.3.10. Suppose that σ_t^2 is assumed to be proportional to the observations on some variable X. There is nothing to prevent us from defining Z to be the logarithm of the variable X and writing

$$\begin{aligned} \sigma_t^2 &= \exp{(\delta_1 + \delta_2 Z_t)} \\ &= \exp{(\delta_1 + \delta_2 \log X_t)} \end{aligned} \qquad (4.3.16)$$

With this form, the null hypothesis $\delta_2 = 0$ implies a constant disturbance variance, equal to $\exp{(\delta_1)}$. On the other hand, the value $\delta_2 = 1$ implies that σ^2 is proportional to X. Hence equation 4.3.16 is a slightly more general alternative than simple proportionality, but a test based on the estimated regression

$$\begin{aligned} \hat{e}_t^2 &= \hat{\delta}_1 + \hat{\delta}_2 Z_t \\ &= \hat{\delta}_1 + \hat{\delta}_2 \log X_t \end{aligned}$$

should certainly be capable of detecting heteroscedasticity in the case in which σ^2 is strictly proportional to X.

There is one final comment to make, concerning the detection of heteroscedasticity in the results from a conventional OLS regression. We have suggested a formal test procedure, based on an attempt to 'explain' the observed behaviour of the squared OLS residuals e_t^2; $t = 1, 2, \ldots, n$. Although the Breusch-Pagan test is relatively straightforward, it cannot really be described as a routine procedure to be performed, as a matter of course, on the residuals from any OLS regression, because one does have to give some thought to the variables to which the disturbance variance is to be related. What one can do, routinely, is to examine a graph of residuals, or better still a graph of squared residuals, to see whether there is any apparent pattern to the variability of residuals over the observations in the sample. One could also plot squared residuals against any variable that could be associated with changes in the disturbance variance. Graphical procedures are very simple, but they represent an important source of information that should not be overlooked.

4.4 Serial correlation

We now consider what happens when the assumption of independence is removed and replaced by some specific pattern of correlation between the disturbances. As mentioned earlier, what we have to say would apply equally to the case in which the assumption removed is actually that of zero covariance, or lack of correlation between disturbances. The usual context for this problem is that of a time series of observations and, in this case, the independence assumption would break down if the disturbance in one period does have an influence on the disturbance in the following period. It would be implausible to argue that successive disturbances are exactly determined by the value in the previous period. If this were true for all time periods it would imply that, once the first period disturbance had taken a particular value, the future behaviour of the disturbances would be deterministic. It is more reasonable to suppose that successive disturbances are partly determined by previous values, but that there is also an additional random component to each disturbance. In other words, we could model the disturbance process in a way which is very similar to that previously used for relationships between economic variables, replacing the assumption of independence by a particular hypothesis about the way in which successive disturbances are linked. One novel feature is that such a hypothesis involves a linkage which extends over the divisions between different periods of time.

A simple form of relationship, applied to the disturbances, would be

$$u_t = \rho u_{t-1} + v_t; t = 1, 2, \ldots, n \qquad (4.4.1)$$

where u_t is determined in part by the previous value u_{t-1} and in part by a new random variable v_t. The quantity ρ is a parameter of the relationship. Thus a particular disturbance, say u_2, is determined as

$$u_2 = \rho u_1 + v_2$$

But equation 4.4.1 also implies that u_1 is formed in a similar way,

$$u_1 = \rho u_0 + v_1$$

where u_0 is a starting value for the process by which the disturbances are generated. The value u_0 may in turn have been determined by earlier values, but this is outside the scope of our model. Continuing the analogy with the modelling of economic relationships, we assume that v_t has all the characteristics previously attributed to u_t. So u_t; $t = 1, 2, \ldots, n$ are no longer independent, but the new disturbances v_t; $t = 1, 2, \ldots, n$ are independent, with zero means and constant variance. Because we wish to examine one problem at a time, we have ruled out the possibility that the new disturbances are heteroscedastic.

The process shown in equation 4.4.1 is a particular example of a situation in which there is *serial correlation* (or *autocorrelation*) of the disturbances u_t; $t = 1, 2, \ldots, n$. There are two respects in which 4.4.1 is a specialized example. The first concerns the form of 4.4.1 in which u_t is linked to a past value u_{t-1} by means of a regression type relationship. This is known as an *autoregressive* process. Next, it is a first order process, because u_t is explicitly related to u_{t-1} and not to earlier values such as u_{t-2}, u_{t-3}, etc. There is, of course, an indirect relationship between u_t and earlier values. For a particular time period, say $t = 3$, we have

$$u_3 = \rho u_2 + v_3$$

But it is also true that

$$u_2 = \rho u_1 + v_2$$

and that

$$u_1 = \rho u_0 + v_1$$

Putting these equations together, we have

$$u_3 = \rho u_2 + v_3$$
$$= \rho(\rho u_1 + v_2) + v_3$$
$$= \rho(\rho(\rho u_0 + v_1) + v_2) + v_3$$

or

$$u_3 = \rho^3 u_0 + \rho^2 v_1 + \rho v_2 + v_3$$

More generally, u_t is directly linked to u_{t-1}, but it can also be expressed in terms of any earlier value, as far back as the starting value u_0. The other terms in these expressions are past values of the new disturbances. By analogy with the example above, the relationship between u_t and u_0 is

$$u_t = \rho^t u_0 + [\rho^{t-1} v_1 + \rho^{t-2} v_2 + \ldots + \rho v_{t-1} + v_t]; t = 1, 2, \ldots, n$$

(4.4.2)

Equations 4.4.1 and 4.4.2 are alternative expressions for the *dynamic* process by which the successive values u_t; $t = 1, 2, \ldots, n$ are determined. Whereas previously the disturbances in each time period could be treated quite separately, we now have a hypothesis concerning the evolution of disturbances through time and, as equation 4.4.2 shows, it is possible to establish a relationship between any single disturbance u_t and the starting value u_0. Obviously, we would expect the starting value to have some influence on the process, but it does seem reasonable to assert that this influence should tend to diminish as we move forward in time. Ignoring the effect of the other terms in equation 4.4.2, this will only happen if ρ^t becomes progressively closer to 0 as t is increased, and this in turn requires that ρ should lie between -1 and $+1$ without reaching either extreme value. If this condition is satisfied, the term $\rho^t u_0$ diminishes in importance as we move forward in time. We therefore assume, in what follows, that $-1 < \rho < +1$.

Under ideal conditions, with a properly specified model, it is perhaps difficult to see why there should be serial correlation of the disturbances. At one level, the answer would be that independence of the disturbances is simply an assumption and that equation 4.4.1 is an alternative and less restrictive assumption. Perhaps more relevant is the argument that models are not constructed under ideal conditions and, in particular, the unit time period is largely determined by the frequency of observation of the data. There is no reason why relationships between economic variables should be fully worked through within the chosen time period. This may mean that the main part of the model involves lag relationships, in which linkages between variables extend over the divisions between successive periods of time, and we shall consider this possibility in the next chapter. But given that the disturbances are a summary representation for all the variables that are not included in the main part of the model, it seems reasonable to assert that there can be factors contributing to the disturbances which could influence the behaviour of the model for more than one time period. What this would mean is that successive disturbance terms have common components and they cannot therefore be independent. One other point is that the form of equation used for estimation is not always the same as the original specification, and there are transformations that can induce serial correlation. We shall see examples of this in due course.

There is no reason to suppose that equation 4.4.1 would always represent the correct pattern of serial correlation, but it is equally clear that the assumption of independence between successive disturbances cannot always be maintained. Once this assumption is removed, it is necessary to introduce some specific alternative hypothesis. The first order autoregressive scheme is often used as an approximation. As in the case of heteroscedasticity, we have a form of disturbance behaviour that can arise for a variety of reasons, and it is quite likely that this is not the only problem associated with a given model. Despite this fact, we must start by treating serial correlation as a property of the 'natural' disturbances to a model in which all other assumptions are satisfied.

Returning now to the problems of estimation, we again make use of the simple model

$$Y_t = \beta X_t + u_t; t = 1, 2, \ldots, n \tag{4.4.3}$$

where now

$$u_t = \rho u_{t-1} + v_t; t = 1, 2, \ldots, n$$

If OLS is used to estimate β then, as in the case of heteroscedastic disturbances, the estimator would be linear unbiased, but not best linear unbiased. It is therefore necessary to find a transformation of equation 4.4.3, chosen in such a way that the disturbances in the transformed model are at least uncorrelated. This, together with OLS estimation applied to the transformed model, would define a GLS estimator and, as long as the transformation does not violate any of the other assumptions of the model, the GLS estimator would be best linear unbiased.

If we choose a particular time period, say $t = 2$, then from equation 4.4.3 it follows that

$$Y_2 = \beta X_2 + u_2 \tag{4.4.4}$$

But it is also true that

$$Y_1 = \beta X_1 + u_1 \tag{4.4.5}$$

and, on multiplying both sides of equation 4.4.5 by ρ, that

$$\rho Y_1 = \rho(\beta X_1 + u_1) = \beta \rho X_1 + \rho u_1 \tag{4.4.6}$$

Finally, subtracting equation 4.4.6 from 4.4.4 gives

$$(Y_2 - \rho Y_1) = \beta(X_2 - \rho X_1) + (u_2 - \rho u_1) \qquad (4.4.7)$$

The last statement must be valid: because equation 4.4.6 holds, we are effectively subtracting the same quantity from both sides of equation 4.4.4. More generally, we have that

$$Y_t = \beta X_t + u_t; t = 1, 2, \ldots, n$$

so that

$$Y_{t-1} = \beta X_{t-1} + u_{t-1}; t = 2, 3, \ldots, n$$

and

$$\rho Y_{t-1} = \beta \rho X_{t-1} + \rho u_{t-1}; t = 2, 3, \ldots, n$$

and finally

$$(Y_t - \rho Y_{t-1}) = \beta(X_t - \rho X_{t-1}) + (u_t - \rho u_{t-1}); t = 2, 3, \ldots, n$$
$$(4.4.8)$$

Notice that the last three statements are true for values of t from $t = 2$ to $t = n$. They may also be true for $t = 1$, but we are looking for an operational transformation to be applied to a given set of data Y_t, X_t; $t = 1, 2, \ldots, n$, and the equivalent statements for the period $t = 1$ would involve values represented as Y_0 and X_0, which are not part of the given data.

Equation 4.4.8 does represent a transformed model in which the disturbances are independent, provided that $v_t; t = 1, 2, \ldots, n$ are independent. This follows directly from equation 4.4.1. If

$$u_t = \rho u_{t-1} + v_t; t = 1, 2, \ldots, n$$

then

$$u_t - \rho u_{t-1} = v_t; t = 1, 2, \ldots, n$$

The disturbances in equation 4.4.8 are therefore given by $v_2, v_3, \ldots, v_n$, which are independent by assumption. The only problem with 4.4.8 is that, by carrying out the transformation, we have lost an observation. For this reason, the application of OLS to 4.4.8 does not produce a best linear unbiased estimator, although such a method is often used in practice. To be strictly correct, another observation should be added to the transformed model, based on a different transformation

$$(\rho^* Y_1) = \beta(\rho^* X_1) + (\rho^* u_1) \qquad (4.4.9)$$

where

$$\rho^* = \sqrt{(1 - \rho^2)}$$

The disturbance in equation 4.4.9 has a zero mean, the same variance as $v_2, v_3, \ldots, v_n$ and it is independent of $v_2, v_3, \ldots, v_n$. We can therefore define transformed variables Y^* and X^*, where

$$Y_1^* = \rho^* Y_1 \text{ and } Y_t^* = Y_t - \rho Y_{t-1}; t = 2, 3, \ldots, n$$
$$X_1^* = \rho^* X_1 \text{ and } X_t^* = X_t - \rho X_{t-1}; t = 2, 3, \ldots, n \quad (4.4.10)$$

and a complete transformed model

$$Y_t^* = \beta X_t^* + u_t^*; t = 1, 2, \ldots, n \quad (4.4.11)$$

where

$$u_t^* = \rho^* u_1 \text{ and } u_t^* = v_t; t = 2, 3, \ldots, n$$

The application of OLS to equation 4.4.11 does produce a best linear unbiased estimator of β and, in terms of the original variables Y and X, this is a GLS estimator. Obviously one must know the value of ρ before this method can be used, and we shall have more to say about this in due course.

The procedure that we have described seems to be rather more complicated than that for heteroscedastic disturbances, although the basic approach is similar. In the simplified version, mentioned above, the additional transformed observations Y_1^* and X_1^* are ignored. This is obviously convenient, because it amounts to a regression run on equation 4.4.8 or, equivalently, on

$$Y_t^* = \beta X_t^* + u_t^*; t = 2, 3, \ldots, n \quad (4.4.12)$$

In equation 4.4.12 the $n - 1$ observations on Y^* and X^* are all generated in a similar fashion. The steps involved in creating the transformed variables are summarized in Table 3. In most cases the omission of the first observation on the transformed model makes little difference to the final estimate of β, but one can always find counter-examples. The real reason for the widespread use of the simplified approach is that of convenience.

The methods outlined above can obviously be used with a model containing several explanatory variables. All that we need to do is to apply the transformation to all the variables in the model. If there is an intercept in the original model, the transformation must also be applied to this term. So, for example

$$Y_t = \alpha + \beta X_t + u_t; t = 1, 2, \ldots, n$$

Table 3

	Original variables		Lagged variables		Multiplication by a constant		Subtraction of variables	
	Y_t	X_t	Y_{t-1}	X_{t-1}	ρY_{t-1}	ρX_{t-1}	Y_t^*	X_t^*
t								
2	Y_2	X_2	Y_1	X_1	ρY_1	ρX_1	$Y_2 - \rho Y_1$	$X_2 - \rho X_1$
3	Y_3	X_3	Y_2	X_2	ρY_2	ρX_2	$Y_3 - \rho Y_2$	$X_3 - \rho X_2$
.	.	.	.	.	.	.	.	.
.	.	.	.	.	.	.	.	.
.	.	.	.	.	.	.	.	.
n	Y_n	X_n	Y_{n-1}	X_{n-1}	ρY_{n-1}	ρX_{n-1}	$Y_n - \rho Y_{n-1}$	$X_n - \rho X_{n-1}$

becomes

$$Y_t - \rho Y_{t-1} = \alpha(1 - \rho) + \beta(X_t - \rho X_{t-1}) + v_t; t = 2, 3, \ldots, n$$

with an additional observation

$$\rho^* Y_1 = \alpha\rho^* + \beta\rho^* X_1 + \rho^* u_1$$

in the full GLS method. Using the simplified version, it is possible to treat $\alpha(1 - \rho)$ as a single parameter attached to a 'variable' which is always equal to 1. One can then estimate $\alpha(1 - \rho)$ as a whole and, since the value of ρ is assumed to be known, it is possible to 'unscramble' an estimate of α, the intercept in the original model. In the full GLS method, α is attached to a quantity which differs between the first observation and all other observations and this has to be treated as a true variable, with observations

$$\sqrt{(1 - \rho^2)}, (1 - \rho), (1 - \rho), \ldots, (1 - \rho)$$

The full GLS method therefore involves a regression on k genuine variables, with no additional intercept term.

The most serious difficulty with the methods described so far is that it is necessary to know the value of ρ. This is a parameter of the disturbance process, and disturbance parameters seldom have known values. We should therefore try to find an estimate of ρ and, given the form of the relationship

$$u_t = \rho u_{t-1} + v_t; t = 1, 2, \ldots, n \qquad (4.4.13)$$

one would naturally think in terms of an estimate obtained from a regression run on equation 4.4.13. Unfortunately, the relationship involves the unobservable disturbances u_t; $t = 0, 1, \ldots, n$, and all that we can do is to replace these disturbances by residuals. If the model used is

$$Y_t = \beta X_t + u_t; t = 1, 2, \ldots, n \qquad (4.4.14)$$

the residuals that we would want are

$$e_t = Y_t - \hat{\beta} X_t; t = 1, 2, \ldots, n \qquad (4.4.15)$$

where $\hat{\beta}$ is the OLS estimator for the parameter β. A moment's thought will show that these are the appropriate residuals. We require a set of values to replace the disturbances in the original model 4.4.14, and so we should use residuals based on the original model. And we cannot even approximate a GLS estimate of β, since we do not yet have an estimate of ρ. So it is the OLS estimator that appears in equation 4.4.15.

Instead of a regression of u_t on u_{t-1}, we now consider a regression of e_t on e_{t-1}. We can only use observations for periods $t = 2$ to $t = n$, since we do not have a value for the residual that would be written as e_0. The estimator for ρ is therefore

$$\hat{\rho} = \sum_{t=2}^{t=n} (e_t e_{t-1}) \left/ \sum_{t=2}^{t=n} (e_{t-1}^2) \right. \qquad (4.4.16)$$

At this stage, we shall not worry about the properties of the estimator shown in equation 4.4.16: there is an obvious complication caused by the use of residuals in place of the unobservable disturbances, and there are other problems besides. What we do have is a regression on the residuals that will produce an estimate of ρ and, with this development, we can describe a complete procedure for the estimation of the parameter β in equation 4.4.14. The same method can be applied to a model containing several explanatory variables.

What is suggested here is a two step procedure of the type already mentioned in earlier sections of this chapter. The first step involves regressions based on the original model and the second step involves the transformed model. The first step actually consists of two regressions, one to find an OLS estimate of β and the second, using the residuals, to obtain an estimate of ρ. The second step consists of a regression on the transformed model to provide an approximation to the GLS estimate of β. It is an approximation, because the transformation uses an estimate of ρ rather than the true value. If the simplified transformation is used, a further approximation is involved. The names given to these procedures are the *Cochrane-Orcutt two step method* and the *Prais-Winsten method*. The Cochrane-Orcutt method uses the simplified transformation, ignoring the first observation, whereas the Prais-Winsten method uses the full transformation, including the first observation. As we have said before, the use of estimated disturbance parameters does have implications for the properties of the final estimators obtained from the second step of a two step procedure, and we return to this topic in Section 4.6.

Before leaving this section, we should consider briefly what the result would be if, instead of trying to estimate the value of ρ, we were to proceed as though it were true that $\rho = 1$. This would suggest that the model

$$Y_t = \beta X_t + u_t; t = 1, 2, \ldots, n \tag{4.4.17}$$

should be transformed as

$$(Y_t - Y_{t-1}) = \beta(X_t - X_{t-1}) + (u_t - u_{t-1}); t = 2, 3, \ldots, n \tag{4.4.18}$$

The variables in equation 4.4.18 are first differences of the original variables and, if it were true that $\rho = 1$, the disturbances in the transformed model would be independent. But we have suggested that ρ is usually less than 1 and, if this is the case, the disturbances in equation 4.4.18 will follow a rather complicated pattern, under which they are actually less 'well behaved' than the disturbances to the original model.

We can get some idea of what may happen by considering a related problem. Suppose now that the disturbances in equation 4.4.17 are actually independent, but that the investigator believes that there is serial correlation and proceeds to transform the model accordingly. To emphasize the nature of the 'true' model for this case, we rewrite equation 4.4.17 as

$$Y_t = \beta X_t + v_t; t = 1, 2, \ldots, n \tag{4.4.19}$$

where $v_t; t = 1, 2, \ldots, n$ are independent. Given the specification 4.4.19, the correct value for the parameter ρ would be zero, but we will suppose that the investigator uses some nonzero value, say λ, and transforms as

$$(Y_t - \lambda Y_{t-1}) = \beta(X_t - \lambda X_{t-1}) + (v_t - \lambda v_{t-1}); t = 2, 3, \ldots, n \tag{4.4.20}$$

Far from improving the model, this would actually induce serial correlation, but it is interesting to note that the disturbances in equation

4.4.20 do not follow a first order autoregressive process. Instead, there is a *moving average* disturbance scheme in the transformed model. If we write

$$u_t = v_t - \lambda v_{t-1}; t = 2, 3, \ldots, n \qquad (4.4.21)$$

it is clear that u_t and u_{t-1} cannot be independent, since both involve the term v_{t-1}. If λ is positive, there will actually be a negative correlation between u_t and u_{t-1}. But u_t and u_{t-2} will be independent, so long as $v_t; t = 1, 2, \ldots, n$ are independent. This is not true of an autoregressive process.

We have established the fact that trying to correct for positive serial correlation, when the disturbances are actually independent, will induce negative serial correlation in the form of a moving average process. This suggests that one would get a somewhat similar effect from using the first difference transformation, when the disturbances in the original model follow an autoregressive scheme, with a value of ρ which is considerably less than 1. The other point that emerges from the example above is that we have two possible types of representation for serial correlation of the disturbances. In the example, the moving average process arises as the result of a mistake in the specification, but this is not always true and, in several different contexts, a moving average process would be a more appropriate representation than an autoregressive process. The transformations required with the simplest (first order) moving average scheme consist basically of generating variables of the form

$$Y_t^* = \sum_{s=0}^{s=t-1} \lambda^s Y_{t-s}; t = 1, 2, \ldots, n$$

$$Y_t^* = \sum_{s=0}^{s=t-1} \lambda^s X_{t-s}; t = 1, 2, \ldots, n$$

Beyond this case the moving average transformations do become more complicated, although the approach is still that of trying to generate independent, or at least uncorrelated disturbances in the transformed model.

4.5 Testing for serial correlation

Following the pattern set by our discussion of heteroscedasticity, we have described an estimation procedure for use when the disturbances are serially correlated, without asking how one would know that the disturbances do actually exhibit this behaviour. One possibility would be to assume some form of serial correlation and to estimate accordingly: but if the disturbances are actually independent (or uncorrelated), OLS estimators are best linear unbiased and any other estimator would be inferior to OLS. An alternative would be to ignore the possibility of serial correlation. In this case the OLS estimators would be unbiased (if other assumptions are satisfied) but, if the disturbances are serially correlated, OLS would not give best linear unbiased estimators and, moreover, the standard errors and t ratios would be calculated incorrectly. This suggests that we need a test for the null hypothesis of no serial correlation, against some alternative which does allow for correlation between successive disturbances.

If the alternative to independence is considered to be a first order autoregressive process, both possibilities are covered by the statement

$$u_t = \rho u_{t-1} + v_t; t = 1, 2, \ldots, n \tag{4.5.1}$$

If $\rho = 0$ and $v_t; t = 1, 2, \ldots, n$ are independent, then

$$u_t = v_t; t = 1, 2, \ldots, n \tag{4.5.2}$$

and $u_t; t = 1, 2, \ldots, n$ are also independent. Any other value of ρ means that the disturbances are serially correlated. A suitable test would therefore be concerned with the null hypothesis that $\rho = 0$. One could approach a test of this null hypothesis in a manner which is similar to that used in testing for heteroscedasticity. Taking OLS residuals in place of the unobservable disturbances, one could perform a regression of e_t on e_{t-1}, thereby generating an estimate of ρ. One could then use a regression type test, justified in terms of the large sample properties of the chosen test statistic. Such an approach is entirely feasible, but in the case of serial correlation there is an alternative small sample test, which is so widely used that the value of the test statistic is usually presented as part of the computer output from a standard regression calculation. The test in question is known as the *Durbin-Watson test* and, given the widespread use of this approach, we shall devote this section almost entirely to a discussion of the Durbin-Watson procedure.

The Durbin-Watson test statistic, denoted initially as d, is given by

$$d = \sum_{t=2}^{t=n} (e_t - e_{t-1})^2 \left/ \sum_{t=1}^{t=n} e_t^2 \right. \tag{4.5.3}$$

where e_t; $t = 1, 2, \ldots, n$ are the OLS residuals. Equation 4.5.3 shows that the value of d can be computed directly from a given set of residuals and, as we have said, many computer programs provide a value as part of the output from any regression calculation. When reporting results we shall use the rather more distinctive notation DW, but in this section we use d. Obviously, the next step is to consider the information contained in a given value of d.

The first thing to notice is that d cannot be negative, since it is a ratio of sums of squares. Next, the value of d will tend to be small if successive residuals are close to one another. If we consider a first order autoregressive process

$$u_t = \rho u_{t-1} + v_t; t = 1, 2, \ldots, n$$

then, to the extent that the residuals do represent the behaviour of the disturbances, there will be a progressively greater tendency for successive residuals to be 'close' to each other as ρ is increased from 0 towards 1. If ρ is negative, there will be a tendency for successive residuals to take opposite signs and for the differences $e_t - e_{t-1}$; $t = 2, 3, \ldots, n$ to be relatively large. But of course d is a random variable and any single value of p could give rise to many different values of d. What ρ determines is the probability of finding a value of d within any given interval. If 4.5.3 is used to test the null hypothesis that $\rho = 0$, it is of particular interest to know the probabilities that would apply if the null hypothesis were true.

In earlier examples of test procedures, we have found that the distribution of the test statistic can depend on the number of observations n and the number of explanatory variables k. In the case of the Durbin-Watson test, the distribution also depends on something else. Suppose that we have the model

$$Y_t = \alpha + \beta X_t + u_t; t = 1, 2, \ldots, n \tag{4.5.4}$$

where, as before, the values of the explanatory variables are considered to be nonrandom. The residuals would be

$$e_t = Y_t - \hat{\alpha} - \hat{\beta} X_t; t = 1, 2, \ldots, n \tag{4.5.5}$$

where $\hat{\alpha}$ and $\hat{\beta}$ represent OLS estimators. The Durbin-Watson statistic depends on the residuals, which in turn depend on the particular X values used in any given application. This, in itself, is not remarkable, but unfortunately there is no way of correcting d to make the distribution independent of the X values. This means that, in general, the critical values depend on the explanatory variable observations, as

well as on n and k. It is obviously impossible to tabulate critical values
for all possible sets of explanatory variables and, if we wanted exact
critical values, we would have to compute them for each separate
regression that is run. This hardly qualifies as a simple and routine
test procedure.

Fortunately, it is possible to put bounds on the critical values for
the Durbin-Watson test. This means that an exact critical value, for
any given application, will fall between two extremes, and these bounds
have been tabulated for given n and k and for various levels of significance (probabilities of rejecting the null hypothesis $\rho = 0$ when, in
fact, this is true). The tables for the test are used in the following way.
First, a decision is made as to whether the alternative to $\rho = 0$ is a
positive value of ρ or a negative value of ρ. In either case, there are
three possible outcomes to the test. Suppose that the alternative is
that ρ is positive. If the calculated value of d is less than the lower
bound (usually denoted as d_L), the null hypothesis of independence
is rejected in favour of the alternative of positive serial correlation.
If d is greater than the upper bound (usually denoted as d_U), the null
hypothesis is not rejected. If d falls between the bounds, we simply do
not know the relationship between d and the exact critical value and
the test is inconclusive. The tables do not give bounds for the case in
which the alternative is that ρ is negative, but we can proceed as
follows. If d is greater than $4 - d_L$, the null hypothesis of independence
is rejected in favour of the alternative of negative serial correlation. If
d is less than $4 - d_U$, the null hypothesis is not rejected. If d falls
between $4 - d_U$ and $4 - d_L$, the test is inconclusive. Notice that the
test is used with one or other of the two possible alternatives and not
with both together. We say that this is a one tailed test.

Table E (p. 272) gives bounds for the critical values corresponding
to a 5 per cent significance level, for a selection of values of n and k.
Values which are not explicitly tabulated may be found by interpolation. As a very rough alternative to the explicit use of the tables, one
could use the following rule of thumb. A value of d between 0 and 1
will generally indicate positive serial correlation and a value between
3 and 4 will indicate negative serial correlation. A value between 1
and 3 can, somewhat cautiously, be interpreted as being consistent
with independence of the disturbances: the closer the value is to 2,
the more confidence one would have in drawing this conclusion. It
should be noted that the rule of thumb effectively takes both alternatives together, and so the tables are not strictly appropriate for
checking the accuracy of the rule. It should also be noted that, as

n is increased, the bounds shown in the tables move in towards 2 and this suggests that, for larger values of n, the range of values consistent with the null hypothesis should be more like 1·5–2·5.

Before going any further, two limitations to the Durbin-Watson test should be noted. The theoretical development does assume that the explanatory variables in the model can be considered to be nonrandom and, when this assumption breaks down, there can be definite distortions in the behaviour of the test statistic. We return to this in the next chapter. There is also an implicit assumption that the model contains an intercept term: the table given is not appropriate to a model which does not contain an intercept, although tables do exist which apply to this case.

We now consider the possibility that a first order autoregressive scheme is not a suitable alternative to serial independence of the disturbances. For example, with quarterly data, the disturbance in period t may be related to the disturbance in period $t - 4$, or to all disturbances in the previous four quarters, or perhaps to disturbances as far back as $t - 8$ or $t - 12$. The Durbin-Watson test can sometimes reveal the presence of such alternatives, but it cannot discriminate between the different possibilities, so rejection of serial independence merely tells us that there is serial correlation, rather than the exact form that the serial correlation takes. A full discussion of the methods of testing for higher order schemes is beyond the scope of this book, but there are some comments that can usefully be made here. First, one can modify the Durbin-Watson statistic, in an attempt to improve the ability to detect correlation between u_t and u_{t-s}, by writing

$$d_s = \sum_{t=s+1}^{t=n} (e_t - e_{t-s})^2 \left/ \sum_{t=1}^{t=n} e_t^2 \right. \tag{4.5.6}$$

Strictly speaking, separate tables are needed for each value of s, but one could use the rule of thumb described for $d(= d_1)$ as a rough guide, rejecting the null hypothesis of no association between u_t and u_{t-s} if d_s is either less than 1 or greater than 3, with a rather narrower 'acceptance' region if n is large. An even simpler approach is to examine a graph of e_t against e_{t-s}, for various values of s. If there appears to be a definite relationship between e_t and e_{t-s}, for some value of s, one might use a scheme of the form

$$u_t = \phi_s u_{t-s} + v_t \, ; t = 1, 2, \ldots, n \tag{4.5.7}$$

where ϕ_s is a single unknown parameter, or alternatively one might use

$$u_t = \phi_1 u_{t-1} + \phi_2 u_{t-2} + \ldots + \phi_s u_{t-s} + v_t; t = 1, 2, \ldots, n \qquad (4.5.8)$$

where $\phi_1, \phi_2, \ldots, \phi_s$ are all unknown. In either case, it would be possible to obtain two step approximations to GLS estimates by a suitable modification of the Cochrane-Orcutt method. The implied estimators may not be the best available, but they are relatively easy to implement.

There is one final point to be made concerning the use of OLS residuals in the detection of disturbance problems. As is usually the case, the analysis has been constructed on the assumption that the main part of the model is correctly specified, so that any serial correlation or heteroscedasticity is a property of the 'natural' disturbances. In practice, the apparent existence of a disturbance problem will often indicate that the main part of the model is not correctly specified, and this is particularly true of a model which appears to exhibit serial correlation. At the theoretical level, two distinct cases must be considered. If the explanatory variables are nonrandom, the main effect of an omitted variable is to produce disturbances which do not have zero expectation: as shown in Section 3.9, this leads to bias in the OLS estimators. It can also be shown that the behaviour of the Durbin-Watson statistic is distorted by the presence of a nonrandom component in the disturbances, in such a way that an omitted variable will often lead to rejection of the null hypothesis of serial independence. In this case the correct procedure would be to find the missing variable rather than to treat the symptoms of apparent serial correlation, and this is why the Durbin-Watson statistic is often used as an indicator of potential misspecification. In the case in which the omitted variables are random, the implied disturbances may well be serially correlated, but there can still be omitted variables bias, and experimentation with the main part of the model could still be a more appropriate response than moving directly to some form of GLS estimation.

4.6 Two step and iterative methods

On introducing the GLS method, it was possible to obtain the properties of the estimators directly by noting that GLS estimation applied to the original model is equivalent to OLS estimation applied to an appropriate transformed model. Indeed, this equivalence was actually used to define the GLS estimators. But in most cases it is not possible to obtain GLS estimates directly, because the necessary transformation involves at least one unknown disturbance parameter. In this situation we have suggested the use of a two step procedure, in which the first step involves the estimation of one or more disturbance parameters from OLS residuals and the second step involves a GLS type transformation, using the estimated disturbance parameters in place of the unknown true values. Such a procedure is an approximation to GLS, but the two step estimators are not the same as the GLS estimators and we cannot assume that the estimator properties are exactly the same.

The crucial difference between a known disturbance parameter and an estimate is that a known parameter is nonrandom, whereas an estimate is a particular value taken by a random variable. Suppose that we have an original model

$$Y_t = \beta X_t + u_t; t = 1, 2, \ldots, n \tag{4.6.1}$$

and a transformed model

$$Y_t^* = \beta X_t^* + u_t^*; t = 1, 2, \ldots, n \tag{4.6.2}$$

It may be perfectly reasonable to treat $X_t; t = 1, 2, \ldots, n$ as a set of nonrandom quantities, but if equation 4.6.2 is formed by a transformation which uses an estimate of a disturbance parameter, it is not true that $X_t^*; t = 1, 2, \ldots, n$ represents a set of nonrandom quantities. If we had some general small sample properties for OLS estimators obtained from models with random explanatory variables, we could still make use of the fact that a two step procedure is equivalent to OLS applied to a transformed model. In fact, this approach is not particularly fruitful. When the appropriate disturbance parameters are known, we have essentially the same estimation problem for each different type of disturbance specification, but when the disturbance parameters are unknown, there is an additional estimation problem which varies somewhat from case to case. So there is a distinction between the estimation of a disturbance variance, required for the transformation appropriate to heteroscedasticity, and the estimation of the parameters of an autoregressive process, required for the transformation appropriate to serial correlation. The essential difference is the dynamic nature of the serial correlation problem: it is generally true that the analysis of estimator properties is more complicated in the context of a dynamic model, and the results obtained may well be weaker in the dynamic case.

The implication of all this is that the rules governing estimator choice are not quite as simple as before. It is often possible to show that the two step estimators are asymptotically equivalent to the pure GLS estimators, which means that when the GLS estimators are optimal the two step estimators are, in terms of asymptotic properties, an acceptable alternative. Among other things, this would indicate consistency of the two step estimators and would suggest that, in a large sample, it would be reasonable to use the methods appropriate to GLS for such purposes as the calculation of standard errors and test statistics. It should be remembered that the whole point of introducing GLS was to improve the efficiency of estimation − that is, to reduce the estimator variances. If we were simply concerned about unbiased estimation and if assumptions other than those concerned with the independence and constant variance of the disturbances continue to hold, one could simply use OLS on the original model. To replace unbiased but inefficient OLS estimators by two step estimators, which are merely consistent, may seem to be a rather poor bargain, but there are several points to note. First, we have not said that the two step estimators are biased. To answer this question, one has to distinguish between the different types of disturbance problem to a greater extent than has hitherto been necessary, and the analysis does become more difficult. If there is a bias, it need not be large, and it may be outweighed by a gain in efficiency from using the two step procedure. It seems likely that a two step method will usually produce a gain in efficiency, first because of the asymptotic results mentioned above and, intuitively, because the two step procedure is an approximation to GLS. But again, we do not know for sure that there will be an actual efficiency gain in a finite sample. Moreover, if we allow for the relaxation of other assumptions, there will be cases in which OLS does not give unbiased estimators, so the option of choosing OLS for unbiasedness would no longer exist.

If there is some uncertainty as to whether a suggested method of estimation is a sensible choice, one should obviously be prepared to consider a wider class of alternatives. One possibility is a natural extension of the two step method. Suppose that we have the model

$$Y_t = \beta X_t + u_t; t = 1, 2, \ldots, n \qquad (4.6.3)$$

$$u_t = \rho u_{t-1} + v_t; t = 1, 2, \ldots, n \qquad (4.6.4)$$

where the disturbances $v_t; t = 1, 2, \ldots, n$ are 'well behaved'. In the two step method we would first apply OLS to equation 4.6.3, to produce a preliminary estimate of β. We would then use the residuals to obtain an estimate of ρ and, using this estimate in place of the unknown true value, we would transform 4.6.3 in the usual way. Finally, by the application of OLS to the transformed model, we would produce a revised estimate of β. But the complete model involves at least two unknown parameters, β and ρ, and one might wish to improve the estimate of ρ by using the revised estimate of β to generate a new set of residuals. This, in turn, would allow us to find a new estimate of β, and so the process would continue. This describes an iterative method for the estimation of β and ρ, and we can summarize the steps as follows. Let $\beta_{(i)}$ and $\rho_{(i)}$ be the estimates of β and ρ obtained during step i, and let

$$e_{(i)t} = Y_t - \beta_{(i)}X_t \, ; t = 1, 2, \ldots, n \qquad (4.6.5)$$

be the residuals obtained by using the estimate $\beta_{(i)}$. With $\rho_{(0)} = 0$ as the starting point, each step then consists of

1 A transformation

$$(Y_t - \rho_{(i-1)}Y_{t-1}) = \beta(X_t - \rho_{(i-1)}X_{t-1}) + (u_t - \rho_{(i-1)}u_{t-1});$$
$$t = 2, 3, \ldots, n \qquad (4.6.6)$$

or, alternatively, a full transformation, to include the first observation.

2 A regression on the transformed model, to produce an estimate $\beta_{(i)}$. This estimate is used in equation 4.6.5 to produce residuals $e_{(i)t}$; $t = 1, 2, \ldots, n$.

3 A regression of $e_{(i)t}$ on $e_{(i)t-1}$, to produce an estimate $\rho_{(i)}$.

Since $\rho_{(0)} = 0$, the transformation has no effect during step 1 and the first observation can be used. Notice also that the residuals are based on the original variables and that, at each step, the transformation starts again from the original variables.

At some point we have to stop the iterations and, with any iterative process, we must consider whether the estimates will converge so that there is no longer any appreciable difference between successive values. In this case it can be shown that convergence should occur, but this is not true of all iterative methods and, even when convergence can be guaranteed, the number of iterations needed can sometimes be rather large. Although it would be possible to carry out this particular iterative procedure by repeated runs of an OLS regression program, it could be tedious to do so and, in general, special computer programs are needed for iterative calculations.

There is another way of looking at the method that we have described. Suppose that we consider the application of least squares to the transformed model

$$(Y_t - \rho Y_{t-1}) = \beta(X_t - \rho X_{t-1}) + (u_t - \rho u_{t-1}); t = 2, 3, \ldots, n \tag{4.6.7}$$

where β and ρ are the unknown true values. The least squares principle would suggest that we should choose that value for β that minimizes the sum of squares

$$\sum_{t=2}^{t=n} [(Y_t - \rho Y_{t-1}) - \beta(X_t - \rho X_{t-1})]^2 \tag{4.6.8}$$

and that we should use the resulting value as an estimate of β. But ρ is also an unknown parameter and, instead of substituting a prior estimate of ρ, we could minimize 4.6.8 with respect to both β and ρ. The parameters would then be estimated together. Unfortunately this is a non-linear least squares problem, and an iterative method has to be used to obtain the solution. The particular iterations described earlier represent one possible approach.

Intuitively, one ought to gain something from using an iterative rather than a two step method. It is difficult to generalize, but one can often show that two step and iterative approaches are asymptotically equivalent, so any gain from using an iterative method would follow from the fact that asymptotic properties do not tell the whole story about the estimator behaviour in a finite sample. In a very general sense, it does seem likely that one would improve the quality of estimation by allowing iterations to continue to convergence.

Finally, we should consider the possibility that the least squares criterion itself is no longer the best approach to estimation. The criterion was first suggested as an intuitively plausible method for fitting a line to a two dimensional scatter of points, and this was subsequently reinforced by the fact that the estimators have desirable properties under certain conditions. But, if these conditions no longer hold, the criterion itself is called into question. We mention this because there are alternative criteria, of which the most widely used is the *maximum likelihood principle*.

The technical details of the maximum likelihood (ML) approach are beyond the scope of this book, but we can explain the principle by making use of a simple example. Suppose that we have the model

$$Y_t = \beta X_t + u_t; t = 1, 2, \ldots, n \tag{4.6.9}$$

where, for simplicity, the explanatory variable observations are taken to be nonrandom. According to the model, the dependent variable observations are particular values taken by a set of random variables. This follows from the direct linkage between the dependent variable observations and the random disturbances. If we assume some particular probability distribution for each disturbance, it is possible to derive the implied probability distribution for each dependent variable observation. These distributions will involve the unknown parameter β. Now our data consist of one set of observations on the dependent variable and, for any given value of β, there would be a certain probability of obtaining this set of observations. Strictly speaking, we should say that there would be a certain probability of obtaining values in a small range around those which are observed, since the dependent variable observations are treated as continuous random variables, but this is a technicality. The maximum likelihood principle suggests that we should choose that value of β that gives the maximum probability of observing what we have actually observed, and this value of β is used as the ML estimate.

It should be noted that we do have to assume a specific form of distribution for each disturbance and, not surprisingly, the normal distribution is almost invariably the form that is chosen. If this is the case and 4.6.9 has 'well behaved' disturbances, the ML estimator for β is identical to the OLS estimator. In more complicated forms of model, the two estimators may well be different. If, for example, we have a first order autoregressive scheme for the disturbances to equation 4.6.9, with an unknown value for ρ, the ML principle can be used to obtain estimates of β and ρ and the ML estimators are not the same as the least squares estimators defined by the minimization of 4.6.8, although the asymptotic properties of the estimators are the same. The usual reason given for using the maximum likelihood method is in fact concerned with asymptotic properties. For a wide variety of models, the ML estimators can be shown to be consistent, asymptotically efficient and to have asymptotic normal distributions. But establishing the validity of such results for specific models is not always that easy, and statements concerning ML estimation are sometimes based on the folklore of econometrics rather than on careful analysis.

4.7 Some further disturbance problems

In Section 3.11 we introduced the idea of a model in which a given form of relationship may have different parameter values in different regions.

Despite the basic similarity of the individual relationships, this was actually our first example of a multiple equation model. If the parameters are all different, it was suggested that one could treat each equation in isolation and run a separate regression on the data for each region. If, on the other hand, some parameters take the same value in different regions, there are restrictions which apply between equations and, in order to impose these restrictions, it is necessary to find a way of combining all the individual equations into a single relationship. We showed how this can be done by making use of dummy variables and, for the purposes of estimation, we can treat a model with several equations as though it were a model with just one equation, applied to some overall set of data.

As soon as we take the step of combining the equations, we introduce the possibility of heteroscedasticity. In the case described above, it may well be that, within each region, we have a constant disturbance variance, but there may be a different constant variance appropriate to each region. If this is so, combining the equations to give a single relationship will introduce heteroscedasticity. The reason for combining equations would be to enable cross-equation restrictions to be imposed, and so what we would have is a problem of restricted estimation with heteroscedastic disturbances. We can handle this by treating each component problem in turn. Suppose that there are two regions, with disturbance variances given by

$$\text{var } (u_t) = \sigma^2 \lambda_1^2; \text{ in region 1}$$
$$= \sigma^2 \lambda_2^2; \text{ in region 2} \tag{4.7.1}$$

The first step would be to create the dummy variables. In theory, one would introduce a full set of dummies and then the restrictions would be imposed by making the appropriate deletions. In practice, one would simply fail to insert those dummies which are not needed under the restrictions. Then, if λ_1 and λ_2 are known, all observations relating to region 1 would be divided by λ_1, including observations on the dummy variables and, where appropriate, those on the artificial variable which allows for an intercept term. All observations relating to region 2 would be divided by λ_2. After all these preliminary transformations, the application of OLS to the transformed model would produce restricted GLS estimates. Notice that we do not need to know the value of σ^2, the common scale factor in 4.7.1.

It should be remembered that the purpose of using any available restrictions is to improve the efficiency of estimation — that is, to reduce the variance of the estimators. But combining the equations introduces heteroscedasticity and, if heteroscedasticity is present, GLS estimation is more efficient than OLS estimation. So we have the result that the restricted GLS estimators are generally more efficient than the restricted OLS estimators which, in turn, are more efficient than the unrestricted OLS estimators. In this example, two separate problems are dealt with by a combination of the methods appropriate to the individual problems.

If λ_1 and λ_2 are not known, a two step procedure could be used. There would no longer be any point in writing the disturbance variances in terms of two components, since both σ^2 and the λ values are unknown. So 4.7.1 is now written as

$$\text{var}\,(u_t) = \sigma_1^2;\, \text{in region 1}$$
$$= \sigma_2^2;\, \text{in region 2} \tag{4.7.2}$$

and the GLS procedure that we are trying to approximate would involve division by σ_1 and σ_2, respectively, rather than λ_1 and λ_2. The two step procedure would be as follows. Fitting separate unrestricted regressions to each region would produce a set of residuals for each region and the disturbance variances could then be estimated in the usual way. These estimates are denoted as $\hat{\sigma}_1^2$ and $\hat{\sigma}_2^2$. The equations for the two regions would then be combined, as before, and the appropriate restrictions imposed, but the transformation for heteroscedasticity would involve division by $\hat{\sigma}_1$ and $\hat{\sigma}_2$ instead of the unknown values σ_1 and σ_2. The final estimates of the parameters of the main part of the model would then be approximations to the restricted GLS estimates.

The argument above illustrates an important point. One can have an absolutely standard disturbance specification for the individual equations in a model, but the very fact that there is more than one equation means that there are additional possibilities to consider. So, within each equation, there may be a constant disturbance variance, but this does not necessarily mean that the disturbance variance is the same for each equation. Similarly, one may rule out the possibility of serial correlation within the individual equations, but there can be various patterns of correlation between disturbances taken from different equations.

To illustrate this point, suppose that time series data are available, at the regional level, on aggregate consumers' expenditure C and aggregate disposable income D. Suppose also that there are two regions, with m observations for each region, and that the model is

$$C_t = \alpha_1 + \beta_1 D_t + u_t; \text{ in region 1}$$
$$C_t = \alpha_2 + \beta_2 D_t + v_t; \text{ in region 2} \qquad (4.7.3)$$

where $v_t; t = 1, 2, \ldots, m$ is now used to represent the disturbances for region 2, as distinct from $u_t; t = 1, 2, \ldots, m$, the disturbances for region 1. Now consider a particular disturbance term, say u_1. It may be that u_1 is independent of $u_2, u_3, \ldots, u_m$ and of $v_2, v_3, \ldots, v_m$. Similarly, u_2 may be independent of $u_1, u_3, \ldots, u_m$ and of $v_1, v_3, \ldots, v_m$. If this pattern is repeated, there is no serial correlation in the model, but there can still be what is known as *contemporaneous correlation*, between disturbances to different equations, during the same period of time. This would mean that u_1 is correlated with v_1, u_2 with v_2, and so on. The distinction between serial correlation and contemporaneous correlation is illustrated in Figure 11: in each case, there are arrows linking certain disturbances and, where linkage exists, it is impossible to assume independence between those particular disturbance terms.

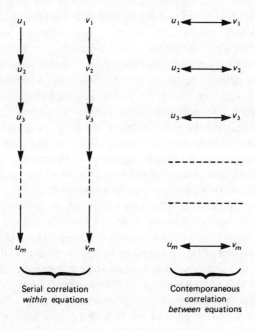

Serial correlation
within equations

Contemporaneous correlation
between equations

Figure 11

If there is contemporaneous correlation in the model, it would generally be assumed that the same pattern of correlation holds between each pair of disturbances, and this assumption would usually be expressed in terms of the covariance between each pair. The assumption of a constant pattern of contemporaneous correlation would therefore be expressed as

$$\text{cov}\,(u_t, v_t) = \sigma_{uv}; t = 1, 2, \ldots, m \qquad (4.7.4)$$

This says that there is a constant covariance for all values of t, the constant value being written as σ_{uv}. If this covariance is not equal to zero, there is contemporaneous correlation in the model. Notice the analogy between 4.7.4 and the assumption of constant variance within each equation. In both cases it is assumed that there are disturbance parameters which do not change through time.

Now consider a possible reason for contemporaneous correlation of the disturbances in model 4.7.3. The disturbances represent all influences on consumption except for disposable income and, in any given time period, it is quite possible that disturbances in the two regions have at least some components in common. This could be the case if the disturbances include factors which represent national rather than regional characteristics. Such factors would tend to affect consumption in both regions in the same way, and this would perhaps suggest a positive correlation between the disturbances. But our example is purely illustrative: in other, more complex models there can be a very definite reason for contemporaneous correlation of the disturbances. The important point is that, in considering a multiple equation model, one must make some assumption concerning the relationship between the disturbances to the different equations. If the assumption of independence is acceptable, well and good. But if the theory underlying the model suggests contemporaneous correlation, or if there is no clear indication one way or another, the existence of a possible disturbance problem must be recognized.

If the two equations in 4.7.3 were combined, the existence of contemporaneous correlation would mean that the complete set of disturbances could not be considered to be independent and this would suggest some form of GLS estimation, to ensure efficiency. But this leaves unanswered the question as to whether it is actually necessary to combine the individual equations. In the previous example, it was suggested that the equations would be combined if there were cross-equation restrictions to be imposed. In such a case, it is the existence of cross-equation restrictions that establishes a connection between the individual equations. The fact that the disturbance variance might differ between equations does not, of itself, establish any such connection. In 4.7.3 it is implicit that the parameters are different as between regions 1 and 2 and so there are no cross-equation restrictions. However, taking the two equations together, there is a restriction of a rather subtle kind. In the context of this model, one should really interpret income in region 1 as a variable which is distinct from income in region 2. We can then say that the variable 'income in region 2' does not appear in the equation representing consumer behaviour in region 1, and vice versa. The significance of this observation is that, although there are no cross-equation restrictions, there are implicit exclusion restrictions, whereby income in region 2 is excluded from the equation for region 1 and income for region 1 is excluded from the equation for region 2. If there is also contemporaneous correlation in the model, there is a connection between the equations, and it can be shown that the combination of contemporaneous correlation and the presence of at least one restriction, somewhere in the model, is a sufficient reason for combining the equations for the purposes of estimation.

A model of the kind described above is said to consist of 'seemingly unrelated regressions': there does not appear to be any connection between the equations, but closer inspection of the disturbance specification shows that a connection does exist. Unless the explanatory variable observations are absolutely identical in all equations, the correct estimation procedure is to combine the equations and then to apply GLS to the resulting single relationship. The transformations appropriate to this particular problem are complicated and we shall not give details, but the principles which lie behind the choice of GLS can be understood. The contemporaneous correlation establishes a connection between the equations and, because of this, a restriction in any equation can, in principle, be used to improve the efficiency of estimation of all the parameters in the model. The one exception is the case mentioned above, in which the explanatory variable observations are identical for all equations: this implies that there is no information available in one equation that is not already available elsewhere. In any other case, the model must be taken as a whole for the purposes of estimation. Because the complete set of disturbances cannot be mutually independent, some form of GLS estimation has to be applied to the combined equation.

The model shown in 4.7.3 is a perfectly valid example of a multiple equation model, but it is not entirely typical. Both equations have consumption as the dependent variable and income as the explanatory variable, and although we have suggested that income in region 1 should be treated as a variable which is formally distinct from income in region 2, it does still seem more natural to combine equations which relate to the same economic phenomenon. In fact, one can combine equations which relate to totally different variables and one should definitely do this if there are cross-equation restrictions or if there are within equation restrictions, in the presence of contemporaneous correlation. This idea is very useful when we consider the estimation of complete models in a more general context, and we shall explain the methodology in more detail in Section 6.5.

4.8　Exercises (solutions on p. 281)

4.1　(a) If

$$Y_t = \beta_1 + \beta_2 X_{2t} + \ldots + \beta_k X_{kt} + u_t;$$
$$E(u_t) = 0; \operatorname{var}(u_t) = \sigma^2; \operatorname{cov}(u_t, u_s) = 0; s \neq t;$$
$$s, t = 1, 2, \ldots, n$$

is the 'true' model, where X_2 to X_k are nonrandom and all variables are measured in constant price terms, what disturbance 'problem' would you expect to observe on multiplying both sides of the equation by a (nonrandom) price index P_t; $t = 1, 2, \ldots, n$?

(b) Using quarterly data for the UK economy 1963–80, an investigator uses OLS to estimate the parameters of a consumption function in current price terms. Among other results, he obtains $n = 72, k = 8$, RSS = 2·635, DW = 2·085, $R^2 = 0·999$. Then, using squared residuals e_t^2; $t = 1, 2, \ldots, n$, two further regressions are performed

$$\hat{e}^2 = 0·060 + 0·036 \log (P^2)$$
$$\phantom{\hat{e}^2 = } (0·007)\ (0·006)$$

explained SS = 0·0928

$$\log (\hat{e}^2) = -4·54 + 0·95 \log (P^2)$$
$$\phantom{\log (\hat{e}^2) = } (0·35)\ (0·29)$$

explained SS = 63·98

Comment on these results in the light of your answer to part (a).

4.2　(a) From a sample of 24 observations, each representing a group of households, taken from the UK Family Expenditure Survey 1979, an investigator obtains the equation

$$\hat{Y} = 10\cdot11 + 0\cdot144X_2$$
$$\quad\; (2\cdot815)\;(0\cdot026)$$

RSS $= 334\cdot78$ DW $= 0\cdot420$ $R^2 = 0\cdot588$ $\chi^2 = 7\cdot80$

where Y is expenditure on food and X_2 is total expenditure. The χ^2 statistic refers to the Breusch-Pagan test of

$$H_0: \sigma_t^2 = \exp(\delta_1) \qquad \text{against}$$
$$H_a: \sigma_t^2 = \exp(\delta_1 + \delta_2 \log Z_2 + \delta_3 \log Z_3)$$

where $Z_2 = X_2$ and Z_3 is the reciprocal of the group size. Since $\chi_2^{2(0\cdot05)} = 5\cdot99$, the investigator concludes that the disturbance variance is related both to total expenditure and to the reciprocal of the group size. Comment on the validity of this procedure.

(b) The investigator then adds X_3 to the model, where X_3 is the average number of children per household group. The result is

$$\hat{Y} = 9\cdot26 + 0\cdot115X_2 + 2\cdot75X_3$$
$$\quad\; (0\cdot74)\;(0\cdot007)\quad(0\cdot16)$$

RSS $= 21\cdot915$ DW $= 1\cdot904$ $R^2 = 0\cdot973$ $\chi^2 = 0\cdot093$

Comment on these results in the light of your answer to part (a).

4.3 Can one impose the stochastic constraint

$$0\cdot5 = \beta + v; \text{var}(v) = 0\cdot1$$

on the model

$$Y_t = \alpha + \beta X_t + u_t; t = 1, 2, \ldots, n$$

using only a standard least squares program?

4.4 The model

$$Y_t = \alpha + \beta X_t + u_t; t = 1, 2, \ldots, n$$

is applied to quarterly data and it is thought that disturbances in the same quarters of successive years are serially correlated:

$$u_t = \rho u_{t-4} + v_t; t = 1, 2, \ldots, n$$

If the value of ρ were known, how could one transform the model to remove serial correlation? Would OLS applied to the transformed model produce a best linear unbiased estimator?

5 Distributed lags and dynamic economic models

5.1 Introduction

In moving towards more realistic forms of economic model, an important step is to allow for *lags* in the relationship between economic variables. We have already considered the use of lags in the disturbance specification: we now consider the implications of including lags in the main part of the model.

The simplest case is that in which Y and X represent two economic variables, connected by a relationship which shows that the current value of Y is linked to a past value of X. A specific example is

$$Y_t = \beta X_{t-1} + u_t; t = 1, 2, \ldots, n \tag{5.1.1}$$

There is no particular reason why this model should not satisfy the full list of assumptions under which the OLS estimator would be best linear unbiased. Indeed, the only difference between 5.1.1 and

$$Y_t = \beta X_t + u_t; t = 1, 2, \ldots, n \tag{5.1.2}$$

lies in the data requirement: the observations $X_{t-1}; t = 1, 2, \ldots, n$ are equivalent to the observations $X_t; t = 0, 1, \ldots, n - 1$. But it is possible to extend equation 5.1.1 in such a way that the dependent variable reacts to several past values of the explanatory variable: although this does not necessarily lead to the violation of assumptions, there are some practical problems of estimation, which are discussed in Section 5.2 under the heading of *distributed lags*.

With the introduction of lags, there is another possibility. The current value of the dependent variable may be determined in part by its own past values. We shall give reasons for such a hypothesis in due course. The immediate objective is to identify the characteristics of this new type of model. The simplest formal example is that in which we use a first order autoregressive process, applied now to the dependent variable observations

$$Y_t = \beta Y_{t-1} + u_t; t = 1, 2, \ldots, n \tag{5.1.3}$$

The only explanatory variable in equation 5.1.3 is the lagged dependent variable and, apart from the random disturbance terms, the current values of the dependent variable are determined entirely by past values. In practice there would be some other explanatory variables, but equation 5.1.3 does serve to illustrate the ways in which this type of model is different from those considered earlier.

The first point to note is that we have a problem of terminology. In equation 5.1.3 there is only one economic variable, which is both 'dependent' and 'explanatory'. As variables in a standard form of statistical model, the current and lagged versions of Y are distinct: but both represent the same economic variable and, if the model is designed to explain the behaviour of this variable, it is inevitable that the behaviour of the 'explanatory' variable is also explained.

Now consider the model shown in equation 5.1.1. In this case there are two quite distinct economic variables and, although the model attempts to explain the behaviour of Y, there is no attempt to explain the behaviour of X. In terms of the underlying economic model, Y would be described as an *endogenous variable* and X as an *exogenous variable*. We have not needed to make use of these terms before: the dependent variable is, by definition, endogenous and it has hitherto been assumed, in formulating the model, that all explanatory variables can be treated as exogenous. This assumption has been implicit, in the sense that the characteristics assumed to hold for explanatory variables are those which, in a more general context, one would assume for exogenous variables only. The terms 'dependent' and 'explanatory' can still be used to refer to 'left hand side' and 'right hand side' variables, respectively, but now 'explanatory' variables can be either exogenous or lagged endogenous variables.

The use of a lagged endogenous variable does lead to problems of estimation. In a model which contains random disturbances, each dependent variable observation must be treated as a particular value taken by a random variable. But, if Y_t; $t = 1, 2, \ldots, n$ represents a set of random quantities, so does Y_{t-1}; $t = 2, 3, \ldots, n$. Note that the starting value Y_0 is not determined within the model, and this could be considered to be nonrandom. The implication is that we have a model in which all but one of the explanatory variable observations must be particular values taken by a set of random variables. We have already come across this problem in the context of a transformed model, when the transformation involves an estimated disturbance parameter. In the lagged endogenous variable case, the fact that the explanatory variable observations are random is an inherent property of the model.

Fortunately we do have specific information as to the nature of the random process, and this can be used in looking at the estimator properties. These properties are discussed in Sections 5.3 and 5.4.

The other novel feature of equation 5.1.3 is that it is a simple example of a *dynamic model*. Ignoring the random disturbances, we can say that a dynamic model is one which is designed to show how an endogenous variable can change through time, even though any exogenous variables that are present may not change at all. In equation 5.1.3 there are no exogenous variables, but each successive value of the endogenous variable is determined by the previous value and, in this way, the model does generate a complete time path for the endogenous variable. The decision as to whether equation 5.1.1 is also a dynamic model is less straightforward. The concept of time is certainly used in specifying the relationship between Y and X but, apart from the effect of the random disturbances, Y can only change in response to a past change in the value of X. It is convenient, for our purposes, to say that a dynamic model should contain at least one lagged endogenous variable. This is slightly restrictive, but it does serve to identify a class of models associated with a specific type of estimation problem.

There is one further complication. If the disturbances are serially correlated, a dynamic element is added to what may otherwise be an essentially static economic model. We shall not pursue this point, beyond noting that the theoretical problems associated with the estimation of unknown parameters in a dynamic disturbance process are very similar to those that arise in the context of a dynamic economic model. Before we consider what those problems are, we return to the case in which the model involves only lagged exogenous variables.

5.2　Distributed lags

In the model shown in equation 5.1.1, the explicit assumption that Y_t is related to X_t is replaced by the equally explicit assumption that Y_t is related to X_{t-1}. There are, of course, many other possibilities. The one period lag could be replaced by a lag of two or more periods. Alternatively, we may have a distributed lag, in which the current value of Y is related to several past values of X. The most commonly quoted example for this type of model is that of investment in plant and machinery, where the flows of investment expenditure during any given period result from the investment decisions of earlier periods. The explanatory variables will primarily be those which affect investment decisions, but there can be many types of lag in the translation of decisions into actual flows of investment expenditure. If the example relates to aggregate investment, at the level of the national economy, the aggregate is taken over many firms, each of which may, in any period, have several projects at different stages of completion. If this is the case, it is not difficult to see why a distributed lag formulation is appropriate.

If we knew exactly which past values of X were relevant in determining the behaviour of Y, it would be possible to specify the lag model precisely. But, typically, there is some uncertainty as to which lagged values of X should be included, and the model could then be specified by choosing a maximum lag and a minimum lag and including all lagged values of X between these extremes. To simplify, we shall assume that the minimum lag is 0 and we shall represent the maximum lag as s. This would give a model in the form

$$Y_t = \beta_0 X_t + \beta_1 X_{t-1} + \ldots + \beta_s X_{t-s} + u_t; t = 1, 2, \ldots, n \qquad (5.2.1)$$

Again, in practice, there would be other explanatory variables and an intercept term, but our concern here is with the estimation of the parameters of the distributed lag relationship and, for this purpose, equation 5.2.1 is an adequate representation.

The first point to note is that equation 5.2.1 is in the form of a k variable model, with $k = s + 1$. The explanatory variables are actually current and lagged versions of the same economic variable, but the parameters can be estimated by treating each version of X as a distinct variable for the purposes of the regression calculation. If the computer program allows for a lag transformation, it is obviously convenient to generate the lagged variable observations directly from a single set of observations on the variable X. The necessary data would then consist of n observations on Y and X, together with some additional observations on the values of X for the s periods immediately prior to $t = 1$. After executing the required lag transformations, the data for the regression calculation would consist of the observations

$$Y_t; t = 1, 2, \ldots, n \qquad X_t; t = 1, 2, \ldots, n \qquad X_{t-1}; t = 1, 2, \ldots, n$$
$$\text{etc.}$$

If X is taken to be nonrandom, the model is correctly specified and the disturbances are well behaved, the OLS estimators would be best linear unbiased. Of course, if there is a particular disturbance problem, the appropriate GLS estimators would be used instead, but there is no inherent property of the model that suggests a violation of assumptions.

Although OLS can be applied to equation 5.2.1, the practical difficulty that we referred to earlier is that there will inevitably be some degree of intercorrelation between the current and lagged versions of X. If the various sets of observations on X are treated as nonrandom quantities, the explicit modelling of any association between successive values of X is not within the scope of the present model. However, some measured correlation would invariably be found, and if there is any regularity in the behaviour of X over time, the degree of intercorrelation between the explanatory variables in equation 5.2.1 can be very high. So we would, in general, have a problem of severe multicollinearity, and this means that we would tend to get rather imprecise estimates of the individual parameters.

From the discussion in Sections 3.9 and 3.10 we know that estimator variances can be reduced by imposing restrictions on the model. If equation 5.2.1 is specified in an attempt to cover all possible lags, there may well be scope for restrictions. One possibility would be to delete some of the lagged variables altogether, but unfortunately, under conditions of severe multicollinearity, the t test applied to individual coefficients would not give a very reliable method for choosing the variables to be deleted and, in the context of a distributed lag model, there are other forms of restriction that can be used.

Equation 5.2.1 shows how the current value of Y reacts to several past values of X, but the model also shows how Y would adjust, over time, to a given change in X. Ignoring the effect of the random disturbances, consider an extremely simple example:

$$Y_t = \beta_0 X_t + \beta_1 X_{t-1} ; t = 1, 2, \ldots, n \qquad (5.2.2)$$

Now suppose that

$$X_t = 0; \text{for all values prior to } t = 1$$

and

$$X_t = X_c; t = 1, 2, \ldots, n$$

where X_c is a single fixed value of X. This implies that X does not change after the value X_c is established in period $t = 1$. The behaviour of Y is then given by

$$Y_1 = \beta_0 X_c + \beta_1 0 = \beta_0 X_c$$
$$Y_2 = \beta_0 X_c + \beta_1 X_c = (\beta_0 + \beta_1) X_c$$
$$Y_3 = \beta_0 X_c + \beta_1 X_c = (\beta_0 + \beta_1) X_c \qquad \text{etc.}$$

After an initial period of adjustment there is no further change in the value of Y, and we can write

$$Y_t = Y_c = (\beta_0 + \beta_1) X_c ; t = 2, 3, \ldots, n$$

If X_c is set to 1, it becomes obvious that the parameter β_0 measures the immediate response of Y to a unit change in X and that the parameter β_1 measures the additional response after a lag of one period. The sum $\beta_0 + \beta_1$ measures the *total* or *long run* response.

With a maximum lag of s periods, we would have a set of response coefficients β_i; $i = 0, 1, \ldots, s$ and the long run response would be measured by

$$\beta = \beta_0 + \beta_1 + \ldots + \beta_s \tag{5.2.3}$$

We could then express the individual coefficients as

$$\beta_i = \beta w_i; i = 0, 1, \ldots, s \tag{5.2.4}$$

where

$$w_i = \beta_i/\beta; i = 0, 1, \ldots, s \tag{5.2.5}$$

The weights defined in equation 5.2.5 show how the total response is distributed through time. If all nonzero response coefficients are positive, β is positive. If all nonzero response coefficients are negative, β is negative. In either case, the weights are either positive or zero. If the response coefficients change in sign, the weights will still be predominantly positive but one or two negative values will occur. As we shall shortly discover, it is very convenient to be able to express the response pattern in a way which is independent of the sign of the long run coefficient, and we can still do this if one or two of the individual coefficients are of a different sign to the rest.

Suppose now that we were to draw a graph showing how the weights change with the value of the lag length i. Figure 12 shows an example in which the largest weight corresponds to a lag of 2 periods, with smaller weights on lags of 0, 1, 3 and 4 periods. This indicates that the peak response of Y to X occurs with a lag of 2 periods, with smaller responses for other lag lengths up to a maximum lag of 4 periods. We could represent this pattern by means of a graph of β_i against i, but if the long run coefficient β is negative, the pattern shown would be the inverse of that on the graph of weights. It does seem more satisfactory to represent the peak response as the highest point on a graph irrespective of the sign of the overall effect, and this is the advantage of using the weights rather than the original response coefficients.

The information shown on the graph of weights is described as the *lag distribution*. The graph actually consists of a set of points but the points do trace out a shape and, although it is unrealistic to suppose that the values of the weights should be known exactly, one may have

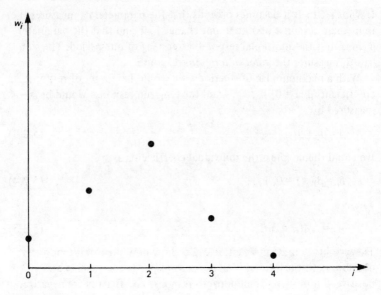

Figure 12

some rough idea of the shape appropriate to a particular application. In the distribution shown in Figure 12, the weights rise and then fall as the lag length is increased. If we knew this, without knowing the exact pattern, we could choose the weights accordingly. For example, we could set

$$w_0 = 1/9, w_1 = 2/9, w_2 = 3/9, w_3 = 2/9, w_4 = 1/9 \qquad (5.2.6)$$

where the scale is chosen to ensure that the weights add to one. These weights trace out an 'inverted V' shape and, if this was thought to be appropriate, equation 5.2.1 could be rewritten as

$$Y_t = \beta[(1/9)X_t + (2/9)X_{t-1} + (3/9)X_{t-2} + (2/9)X_{t-3} + (1/9)X_{t-4}] \\ + u_t; t = 1, 2, \ldots, n \qquad (5.2.7)$$

or as

$$Y_t = \beta X_t^* + u_t; t = 1, 2, \ldots, n \qquad (5.2.8)$$

where X_t^* represents the term in the square brackets on the right of equation 5.2.7. The observations on X^* can be formed from the observations on the original lagged variables and the regression of Y on X^*

would produce an estimate of β, which is now the only unknown parameter.

The imposition of a certain shape on the lag distribution amounts to the use of a set of restrictions on the parameters of the original model and, by using these restrictions, we have apparently overcome the effects of multicollinearity. But the chosen weights are unlikely to correspond exactly to the 'true' values and, as a result, the implicit estimators

$$\hat{\beta}_0 = (1/9)\hat{\beta}, \ \hat{\beta}_1 = (2/9)\hat{\beta}, \ldots, \ \hat{\beta}_4 = (1/9)\hat{\beta}$$

will be subject to a certain amount of bias. This price would be acceptable if the inverted V shape is a reasonably good approximation, for then the bias would tend to be small. Otherwise the bias may be very serious and, in the absence of any firm information as to the shape of the lag distribution, we would have to find another way of choosing the restrictions to be imposed. The discussion that follows is based on a simplified version of what is known as the *Almon method.*

In Figure 12 the lag distribution is represented by a set of points and, as we have said, a similar representation could be used for the original response coefficients. If we consider the latter case, an alternative way of expressing the linkage between the response coefficients and the lag length would be to find the equation of a curve passing through all the points. There is, however, a difficulty. The coefficients are only defined for the lag lengths $i = 0, 1, \ldots, 4$ or, more generally, for $i = 0, 1, \ldots, s$, but the equation of a curve must involve continuous variables. To get round the problem, we treat i as a continuous variable and we define a second continuous variable b, the value of which is determined by the value of i. If an equation linking b to i is to pass through all the points on a graph of β_i against i, the value of b at any of the lag lengths $i = 0, 1, \ldots, s$ must be equal to the corresponding coefficient β_i. So, as part of the definition of b, we have

$$b = \beta_i; i = 0, 1, \ldots, s \tag{5.2.9}$$

If there were just two response coefficients there would only be two points on a graph of β_i against i, and a straight line would be a suitable form for an equation passing through the points. But three or more points would be unlikely to lie exactly along a single straight line, and the equation of a curve would have to be used instead. There is actually a general rule concerning a type of equation that can be guaranteed to fit exactly to a given number of points. For just two points, a straight line

$$b = a_0 + a_1 i \tag{5.2.10}$$

would be sufficient but, for three points, we would need

$$b = a_0 + a_1 i + a_2 i^2 \qquad (5.2.11)$$

and, for $s + 1$ points, we would need

$$b = a_0 + a_1 i + \ldots + a_s i^s \qquad (5.2.12)$$

In each case, a_0, a_1 etc. are parameters of the equation form and these would take particular values for particular examples of lag distributions. Equations 5.2.10, 5.2.11, and 5.2.12 are polynomials of degree 1, 2, and s, respectively. When the maximum length is s, equation 5.2.12 is a general form for the equation of a curve passing through all the points on a graph of β_i against i. Having defined b in order to write down the equation, our interest centres on the particular values of b which correspond to $\beta_i; i = 0, 1, \ldots, s$ and, for these values, we can write

$$\beta_i = a_0 + a_1 i + \ldots + a_s i^s \qquad (5.2.13)$$

If the $s + 1$ values $a_0, a_1, \ldots, a_s$ were known, we could derive the value of β_i appropriate to any of the lag lengths $i = 0, 1, \ldots, s$. Thus we would have

$$i = 0: \ \beta_0 = a_0 + a_1(0) + \ldots + a_s(0)^s = a_0$$
$$i = 1: \ \beta_1 = a_0 + a_1(1) + \ldots + a_s(1)^s = a_0 + a_1 + \ldots + a_s$$
$$i = 2: \ \beta_2 = a_0 + a_1(2) + \ldots + a_s(2)^s \text{ etc.} \qquad (5.2.14)$$

But we are trying to establish a technique that can be used when nothing is known about the lag distribution except for the value of the maximum lag length s, and so $a_0, a_1, \ldots, a_s$ represent a set of unknown parameters. In fact we have expressed the unknown values $\beta_i; i = 0, 1, \ldots, s$ in terms of an equal number of unknown values $a_i; i = 0, 1, \ldots, s$. The substitution does, however, have an advantage, which can best be understood by means of a particular example.

Suppose that we have the model

$$Y_t = \beta_0 X_t + \beta_1 X_{t-1} + \beta_2 X_{t-2} + \beta_3 X_{t-3} + u_t; t = 1, 2, \ldots, n \qquad (5.2.15)$$

In this case $s = 3$, and we would need a third degree polynomial

$$b = a_0 + a_1 i + a_2 i^2 + a_3 i^3 \qquad (5.2.16)$$

to give an exact fit through the four points corresponding to the values $\beta_i; i = 0, 1, 2, 3$.

Equations 5.2.14 would then give

$$\beta_0 = a_0$$
$$\beta_1 = a_0 + a_1 + a_2 + a_3$$
$$\beta_2 = a_0 + 2a_1 + 4a_2 + 8a_3$$
$$\beta_3 = a_0 + 3a_1 + 9a_2 + 27a_3 \qquad (5.2.17)$$

So equation 5.2.15 becomes

$$Y_t = a_0 X_t + (a_0 + a_1 + a_2 + a_3)X_{t-1} + (a_0 + 2a_1 + 4a_2 + 8a_3)X_{t-2}$$
$$+ (a_0 + 3a_1 + 9a_2 + 27a_3)X_{t-3} + u_t; t = 1, 2, \ldots, n$$

Rearranging this equation, we obtain

$$Y_t = a_0(X_t + X_{t-1} + X_{t-2} + X_{t-3})$$
$$+ a_1(X_{t-1} + 2X_{t-2} + 3X_{t-3})$$
$$+ a_2(X_{t-1} + 4X_{t-2} + 9X_{t-3})$$
$$+ a_3(X_{t-1} + 8X_{t-2} + 27X_{t-3}) + u_t; t = 1, 2, \ldots, n \qquad (5.2.18)$$

or

$$Y_t = a_0 X_{0t}^* + a_1 X_{1t}^* + a_2 X_{2t}^* + a_3 X_{3t}^* + u_t; t = 1, 2, \ldots, n$$
$$\qquad (5.2.19)$$

where $X_{it}^*; i = 0, 1, 2, 3$ represent the bracketed terms in equation 5.2.18. What we have done is to define a new set of explanatory variables, which are actually linear combinations of the original lagged variables. The parameters attached to these new variables are $a_0, a_1,$ a_2, a_3. The advantage of having carried out the rearrangement is that there is now a restriction which may be appropriate. A third degree polynomial is needed to guarantee an exact fit to the points on the graph of β_i against i, but a second degree polynomial could be used as an approximation. Equation 5.2.16 can be converted into a second degree polynomial by deleting the last term — that is, by setting $a_3 = 0$. The values a_0, a_1 and a_2 would no longer be unique because there are many different second degree polynomials that could be used to provide an approximation, but we shall see that this does not matter. If a_3 is set to zero then, following through to equation 5.2.19, we see that one of the new explanatory variables is completely removed. There would then only be three unknown parameters, and a regression of Y on X_0^*, X_1^* and X_2^* would provide estimates of a_0, a_1 and a_2. If these estimates are used in equation 5.2.17, together with $a_3 = 0$, it is possible to obtain estimates of the four parameters $\beta_0, \beta_1, \beta_2$ and β_3. The deletion of X_3^* implies a restriction on equation 5.2.19 and, indirectly, a restriction on the original response coefficients. The estimators obtained in this way are thus restricted estimators, which will generally have lower variances than the corresponding unrestricted estimators. The rationale for the restriction is that a polynomial of relatively high degree can be approximated by a polynomial of some lower degree. To the extent that this can be done successfully, the implied restrictions on the response coefficients will be 'almost true', the bias introduced will be relatively small and the reduction in variance should more than compensate for the bias.

The example above was chosen for relative simplicity, and two comments are in order. With quarterly data it is not uncommon to find maximum lags of eight or twelve quarters, so there is scope for increasing the degree of the approximating polynomial. A second degree polynomial is too restrictive for general use, but a third, fourth or fifth degree polynomial will often be a reasonable approximation for the order of maximum lag likely to arise in practice. In principle, one could test the approximation by conducting t tests on the coefficients of a transformed relationship similar to equation 5.2.19. But the results would have to be treated with caution, because the transformed model will still be subject to multicollinearity. The real advantage of using the Almon method is that it suggests restrictions that can be justified on a priori grounds, and it is on this basis that we argue that a suitably chosen polynomial approximation will be adequate.

The other point to be made concerns the practical implementation of the Almon method. Although, in principle, one could carry out the calculations described above with a standard regression program, this would not provide variance estimates for the original response coefficients and, in fact, the version of the method that we have described does give rise to rather severe numerical problems. It is therefore recommended that, for practical purposes, one should use a program with a properly designed Almon subroutine. What we have done in this section is to provide sufficient information to enable the reader to understand the basic principles of the Almon method and to appreciate the significance of any reference to the method which may be found in the literature.

To conclude our discussion of the methods used to estimate the parameters of a distributed lag model, we consider a case in which an *infinite* lag distribution is used. Instead of assuming that there is a maximum lag length s, we impose a pattern under which the weights in the lag distribution decline as the lag length is increased, but except in one special case the weights never become exactly zero. To achieve this, the weights are expressed as

$$w_0 = 1 - \lambda; w_1 = (1 - \lambda)\lambda; w_2 = (1 - \lambda)\lambda^2; \text{etc.} \qquad (5.2.20)$$

where λ is a single unknown parameter. We shall exclude the special case in which $\lambda = 0$, for then $w_0 = 1$, all other weights are zero and, effectively, there is no lag distribution. For any other value of λ, the sequence of weights is assumed to continue indefinitely. To ensure that the weights are positive and steadily declining, λ must be positive and less than 1. Under these conditions, the infinite series

$$1 + \lambda + \lambda^2 + \lambda^3 + \ldots$$

converges to the value $1/(1 - \lambda)$. By including the term $1 - \lambda$ in each of the weights, we ensure that the weights add to 1.

The implication of the lag distribution shown in 5.2.20 is that the current value of Y is determined by all past values of X, going back indefinitely. As an original hypothesis this seems to be rather bizarre, and a better approach might be to argue that 5.2.20 is an approximation to a finite lag distribution. As such it could obviously be useful, because the unknown weights are expressed in terms of a single unknown parameter and, given that λ is less than 1, the weights do become close to zero as the lag length is increased. If the response coefficients are constrained to follow the infinite lag distribution, we would have

$$\beta_0 = \beta(1 - \lambda); \beta_1 = \beta(1 - \lambda)\lambda; \beta_2 = \beta(1 - \lambda)\lambda^2; \text{etc.}$$

As before, β is a single parameter measuring the total or long run response. The distributed lag model could then be written as

$$Y_t = \beta(1 - \lambda)[X_t + \lambda X_{t-1} + \lambda^2 X_{t-2} + \ldots] + u_t; t = 1, 2, \ldots, n \qquad (5.2.21)$$

The main part of equation 5.2.21 involves just two parameters but, given that λ is unknown, 5.2.21 is certainly not in the standard form for a linear model. The parameter λ actually enters the model in a highly nonlinear fashion. Moreover, a strict interpretation of the infinite lag distribution means that the data requirement would be an infinitely long run of past values of X. As a matter of fact, neither of these problems is insurmountable. One can treat the values of X for which no observations are available as a type of nuisance effect for which an allowance can be made, and it is possible to solve nonlinear problems by iterative methods. But the approach that has been most widely used in practice is based on a transformation of equation 5.2.21.

The transformation in question is actually that applied to the case in which the disturbances follow a first order autoregressive scheme. In the present context, it is often described as a *Koyck transformation*. Equation 5.2.21 implies that we can now write

$$Y_{t-1} = \beta(1 - \lambda)[X_{t-1} + \lambda X_{t-2} + \ldots] + u_{t-1}; t = 2, 3, \ldots, n$$
(5.2.22)

and

$$\lambda Y_{t-1} = \beta(1 - \lambda)[\lambda X_{t-1} + \lambda^2 X_{t-2} + \ldots] + \lambda u_{t-1}; t = 2, 3, \ldots, n$$
(5.2.23)

The subtraction of equation 5.2.23 from 5.2.21 gives

$$Y_t - \lambda Y_{t-1} = \beta(1 - \lambda)X_t + u_t - \lambda u_{t-1}; t = 2, 3, \ldots, n \qquad (5.2.24)$$

All other terms cancel out and a final rearrangement gives

$$Y_t = \lambda Y_{t-1} + \beta(1 - \lambda)X_t + u_t - \lambda u_{t-1}; t = 2, 3, \ldots, n \qquad (5.2.25)$$

In principle, would could treat Y_{t-1} and X_t; $t = 2, 3, \ldots, n$ as explanatory variable observations, associated with parameters

$$\beta_1^* = \lambda; \ \beta_2^* = \beta(1 - \lambda)$$

A regression run on 5.2.25 would then provide estimates of β_1^* and β_2^*, from which estimates of λ and β could be obtained. But one of the explanatory variables is actually a lagged endogenous variable, and the disturbances in the transformed model follow a moving average scheme. As we shall see in Section 5.4, the use of OLS under these conditions leads to estimators which are actually inconsistent. We could, of course, take steps to correct for the moving average disturbances: but to do this we would actually have to transform back to equation 5.2.21. The one advantage of the Koyck transformation, followed by OLS estimation applied to the transformed model, is the relative simplicity of the calculation, and this is the historical reason for the widespread use of the method. The apparent simplicity does, however, have a cost. Apart from anything else, the shape of the lag distribution is severely constrained and, although it is possible to use alternative forms of infinite lag, the application of a Koyck type transformation will still produce a combination of lagged endogenous variables and moving average disturbances.

5.3 Estimation in dynamic models I

The first order autoregressive process

$$Y_t = \beta Y_{t-1} + u_t; t = 1, 2, \ldots, n \qquad (5.3.1)$$

is a special case, but it does serve to illustrate the nature of the estimation problem in a dynamic model. Initially, it is assumed that the disturbances $u_t; t = 1, 2, \ldots, n$ are serially independent, with zero means and constant variance. Since the model explicitly involves the observations $Y_t; t = 1, 2, \ldots, n$ and the starting value Y_0, it is assumed that all $n + 1$ observations on Y are available. If this is the case then, given that there is no intercept in equation 5.3.1, the OLS estimator for β would be

$$\hat{\beta} = \sum_{t=1}^{t=n} Y_{t-1} Y_t \bigg/ \sum_{t=1}^{t=n} Y_{t-1}^2 \qquad (5.3.2)$$

Having established the range of summation in equation 5.3.2, the range is excluded from subsequent statements.

To investigate the properties of the estimator, it is necessary to consider the nature of the random variable $\hat{\beta}$. If equation 5.3.1 is used to substitute for Y_t, equation 5.3.2 can be written as

$$\hat{\beta} = \Sigma Y_{t-1} (\beta Y_{t-1} + u_t) / \Sigma Y_{t-1}^2$$
$$= \beta \Sigma Y_{t-1}^2 / \Sigma Y_{t-1}^2 + \Sigma Y_{t-1} u_t / \Sigma Y_{t-1}^2$$

or

$$\hat{\beta} = \beta + \Sigma Y_{t-1} u_t / \Sigma Y_{t-1}^2 \qquad (5.3.3)$$

This expression is different, in two respects, from that first introduced in Section 2.3. Because there is no intercept in the model, the observations $Y_{t-1}; t = 1, 2, \ldots, n$ are not expressed in terms of deviations from the sample mean. Of far more fundamental importance is the fact that $Y_{t-1}; t = 1, 2, \ldots, n$ cannot be considered to be nonrandom, or to be completely independent of the disturbances $u_t; t = 1, 2, \ldots, n$. Hence we cannot use the methods of Section 2.3, or the alternative arguments suggested in Section 2.10, under which the OLS slope estimator would be unbiased. To see exactly why this is so, we look a little more closely at the nature of the autoregressive process.

From equation 5.3.1 we have that

$$Y_t = \beta Y_{t-1} + u_t; t = 1, 2, \ldots, n$$

and, by implication, that

$$Y_{t-1} = \beta Y_{t-2} + u_{t-1}; t = 2, 3, \ldots, n \tag{5.3.4}$$

It follows that Y_{t-1} depends directly on the random disturbance u_{t-1} and this is sufficient to suggest that, with the possible exception of $Y_0(Y_{t-1}$ when $t = 1)$, the observations $Y_{t-1}; t = 1, 2, \ldots, n$ must be random. However, to analyse the process properly we should express the endogenous variable observations entirely in terms of disturbances, apart from a term in the starting value Y_0. To do this, we write

$$\begin{aligned} Y_t &= \beta Y_{t-1} + u_t \\ &= \beta(\beta Y_{t-2} + u_{t-1}) + u_t \\ &= \beta[\beta(\beta Y_{t-3} + u_{t-2}) + u_{t-1}] + u_t \end{aligned}$$

$$= \beta^t Y_0 + \beta^{t-1} u_1 + \ldots + \beta u_{t-1} + u_t \tag{5.3.5}$$

Equation 5.3.5 shows that Y_t depends on u_t, u_{t-1}, u_{t-2} etc. and, by implication, that Y_{t-1} depends on $u_{t-1}, u_{t-2}, u_{t-3}$ etc. On the other hand, if the disturbances are serially independent, Y_t is independent of u_{t+1}, u_{t+2}, u_{t+3} etc. or, equivalently, Y_{t-1} is independent of u_t, u_{t+1}, u_{t+2} etc. In particular, because Y_{t-1} is independent of u_t, it is possible to argue that

$$E(Y_{t-1} u_t) = E(Y_{t-1})E(u_t) = 0; t = 1, 2, \ldots, n$$

and

$$E(\Sigma Y_{t-1} u_t) = \Sigma E(Y_{t-1} u_t) = 0$$

This is an important result, but it is not sufficient to enable us to argue that $\hat{\beta}$ is an unbiased estimator. From equation 5.3.3 we have

$$\hat{\beta} = \beta + \Sigma Y_{t-1} u_t / \Sigma Y_{t-1}^2 \tag{5.3.6}$$

or, rearranging slightly,

$$\begin{aligned} \hat{\beta} &= \beta + \Sigma(Y_{t-1}/\Sigma Y_{t-1}^2) u_t \\ &= \beta + \Sigma w_t u_t \end{aligned} \tag{5.3.7}$$

where

$$w_t = Y_{t-1}/\Sigma Y_{t-1}^2; t = 1, 2, \ldots, n$$

It is not true that w_t is independent of u_t, because each weight involves ΣY_{t-1}^2, which includes all observations on Y except for Y_n. The result is that the right hand term in equation 5.3.6 cannot be shown to have an expectation equal to zero and, in the autoregressive model, the estimator $\hat\beta$ is generally biased.

Given that the origin of the bias lies in the connection between each disturbance u_t and some of the terms in ΣY_{t-1}^2, we now consider what happens when the number of observations is large. For this purpose it is convenient to look at a particular disturbance term. A given disturbance, say u_3, would influence Y_3 and, indirectly, Y_4, Y_5, Y_6 etc.: but whereas Y_3 depends directly on u_3, Y_4 depends on βu_3, Y_5 depends on $\beta^2 u_3$ and so on. If β lies between -1 and $+1$, without reaching either extreme value, the influence of u_3 would diminish over time. If n is very large and $-1 < \beta < 1$, those values of Y which are strongly influenced by u_3 make a relatively unimportant contribution to the sum ΣY_{t-1}^2. Moreover, u_3 does not influence the numerator of the weight w_3, since $w_3 = Y_2/\Sigma Y_{t-1}^2$. So, in the limit, the influence of u_3 on w_3 would be negligible. This argument is merely indicative but it does suggest that, in some limiting sense, the problem of association between w_t and u_t will disappear. Given the conditions used so far, together with an easily satisfied restriction on the nature of the disturbance distributions, it is possible to show that plim $(\Sigma Y_{t-1}^2/n)$ exists and is nonzero, whereas plim $(\Sigma Y_{t-1}u_t/n)$ exists and is zero. Hence, using the rules for manipulating probability limits, given Section 2.10, we have

$$\begin{aligned}
\text{plim } (\hat\beta) &= \text{plim } [\beta + \Sigma w_t u_t] \\
&= \text{plim } [\beta + (\Sigma Y_{t-1}u_t/n)/(\Sigma Y_{t-1}^2/n)] \\
&= \beta + \text{plim } (\Sigma Y_{t-1}u_t/n)/\text{plim } (\Sigma Y_{t-1}^2/n) \\
&= \beta + 0/\text{plim } (\Sigma Y_{t-1}^2/n) = \beta
\end{aligned} \tag{5.3.8}$$

This shows that $\hat\beta$ is consistent, but the argument does depend critically on the assumption that the disturbances are serially independent. We have also made use of a *stability condition*, represented here by the restriction $-1 < \beta < +1$. As it happens, the stability condition is not strictly necessary to a proof of consistency, but it is difficult to obtain other asymptotic properties without such a condition and, in all future discussion of estimation in dynamic models, stability conditions will be assumed to hold.

There is in fact no practical method of estimation which gives unbiased estimators of the parameters of a model containing one or more lagged endogenous variables. On the other hand, OLS estimators are consistent and, in terms of asymptotic properties, there is no reason why one should not continue to use ordinary least squares. Under conditions such as those used above, it can be shown that the OLS estimators are asymptotically normal and that the asymptotic variances are correctly estimated by treating lagged endogenous variables exactly as one would treat any other variable in an OLS regression calculation. Thus, in the particular case of the autoregressive model shown in equation 5.3.1, the estimator for $\hat{\beta}$ would be that shown in equation 5.3.2 and the asymptotic variance would suggest the approximation

$$\text{var}\,(\hat{\beta}) = \sigma^2/\Sigma Y_{t-1}^2 \qquad (5.3.9)$$

Since $\hat{\beta}$ is also asymptotically normal, we can say that standard OLS procedures do represent a valid approximation as long as the number of observations is large. It is also of interest to know what would happen if n is relatively small: some analytic results are available and these suggest that, if β is positive, the OLS estimator tends to systematically underestimate the true value. Beyond this the analysis does become difficult, and an alternative source of information is that taken from *simulation* experiments.

In Chapter 2 the nature of an estimator was explained by considering what would happen if the estimation could be repeated for different sets of disturbance values. Using a computer, it is possible to generate a number of different sets of artificial disturbances, in such a way that the values look as though they could have been generated from independent normal distributions, with zero means and constant variance. Alternatively, some other pattern of disturbance behaviour could be imposed.

Suppose now that we wished to investigate the properties of the OLS estimator, under the conditions of the simple autoregressive model 5.3.1. For given values of Y_0 and β, a single set of disturbances could be used to produce an artificial set of observations $Y_t; t = 1, 2, \ldots, n$. The procedure would be to use Y_0 and u_1 to generate Y_1, Y_1 and u_2 to generate Y_2, and so on:

$$Y_1 = \beta Y_0 + u_1,\; Y_2 = \beta Y_1 + u_2, \ldots, Y_n = \beta Y_{n-1} + u_n$$

For each set of observations that is generated in this way, one would obtain a single estimate of β, that is, a single value for $\hat{\beta}$. If the process is repeated sufficiently often, the shape of the experimental spread of values for $\hat{\beta}$ should provide an approximation to the shape of the probability distribution. This distribution corresponds to a single value of β, and so the entire experiment would now be repeated for a number of different parameter values. In the case of the simple autoregressive model, one might use the sequence $-0\cdot 8, -0\cdot 6, -0\cdot 4, -0\cdot 2, 0, 0\cdot 2, 0\cdot 4,$

0·6, 0·8. Having tried all these experiments, one would have a reasonably good indication of the behaviour of $\hat{\beta}$ under the specified disturbance conditions. One might also wish to vary the number of observations, and this would require further sets of experiments.

Simulation is expensive in terms of computer time, but if the analysis of estimator properties is difficult, simulation does at least give some indication as to how an estimator would behave under certain specified conditions. The use of simulation is not limited to cases in which the number of observations is small: it can also provide a check on whether the asymptotic properties give a reliable indication of estimator behaviour when the number of observations is large. Experiments which have been carried out on the autoregressive model do tend to confirm the analytic results. If the disturbances are serially independent, there is a bias for small values of n, but the bias tends to disappear as the number of observations is increased. One other important fact that emerges is that there are regions close to $\beta = -1$ and $\beta = +1$ in which estimator behaviour does become rather distorted. The practical implication is that one should treat parameter estimates close to the boundary of the stability region as representing something of a danger signal.

5.4 Estimation in dynamic models II

The assumption of serial independence is clearly important to the arguments laid out in the previous section, and we now consider the case in which the disturbances are serially correlated. As before, we shall use the simple autoregressive model for the behaviour of the endogenous variable, but now the disturbances u_t; $t = 1, 2, \ldots, n$ also follow a first order autoregressive process. The complete model is thus

$$Y_t = \beta Y_{t-1} + u_t; t = 1, 2, \ldots, n \qquad -1 < \beta < +1 \qquad (5.4.1)$$
$$u_t = \rho u_{t-1} + v_t; t = 1, 2, \ldots, n \qquad -1 < \rho < +1 \qquad (5.4.2)$$

where v_t; $t = 1, 2, \ldots, n$ represent a new set of random variables, which are serially independent, with zero means and constant variance. The restrictions on β and ρ ensure that both processes are stable. The other possibility that we shall consider is that the disturbances to equation 5.4.1 follow the first order moving average process

$$u_t = v_t - \lambda v_{t-1}; t = 1, 2, \ldots, n \qquad -1 < \lambda < +1 \qquad (5.4.3)$$

In the presence of either of these forms of serial correlation of the disturbances, the properties of the OLS estimator are radically altered. The relationship between the estimator $\hat{\beta}$ and the disturbances to 5.4.1 is still given by the equation

$$\hat{\beta} = \beta + \Sigma Y_{t-1} u_t / \Sigma Y_{t-1}^2 \qquad (5.4.4)$$

but there is now a definite connection between u_t and Y_{t-1} and, with either pattern of serial correlation, it can be shown that $\hat{\beta}$ is no longer a consistent estimator. To analyse this problem properly, we should express the processes generating u_t and Y_{t-1} in terms of starting values and current and past values of what is really the fundamental source of random variation, namely the series $v_1, v_2, \ldots, v_n$. However, essentially correct conclusions can be drawn by looking at equations of the kind used in writing down the model.

From equation 5.4.1 we have that

$$Y_t = \beta Y_{t-1} + u_t ; t = 1, 2, \ldots, n$$

and, by implication, that

$$Y_{t-1} = \beta Y_{t-2} + u_{t-1} ; t = 2, 3, \ldots, n \qquad (5.4.5)$$

If the disturbances follow the autoregressive form 5.4.2, we also have

$$u_t = \rho u_{t-1} + v_t ; t = 1, 2, \ldots, n \qquad (5.4.6)$$

By inspection of these equations, it can be seen that both Y_{t-1} and u_t depend directly on u_{t-1}. Moreover, if ρ is positive, both Y_{t-1} and u_t will be positively related to u_{t-1} and so it seems likely that Y_{t-1} and u_t will themselves be positively related. If ρ is negative, it seems likely that Y_{t-1} and u_t would be negatively related. Under suitable conditions, this rather vague suggestion can be translated into the specific result that plim $(\Sigma Y_{t-1} u_t / n)$ is positive if ρ is positive and negative if ρ is negative. Either way, plim $(\Sigma Y_{t-1} u_t / n)$ is nonzero, so the argument for consistency used in the previous section now breaks down. Provided that plim $(\Sigma Y_{t-1}^2 / n)$ exists and is nonzero, we have

$$\text{plim } (\hat{\beta}) = \beta + \text{plim } (\Sigma Y_{t-1} u_t / n) / \text{plim } (\Sigma Y_{t-1}^2 / n)$$
$$\neq \beta \qquad (5.4.7)$$

This shows that $\hat{\beta}$ is not a consistent estimator and also provides information on the sign of the inconsistency. The denominator probability limit involves a sum of squares and is therefore positive or zero. Since we have assumed a nonzero value, it follows that the sign of the inconsistency depends only on the sign of the numerator probability limit.

By the argument above, this depends only on the sign of ρ, provided that both processes satisfy the stability conditions. If ρ is positive, plim $(\hat{\beta})$ is greater than β and the OLS estimator systematically over-estimates the true parameter value. If ρ is negative, plim $(\hat{\beta})$ is less than β and the OLS estimator systematically underestimates the true parameter. Thus, whereas the extent of the inconsistency depends on the true values of β and ρ, the sign of the inconsistency depends only on the sign of ρ.

If the serial correlation of disturbances follows the moving average scheme shown in equation 5.4.3, one can use a similar argument to suggest that $\hat{\beta}$ will again be inconsistent. Given the way in which we have written the moving average process, a positive value for λ suggests a negative inconsistency; that is, the probability limit of $\hat{\beta}$ will be less than the true value. This is not surprising, since a positive value of λ implies negative serial correlation between successive pairs of disturbances $u_t, u_{t-1}; t = 2, 3, \ldots, n$.

The fact that OLS estimators are inconsistent will, in principle, generalize to any model in which lagged dependent variable observations appear on the right hand side of the equation, together with serial correlation of the disturbances. This suggests that there will be a systematic distortion in the behaviour of the estimators in a finite sample, a distortion which does not disappear as the number of observations is increased. Strictly speaking we should not refer to this finite sample effect as a bias, because we have not established that the expectation of the estimator exists and is different from the true parameter. We shall respect this theoretical nicety by using the phrase 'apparent bias' to describe the finite sample behaviour of an estimator that has been shown to be inconsistent. From the results of simulation experiments, it is clear that, under the conditions described above, there is an apparent bias in the OLS estimators, which can sometimes be very

---

Technical note 7

The argument used above is merely suggestive, and does in fact contain a logical flaw. In equation 5.4.5, Y_{t-1} is determined by both u_{t-1} and Y_{t-2} and, in order to see how these terms interact to produce a value for Y_{t-1}, we need to know the nature of the correlation between Y_{t-2} and u_{t-1}. But this is exactly the same phenomenon as the correlation between Y_{t-1} and u_t, which is what we are trying to establish. To conduct the argument properly, we should really reduce both processes to expressions involving the independent series $v_1, v_2, \ldots, v_n$.

serious. It is also the case that, for a given model, the direction of the apparent bias is usually that suggested by the direction of the inconsistency.

If OLS estimators are inconsistent under the conditions described above, there is obviously an incentive to look for some alternative method of estimation. The methods proposed divide roughly into two groups, depending on whether the objective is merely to attain consistency, or whether there is also an attempt to improve asymptotic efficiency by recognizing the existence of a disturbance problem. In both groups we find estimators which make use of *instrumental variables,* and we now consider what this means.

In order to show the form of an instrumental variable (IV) estimator, we use the simple model

$$Y_t = \beta X_t + u_t; t = 1, 2, \ldots, n \tag{5.4.8}$$

where, initially, the properties of the observations $X_t; t = 1, 2, \ldots, n$ are left undefined. The OLS estimator for β is obtained as the solution to the equation

$$\hat{\beta}\Sigma X_t^2 = \Sigma X_t Y_t \tag{5.4.9}$$

In contrast, the IV estimator $\hat{\beta}_I$ is obtained as the solution to

$$\hat{\beta}_I \Sigma Z_t X_t = \Sigma Z_t Y_t \tag{5.4.10}$$

where the observations $Z_t; t = 1, 2, \ldots, n$ are also undefined, except for the fact that Z is to be known as an instrumental variable. Provided that $\Sigma Z_t X_t$ is nonzero, equation 5.4.10 can be solved to give

$$\hat{\beta}_I = \Sigma Z_t Y_t / \Sigma Z_t X_t \tag{5.4.11}$$

Equation 5.4.8 can then be used to substitute for Y_t, to give

$$\hat{\beta}_I = \Sigma Z_t (\beta X_t + u_t) / \Sigma Z_t X_t$$
$$= \beta \Sigma Z_t X_t / \Sigma Z_t X_t + \Sigma Z_t u_t / \Sigma Z_t X_t$$

or

$$\hat{\beta}_I = \beta + \Sigma Z_t u_t / \Sigma Z_t X_t \tag{5.4.12}$$

If the variable Z is chosen in such a way that

$$\text{plim} \left(\Sigma Z_t u_t / n \right) = 0 \tag{5.4.13}$$

and

$$\text{plim} \left(\Sigma Z_t X_t / n \right) \text{ exists and is nonzero} \tag{5.4.14}$$

then $\hat{\beta}_I$ would be a consistent estimator. This seems to be a neat trick, but it is inherently implausible that one has only to satisfy the technical conditions 5.4.13 and 5.4.14 to obtain an acceptable result. Although the IV method does not involve a complete replacement of the observations on X by observations on Z, it does seem likely that there should be some more specific requirement on the degree of association between X and Z, if the IV method is to provide information about a model in which it is X, not Z, that is the explanatory variable in the original equation. To investigate this question, we shall detour slightly from the main purpose of introducing instrumental variables and we shall consider what happens when both IV and OLS estimators are consistent.

For the purpose of this paragraph only, suppose that the disturbances to equation 5.4.8 are independent, with zero expectation and constant variance σ^2. Then suppose that both the OLS estimator $\hat{\beta}$ and the IV estimator $\hat{\beta}_I$ are consistent. Given some rather undemanding additional assumptions, it is possible to show that the asymptotic variance of the OLS estimator suggests the approximation

$$\text{var}\,(\hat{\beta}) = \sigma^2/\Sigma X_t^2 \qquad (5.4.15)$$

whereas the asymptotic variance of the IV estimator suggests the approximation

$$\text{var}\,(\hat{\beta}_I) = \sigma^2 \Sigma Z_t^2/(\Sigma Z_t X_t)^2 \qquad (5.4.16)$$

Combining these equations, we have

$$\text{var}\,(\hat{\beta}_I) = \text{var}\,(\hat{\beta})/r_{ZX}^2$$

where

$$r_{ZX}^2 = (\Sigma Z_t X_t)^2/\Sigma Z_t^2 \Sigma X_t^2 \qquad (5.4.17)$$

Equation 5.4.17 is similar to the square of a simple correlation coefficient between Z and X, the only difference being that the sums of squares and products are not adjusted for means. However, it is true that $0 \leqslant r_{ZX}^2 \leqslant 1$, so it does follow that

$$\text{var}\,(\hat{\beta}_I) \geqslant \text{var}\,(\hat{\beta})$$

with the greatest increase in variance arising in the case in which the measured correlation between Z and X is small, in the sense described above.

It should now be clear that there is no advantage in using an IV estimator when the OLS estimator is consistent. Put slightly differently, one could say that if the IV method is to be used when $\text{plim}\,(\Sigma X_t u_t/n) = 0$, then X should act as its own instrumental variable. Unfortunately, we cannot apply the variance comparison directly to the case in which the

IV estimator is consistent but the OLS estimator is not. However, the argument is indicative and the results of simulation experiments certainly suggest that the consistency of an IV estimator is usually attained at the cost of an increase in the apparent variance, *vis-à-vis* an inconsistent OLS estimator. It is against this background that we now consider the use of IV estimators in a case in which the OLS estimators are definitely inconsistent.

Suppose that we have the model

$$Y_t = \beta_1 Y_{t-1} + \beta_2 X_t + u_t; t = 1, 2, \ldots, n \tag{5.4.18}$$

$$u_t = \rho u_{t-1} + v_t; t = 1, 2, \ldots, n \tag{5.4.19}$$

where the observations X_t; $t = 1, 2, \ldots, n$ are now taken to be non-random, v_t; $t = 1, 2, \ldots, n$ are independent with zero expectation and constant variance, and both β_1 and ρ lie between -1 and $+1$ without reaching either extreme value. Given that there are now two 'explanatory' variables, the expressions for both OLS and IV estimators would change, but the essential characteristics of the two methods do not. The combination of a lagged dependent variable and serial correlation of the disturbances would render the OLS estimators of both β_1 and β_2 inconsistent. This follows from the fact that, after solution of the normal equations

$$\hat\beta_1 \Sigma Y_{t-1}^2 + \hat\beta_2 \Sigma Y_{t-1} X_t = \Sigma Y_{t-1} Y_t$$
$$\hat\beta_1 \Sigma X_t Y_{t-1} + \hat\beta_2 \Sigma X_t^2 = \Sigma X_t Y_t \tag{5.4.20}$$

both $\hat\beta_1$ and $\hat\beta_2$ depend on the term $\Sigma Y_{t-1} u_t$. As before, given suitable assumptions, it can be shown that

$$\text{plim}\,(\Sigma Y_{t-1} u_t / n) \neq 0$$

In contrast, under the same conditions,

$$\text{plim}\,(\Sigma X_t u_t / n) = 0$$

This means that X can act as its own instrumental variable, but the lagged dependent variable cannot. We therefore need an instrumental variable Z, such that $\text{plim}\,(\Sigma Z_t u_t / n) = 0$ and $\text{plim}\,(\Sigma Z_t Y_{t-1} / n) \neq 0$, to serve as an instrument for the lagged endogenous variable. Given such a variable, the equations defining the IV estimators $\hat\beta_{I1}$ and $\hat\beta_{I2}$ would be

$$\hat\beta_{I1} \Sigma Z_t Y_{t-1} + \hat\beta_{I2} \Sigma Z_t X_t = \Sigma Z_t Y_t$$
$$\hat\beta_{I1} \Sigma X_t Y_{t-1} + \hat\beta_{I2} \Sigma X_t^2 = \Sigma X_t Y_t \tag{5.4.21}$$

To obtain these equations from those defining the OLS estimators, one would take the leading term from each sum in the first equation of 5.4.20 and replace Y_{t-1}, in that position only, by Z_t. Thus ΣY_{t-1}^2 becomes $\Sigma Z_t Y_{t-1}$, $\Sigma Y_{t-1} X_t$ becomes $\Sigma Z_t X_t$, and so on. The second equation is unchanged, apart from the notation used for the estimators, because X acts as its own instrumental variable. This rule generalizes in a fairly obvious way. If variable j is a 'source of inconsistency', the leading term in all sums in equation j is replaced by an appropriately chosen instrumental variable. If variable j can act as its own instrument, then equation j is unchanged, apart from the notation used for the estimators.

To complete the example described above, we need a way of choosing the instrumental variable Z. According to the model, the observations Y_t; $t = 1, 2, \ldots, n$ depend partly on the observations X_t; $t = 1, 2, \ldots, n$, which means that Y_{t-1}; $t = 2, 3, \ldots, n$ depend partly on X_{t-1}; $t = 2, 3, \ldots, n$. If we assume that Y_0 also depends partly on X_0 and that the observation X_0 is available, then we can define $Z_t = X_{t-1}$; $t = 1, 2, \ldots, n$. Since the observations on X are nonrandom, it should not be difficult to show that $\text{plim}\,(\Sigma Z_t u_t / n) = \text{plim}\,(\Sigma X_{t-1} u_t / n) = 0$. Moreover, if the model is correct, there is clearly some association between X_{t-1} and Y_{t-1}, for each value of t, so one would expect that $\text{plim}\,(\Sigma X_{t-1} Y_{t-1} / n) \neq 0$. The lagged exogenous variable therefore acts as an instrument for the lagged endogenous variable and the final version of the estimating equations would be

$$\hat{\beta}_{I1} \Sigma X_{t-1} Y_{t-1} + \hat{\beta}_{I2} \Sigma X_{t-1} X_t = \Sigma X_{t-1} Y_t$$
$$\hat{\beta}_{I1} \Sigma X_t Y_{t-1} + \hat{\beta}_{I2} \Sigma X_t^2 = \Sigma X_t Y_t \qquad (5.4.22)$$

It is worth noting that there is an alternative way of obtaining the instrumental variable estimates for the model described above. This consists of two regressions, the first of which generates predicted values $\hat{Y}_{t-1}$; $t = 1, 2, \ldots, n$ from a regression of Y_{t-1} on X_{t-1} and X_t. Using a_1 and a_2 to denote the coefficients of this regression, we may write the predicted values as

$$\hat{Y}_{t-1} = a_1 X_{t-1} + a_2 X_t; \, t = 1, 2, \ldots, n \qquad (5.4.23)$$

The second regression corresponds to equation 5.4.18, except that the observations Y_{t-1}; $t = 1, 2, \ldots, n$ are replaced by $\hat{Y}_{t-1}$; $t = 1, 2, \ldots, n$. It can be shown that the regression of Y_t on $\hat{Y}_{t-1}$ and X_t defines estimators which are identical to $\hat{\beta}_{I1}$ and $\hat{\beta}_{I2}$. This method of generating IV estimates is known as two stage least squares, and we shall encounter the method again in Chapter 6. Note that two stage least squares

estimators are quite distinct from the 'two step' estimators first introduced in Chapter 4. Note also that alternative instrumental variable
estimators can be defined by adding to the number of lagged values of
X that appear in the regression which produces $\bar{Y}_{t-1}$; $t = 1, 2, \ldots, n$.

As described above, the sole motivation for using the IV approach is
to obtain consistency: there is no attempt to correct for the existence
of a disturbance problem. By analogy with the use of GLS for pure
serial correlation, there ought to be a possible efficiency gain from
using a transformation which aims to produce serially independent
disturbances. This leads us to the second group of estimation methods.

If the necessary disturbance parameters were known, it would be
possible to transform the model so as to remove the disturbance
problem. In exercise 5.2 the reader is asked to show that equations
5.4.18 and 5.4.19 together imply

$$Y_t = (\beta_1 + \rho)Y_{t-1} - \beta_1\rho Y_{t-2} + \beta_2 X_t - \beta_2\rho X_{t-1} + v_t \,; t = 2, 3, \ldots, n$$

$$(5.4.24)$$

For a known value of ρ, this could be written as

$$(Y_t - \rho Y_{t-1}) = \beta_1(Y_{t-1} - \rho Y_{t-2}) + \beta_2(X_t - \rho X_{t-1}) + v_t \,;$$
$$t = 2, 3, \ldots, n \qquad (5.4.25)$$

The use of OLS on the transformed model would then be equivalent to
the use of GLS on the original model, except for the treatment of the
first observation. Even though the transformed model still involves
lagged endogenous variables, there would no longer be serial correlation
of the disturbances and, in principle, this approach should give consistent estimators. The difficulty that arises in practice is that the
disturbance parameters are not known. If ρ has to be estimated along
with β_1 and β_2, the application of least squares to 5.4.24 defines a nonlinear least squares problem. It is not enough to treat $\beta_1 + \rho$, $-\beta_1\rho$, β_2
and $-\beta_2\rho$ as composite parameters, because it is only by enforcing a
nonlinear restriction that one can obtain unique estimates of β_1, β_2 and
ρ. We are therefore left with essentially similar options to those discussed
in Section 4.6, the one difference being that two step and iterative procedures should now start with instrumental variable estimates of β_1 and
β_2. In the model described above, this would mean that the 'first round'
estimate of ρ would be based on IV residuals, defined as

$$e_{\mathrm{I}t} = Y_t - \hat{\beta}_{\mathrm{I}1}Y_{t-1} - \hat{\beta}_{\mathrm{I}2}X_t \,; t = 1, 2, \ldots, n$$

A final possibility is to cast the whole problem into the framework of
maximum likelihood estimation. Again, the basic philosophy would be

to exploit all the information provided in the model specification, including the fact that the disturbances are serially correlated. In this way, one obtains an estimator which should be both consistent and asymptotically efficient.

Despite the problems raised in this section, it is the case that OLS is quite frequently used in dynamic models with serially correlated disturbances. In this situation, one must appreciate that the estimators are inconsistent and that the distortion of estimator behaviour in a small sample can be quite serious. The one encouraging result on the application of OLS is that the presence of additional exogenous variables does tend to reduce the apparent bias.

There is still one further problem that we have not yet mentioned. In the presence of a lagged dependent variable, the assumptions underlying the Durbin-Watson test are no longer valid and the value of the test statistic is not a reliable indicator of disturbance behaviour. Specifically, one cannot assume that a value in the region around 2 indicates independence of the disturbances, as is the case in a model with nonrandom explanatory variables. So, with a dynamic model, we need a different procedure, and one possibility is what is often described as the *Durbin h test*. The test statistic is computed as

$$h = (1 - 0.5d)\sqrt{[n/(1 - n \text{ var} (\hat{\beta}_1))]} \qquad (5.4.26)$$

where d is the Durbin-Watson statistic, n is the number of observations and var $(\hat{\beta}_1)$ is the estimated variance of the coefficient attached to Y_{t-1}, as obtained from a standard OLS regression, applied to the original model. Under the null hypothesis of serial independence of the disturbances, h has an asymptotic standard normal distribution and, following the principle of the original Durbin-Watson test, a one-tailed procedure is used. For a significance level of 0.05 and for the alternative of positive serial correlation, the critical value is 1.64 (see Table A, p. 267). If h is greater than 1.64, the null hypothesis of serial independence is rejected in favour of the alternative of positive serial correlation. If the alternative is negative serial correlation, the rejection region consists of values which are less than −1.64. Because the test is based on the asymptotic distribution of 5.4.26, the behaviour of the test in a small sample is somewhat uncertain. There is also a problem associated with the fact that the test statistic is only defined when n var $(\hat{\beta}_1) < 1$. If this condition is not satisfied, the recommended procedure is to perform a regression of OLS residuals on both lagged residuals and all the explanatory variables from the original model: the 't ratio' associated with the variable defined by the lagged residuals is then treated as being equivalent to the h statistic and is tested in the manner described above.

5.5 Alternative dynamic hypotheses

In the previous sections of this chapter, we have seen two somewhat different ways in which one can arrive at a specification involving a lagged endogenous variable. One might choose such a hypothesis directly: alternatively, it could arise as a result of a transformation applied to a model with an infinite distributed lag. If the lag model is

$$Y_t = \beta(1 - \lambda)[X_t + \lambda X_{t-1} + \lambda^2 X_{t-2} + \dots] + u_t; t = 1, 2, \dots, n \quad (5.5.1)$$

then, after transformation, we obtain

$$Y_t = \lambda Y_{t-1} + \beta(1 - \lambda)X_t + u_t - \lambda u_{t-1}; t = 2, 3, \dots, n \quad (5.5.2)$$

The equivalence between these forms is instructive. It is not immediately obvious that a model with an infinite distributed lag is, within our definition, a dynamic model. But it is certainly possible to transform so as to obtain an equation involving a lagged endogenous variable and, ignoring the random disturbances, equation 5.5.1 could generate a time path in which each value $Y_t; t = 1, 2, \dots, n$ is different, without there being any change in the values of X between periods $t = 1$ and $t = n$. This happens because Y reacts to all past values of X and any changes in X prior to period $t = 1$ would have some effect, however small, on the values $Y_1, Y_2, \dots, Y_n$. So the hypothesis of an infinite distributed lag is at least equivalent to a dynamic model and equation 5.5.1 does imply that the current behaviour of the endogenous variable is linked to the immediate past value of that variable. Equally, the direct specification implies that the current value of the endogenous variable is partly determined by past values of any exogenous variables that are present. If the model is

$$Y_t = \beta_1 Y_{t-1} + \beta_2 X_t + v_t; t = 1, 2, \dots, n \quad (5.5.3)$$

then, starting at period $t = 1$, we have

$$Y_1 = \beta_1 Y_0 + \beta_2 X_1 + v_1$$
$$Y_2 = \beta_1 Y_1 + \beta_2 X_2 + v_2$$
$$= \beta_1(\beta_1 Y_0 + \beta_2 X_1 + v_1) + \beta_2 X_2 + v_2$$
$$= \beta_2(X_2 + \beta_1 X_1) + \beta_1^2 Y_0 + (v_2 + \beta_1 v_1)$$

The general form for this expression would be

$$Y_t = \beta_2 [X_t + \beta_1 X_{t-1} + \ldots + \beta_1^{t-1} X_1] + \beta_1^t Y_0 + \text{disturbance terms}$$
(5.5.4)

Given that the parameters are unknown, the only formal difference between equations 5.5.4 and 5.5.1 lies in the treatment of the observations immediately prior to $t = 1$ and, possibly, in the behaviour of the disturbance terms. The infinite lag model would relate Y_t to all past values of X: in equation 5.5.4 we have a term in the starting value, Y_0, and the model does not state explicitly that Y_0 could be replaced by an expression involving values of X prior to period $t = 1$. But, just as equation 5.5.1 can generate a model which is similar to equation 5.5.3, so 5.5.3 can generate a model which is similar to 5.5.1. Indeed, under certain conditions, the two forms of model may be observationally equivalent. To see what this means, consider a specific example.

Suppose that two investigators decide to examine the behaviour of consumers' expenditure C, and that the first postulates an infinite lag reaction to present and past values of disposable income D, whereas the other specifies a model in which consumers' expenditure is linked to the present value of disposable income and to the immediate past value of consumers' expenditure. Then suppose that the first investigator transforms his model, to give a specification equivalent to equation 5.5.2:

$$C_t = \lambda C_{t-1} + \beta(1 - \lambda)D_t + u_t - \lambda u_{t-1}; t = 1, 2, \ldots, n \qquad (5.5.5)$$

The second investigator would write directly

$$C_t = \beta_1 C_{t-1} + \beta_2 D_t + v_t; t = 1, 2, \ldots, n \qquad (5.5.6)$$

For convenience, we have assumed that both investigators have the same set of observations, including C_0, and that the first investigator is prepared to apply the derived model to the period $t = 1$. The obvious question is whether one can actually tell the difference between these hypotheses. As it stands, the only possibility is to exploit the apparent difference in the disturbance behaviour. If u_t; $t = 1, 2, \ldots, n$ and v_t; $t = 1, 2, \ldots, n$ are both serially independent, the disturbances to equation 5.5.5 follow a moving average scheme and there is a formal distinction between the two models. There is then the separate question of whether a test procedure, based on a given set of data, can offer satisfactory discrimination in practice. In our example, this could be somewhat difficult, given the problems of testing for serial correlation in the presence of a lagged endogenous variable. But, in principle, one could solve the problem by using a sufficiently large data set. In contrast, if v_t; $t = 1, 2, \ldots, n$ are, for some reason, considered to follow a moving average scheme, then no amount of data would enable one to distinguish between the two models: it is in this case that the two specifications are said to be observationally equivalent.

If our two investigators agree that they have simply chosen alternative forms for essentially the same hypothesis, there is no particular problem. If, on the other hand, they have somewhat different ideas as to the economic behaviour underlying the formal specification then, as we have seen, it may be difficult, or perhaps impossible, to distinguish between the competing 'theories'. Ideally, the reasoning behind the formal specification should be made explicit and should be made a part of the model that is tested, but this is not always possible. In particular the underlying hypothesis may include unobservable variables, and we now consider some examples in which this is the case.

The first example is the *partial adjustment* hypothesis. In the context of the consumption–income relationship, the argument would be that there exists some desired level of consumption which is determined by the current value of disposable income. For a variety of reasons, it may be impossible to adjust the actual value of C to the desired value within a single time period. It is then necessary to add a second hypothesis about the way in which the actual value is adjusted. For example, one might assume that the desired value C^* is determined as

$$C_t^* = \beta D_t; t = 1, 2, \ldots, n \qquad (5.5.7)$$

and that the actual adjustment between periods is some proportion of the desired adjustment

$$C_t - C_{t-1} = \delta(C_t^* - C_{t-1}); t = 1, 2, \ldots, n \qquad (5.5.8)$$

It is generally very difficult to devise ways in which one might attempt to measure a 'desired' value such as C^*, and so neither of these hypotheses can be tested directly. But equation 5.5.8 implies that

$$C_t = (1 - \delta)C_{t-1} + \delta C_t^*; t = 1, 2, \ldots, n \qquad (5.5.9)$$

and, using equation 5.5.7 to substitute for C_t^*, this becomes

$$C_t = (1 - \delta)C_{t-1} + \delta\beta D_t; t = 1, 2, \ldots, n \qquad (5.5.10)$$

Equation 5.5.10 involves the same explanatory variables as both 5.5.5 and 5.5.6. As yet there are no disturbances in equation 5.5.10, but if disturbance terms were added to either of equations 5.5.7 or 5.5.8 or, for that matter, to both, this would imply a set of disturbances to equation 5.5.10. Note that there is no particular reason to assume that these would follow a moving average scheme.

A second example is one in which the basic hypothesis involves an explanatory variable that is unobservable. Suppose that the behaviour of consumption is believed to be determined by permanent income, excluding any transitory or 'windfall' components. The model for this process might be

$$C_t = \beta D_t^* + u_t; t = 1, 2, \ldots, n \qquad (5.5.11)$$

where D^* represents permanent income. Once again we have a hypothesis which cannot be tested directly, and we need a second hypothesis about the way in which permanent income is derived from measured income. One possibility is to specify that D_t is a weighted average of current and past values of D and, in particular, we might have

$$D_t^* = (1 - \lambda)[D_t + \lambda D_{t-1} + \lambda^2 D_{t-2} + \ldots]; t = 1, 2, \ldots, n \quad (5.5.12)$$

where λ is positive and less than 1. We already know that the weights $1 - \lambda, (1 - \lambda)\lambda, (1 - \lambda)\lambda^2, \ldots$, do add to 1 and so equation 5.5.12 is a weighted average, including all past values, with steadily declining weights. This is, of course, a single possibility, but it does show another way in which one might arrive at our basic dynamic model. If equation 5.5.12 is used to eliminate D_t^* from equation 5.5.11, we would obtain the infinite lag model and, indirectly, a model in the form of equation 5.5.5. In this case, the disturbances to the dynamic model would probably follow a moving average process.

A very similar example arises when the behaviour of the dependent variable is determined by the anticipated value of one or more explanatory variables. Although one could envisage situations in which consumption is determined by anticipated income, the example is not entirely satisfactory, and we revert to a general description in terms of variables Y and X. The model might be

$$Y_t = \beta X_{t+1}^* + u_t; t = 1, 2, \ldots, n \qquad (5.5.13)$$

where the current value of Y is determined by a prediction of the value that X will take in the following period. Yet again we have an unobservable variable which has to be eliminated, and again it might be argued that the predictions are formed as a weighted average of known values of X

$$X_{t+1}^* = (1 - \lambda)[X_t + \lambda X_{t-1} + \lambda^2 X_{t-2} + \ldots]; t = 1, 2, \ldots, n$$
$$(5.5.14)$$

With this secondary hypothesis we obtain a model which, in terms of observable variables, is equivalent to an infinite lag model and thus, indirectly, to our basic dynamic model. The hypothesis shown in equation 5.5.14 is sometimes written as

$$(X_{t+1}^* - X_t^*) = (1 - \lambda)(X_t - X_t^*); t = 1, 2, \ldots, n \qquad (5.5.15)$$

and the process is described as an *adaptive expectations* hypothesis. We can interpret equation 5.5.15 as saying that the prediction of the behaviour of X is revised by taking the change in the prediction as some proportion $1 - \lambda$ of the extent to which anticipations are not realized in the current period. Repeated substitutions for X_t^*, X_{t-1}^* etc. will show that equations 5.5.14 and 5.5.15 are formally equivalent, except possibly for the treatment of the starting value X_1^*.

The example above does illustrate yet another way in which a certain type of dynamic equation may arise. However, in recent years considerable doubt has been expressed as to the validity of this method of modelling expectations, because it implies a curious inability on the part of decision makers to avoid systematic errors of prediction that may have been made in the past. An alternative approach is to represent 'anticipated' values directly in terms of mathematical expectations, formed on the basis of the information available at the time at which the prediction is made. In the case of an exogenous variable, this implies the use of some random process distinct from the model in which the expectations are used. In the case of a model involving the expectation of an endogenous variable, the implication is that expectations are formed by making use of the model itself. Given certain conditions on the process by which expectations are formed, this approach leads to what is known as the *rational expectations* hypothesis.

From the discussion in this section, we have learned that there can be several different reasons for using a certain basic type of estimating equation. This certainly justifies the time spent on considering problems of estimation that will arise quite frequently, but it is rather disturbing to find that the same derived model can be consistent with quite distinct types of underlying hypothesis. Of course, the problem would not arise if we could observe 'desired', 'expected' and 'permanent' versions of the relevant variables: and it would not arise if the theory suggested restrictions which would make one derived model different from the rest. As it is, one has always to be aware of the possibility that there may be alternative justifications for a single formal model.

5.6 Exercises (solutions on p. 282)

5.1 The partial adjustment and adaptive expectations hypotheses can be combined, as in the following simple model:

$$Y_t^* = \beta X_{t+1}^*$$
$$Y_t - Y_{t-1} = \delta(Y_t^* - Y_{t-1}) + u_t$$
$$(X_{t+1}^* - X_t^*) = (1 - \lambda)(X_t - X_t^*); t = 1, 2, \ldots, n$$

where Y_t^* is a desired value and X_{t+1}^* is an anticipated value. Derive an equation which contains only observable variables and point to any problems of estimation associated with this equation.

5.2 Show that the equations

$$Y_t = \beta_1 Y_{t-1} + \beta_2 X_t + u_t; t = 1, 2, \ldots, n$$
$$u_t = \rho u_{t-1} + v_t; t = 1, 2, \ldots, n$$

together imply

$$Y_t = (\beta_1 + \rho)Y_{t-1} - \beta_1 \rho Y_{t-2} + \beta_2 X_t - \beta_2 \rho X_{t-1} + v_t;$$
$$t = 2, 3, \ldots, n$$

5.3 Using annual data for the UK for 1965–81, an investigator estimates the following equation by OLS:

$$\hat{I} = -5 \cdot 22 + 0 \cdot 153 Y - 0 \cdot 194 r + 0 \cdot 431 I_{-1}$$
$$(0 \cdot 99) \quad (0 \cdot 023) \quad (0 \cdot 039) \quad (0 \cdot 099)$$
$$\text{RSS} = 0 \cdot 797 \quad \text{DW} = 2 \cdot 026 \quad R^2 = 0 \cdot 984$$

where I is gross investment, Y is GDP at factor cost, r is a long term interest rate and I_{-1} is lagged investment. I and Y are measured in £ thousand million at 1975 prices.

(*a*) On the basis of the information provided, comment on the evidence for or against the presence of serial correlation.

(*b*) Why is the presence or absence of serial correlation a crucial question here?

(*c*) Can you deduce the nature of the dynamic adjustment process assumed by the investigator?

5.4 Show that the equations

$$\hat{\beta}_{I1} \Sigma Z_t Y_{t-1} + \hat{\beta}_{I2} \Sigma Z_t X_t = \Sigma Z_t Y_t$$
$$\hat{\beta}_{I1} \Sigma X_t Y_{t-1} + \hat{\beta}_{I2} \Sigma X_t^2 = \Sigma X_t Y_t$$

give exactly the same solution when

(a) $Z_t = X_{t-1}$

(b) $Z_t = aX_{t-1}$

(c) $Z_t = a_1X_{t-1} + a_2X_t$

where a, a_1, a_2 are constants. Explain the significance of this result.

6 Simultaneous equation models

6.1 Introduction

Despite all the modifications discussed in previous chapters, there is still a divergence between the type of statistical model that has been described and the way in which one typically envisages the working of an economic system. In particular, we have been concerned almost exclusively with models suitable for partial analysis, designed to explain the behaviour of a single endogenous variable. In those cases in which we have briefly mentioned multiple equation models, all dependent (left hand side) variables have been endogenous and all explanatory (right hand side) variables have been exogenous. But typically, the representation of a complete economic system would involve several equations and the 'dependent' variable in one equation might well appear as an 'explanatory' variable elsewhere. If all left hand side variables are taken to be endogenous, we may have an equation with one endogenous variable on the left and other current endogenous variables on the right. There are two types of analysis in which this can occur. Obviously, it can happen when the intention is to build a model for the complete system. But it is also relevant to the analysis of a single equation, when it is explicitly recognized that this is taken from a larger model.

As is often the case, it is possible to explain the essential points of the argument by using an extremely simple example. Consider a representation of income flow in an economy, in which income is allocated between consumption and nonconsumption expenditure and in which total income is equal to total expenditure. Let C be consumers' expenditure, Z be nonconsumption expenditure and D be total income. The model might then be

$$C_t = \alpha + \beta D_t + u_t; t = 1, 2, \ldots, n \qquad (6.1.1)$$
$$D_t = C_t + Z_t; t = 1, 2, \ldots, n \qquad (6.1.2)$$

The second equation in this model is clearly of a different type to the

first, since it is an exact relationship representing the equality between
income and expenditure. This is essentially a convention of accounting
at the level of macroeconomy. A relationship of this kind is an identity,
as distinct from a behavioural relationship such as the consumption
function.

It is readily apparent that this is a case in which the 'dependent'
variable in one equation is an 'explanatory' variable elsewhere in the
model. From the way in which the equations are written, it also seems
clear that the intention is to have C and D as endogenous variables.
Although it may be natural to think of the consumption function as
determining consumption and of the identity as determining income,
what the model actually says is that both equations together determine the values of the endogenous variables. More precisely, the model
consists of a pair of simultaneous equations in C_t and D_t.

In any given time period and for any particular values of α and β,
Z_t and u_t, there are two linear equations in two unknowns. Since we
can safely rule out those cases in which there is no unique solution, the
model can be assumed to determine unique values for C_t and D_t. In
practice, α, β and u_t would be unknown, but what the model suggests
is that the economic system behaves as though it were a set of simultaneous equations, which together determine the values of the endogenous variables in each time period. The model used here is obviously
not a sufficiently informative representation for the macroeconomy,
but the same logic would apply in a more realistic case.

Several questions remain to be answered. Given that the model is
supposed to generate values of the endogenous variables by the solution
of linear equations, there must be as many equations as there are endogenous variables. This rule determines the number of endogenous
variables for any given set of equations, but the decision as to which
variables are to be endogenous is based on economic reasoning, not
on the mathematics of the model. Ideally, the only exogenous variables
would be those that can really be thought of as imposed from outside
the system. In the context of the national economy, one might think
of variables for which values are determined by policy decision or for
which values are 'imported' from abroad. But policy is not formed
without consideration of signals generated from the operation of the
real economy, and there is considerable interdependence in both the
national and international economic systems. So very few variables are
truly exogenous and, in practical model building, some compromise
must be reached.

In the example above, there are two equations which are intended as a 'theory' of the determination of consumption and income, for given values of nonconsumption expenditure. We have therefore designated C and D as endogenous variables and Z as an exogenous variable. Ideally, we should like to explain the behaviour of some of the components of nonconsumption expenditure but, if the model is limited to two equations, it is clear that the intention would be to treat Z as an exogenous variable. Of course, as a strictly mathematical proposition, it could be argued that the equations determine any two variables from given values of the third, and so there is a distinction between the mathematical statement of the model and the assumed behaviour that lies behind the formal specification. Indeed we must make precisely this distinction in considering what a simultaneous model actually represents.

To an observer, taking measurements relating to a certain time period, consumption and income might appear to be determined simultaneously. The underlying process could be envisaged as a continuous loop, in which changes in income lead to changes in consumption, possibly with some delay, and in which changes in consumption generate changes in income by a process that we have subsumed in the accounting identity. If the lags in the process are shorter than the frequency of observation of the data, we have a situation in which consumption and income do appear to be determined simultaneously. Although there are implicit directions of causality, these are not made explicit in the formal model.

If the frequency of observation could be increased (the unit time period reduced), the situation might be somewhat different. Suppose that there is a delay in the adjustment of consumption to income and that observations are taken more frequently. One might then have

$$C_t = \alpha + \gamma D_{t-1} + u_t ; t = 1, 2, \ldots, n \qquad (6.1.3)$$
$$D_t = C_t + Z_t ; t = 1, 2, \ldots, n \qquad (6.1.4)$$

or, alternatively,

$$C_t = \alpha + \beta D_t + \gamma D_{t-1} + u_t \qquad (6.1.5)$$
$$D_t = C_t + Z_t ; t = 1, 2, \ldots, n \qquad (6.1.6)$$

The first of these models is dynamic, but no longer simultaneous. From a starting value D_0, the model would generate a sequence of values of C and D for given values of Z and for specific values of the disturbances. The process is

$$C_1 = \alpha + \gamma D_0 + u_1$$
$$D_1 = C_1 + Z_1$$
$$C_2 = \alpha + \gamma D_1 + u_2$$
$$D_2 = C_2 + Z_2, \text{ and so on}$$

Hence the determination of endogenous variable values follows a definite sequence

$$D_0 \rightarrow C_1 \rightarrow D_1 \rightarrow C_2 \rightarrow D_2 \rightarrow \ldots$$

The second example is simultaneous, the logic being that in any time period, the values of C_t and D_t are determined by the solution of the equations, for given values of Z_t and D_{t-1}. The value of Z_t is given in the sense that it is determined outside the model, and the value of D_{t-1} is given in the sense that it has already been determined by the operation of the model in the previous period. Exogenous variables and lagged endogenous variables are therefore described collectively as *predetermined* variables.

In the various examples given in this section, we have adopted the convention of writing a current endogenous variable on the left hand side of each equation. However, if there are two or more current endogenous variables in a single equation, there is an element of choice as to which variable to write on the left hand side. To see exactly what is meant by this, start with the version of the consumption function given in equation 6.1.1 and follow through the algebraic manipulation necessary to write D on the left of the equation

$$C_t = \alpha + \beta D_t + u_t; t = 1, 2, \ldots, n$$

or

$$-\beta D_t = \alpha - C_t + u_t; t = 1, 2, \ldots, n$$

so that

$$D_t = (-\alpha/\beta) + (1/\beta)C_t + (-u_t/\beta); t = 1, 2, \ldots, n \qquad (6.1.7)$$

This is still a linear equation subject to disturbance, since $-\alpha/\beta$ and $1/\beta$ represent unknown parameters and $-u_t/\beta$ is a random disturbance term. And there is still an endogenous variable on the left hand side. Equation 6.1.7 is written in a particular way because we started from a conventional specification of the consumption function. This does not alter the fact that the equation is

$$D_t = \text{intercept} + (\text{slope} \times C_t) + \text{disturbance} \qquad (6.1.8)$$

which is a perfectly valid formal statement of the hypothesis that C and D are connected by a linear relationship subject to disturbance, in a situation in which C and D are both endogenous variables in a simultaneous model.

It is clear from this argument that the decision to write C on the left of the consumption function is, in a formal sense, arbitrary. This does not imply that it is undesirable to write C on the left hand side: on the contrary, since it is natural for an economist to write the consumption function in this way and since there is freedom of choice, the original formulation is sensible. The point is just that a choice must be made. In each equation of a simultaneous model, one endogenous variable is chosen to appear on the left hand side. This is known as the *normalization* of the equation.

At this stage, the reader may have anticipated the nature of the estimation problem in a simultaneous model, given that each equation can contain current values of endogenous variables on the right hand side. We shall consider estimation in Sections 6.4 to 6.6, but first there is another aspect of using a simultaneous model, the question of *identification*, to which we now turn.

6.2 Identification

To illustrate the concept of identification, we use a simple model of a single market. Let Q^d be quantity demanded, Q^s be quantity supplied and P be price. The model may then be written as

$$Q_t^d = \alpha + \beta P_t + u_t \,; t = 1, 2, \ldots, n \qquad (6.2.1)$$

$$Q_t^s = \gamma + \delta P_t + v_t \,; t = 1, 2, \ldots, n \qquad (6.2.2)$$

where u_t and v_t are both random disturbances. As it stands, this multiple equation model is not simultaneous, because quantity demanded and quantity supplied are quite distinct concepts represented by two different variables. However, the model is obviously incomplete, because it does not say how demand and supply are to be reconciled. Moreover, it is difficult to see how one could expect to observe quantities demanded and supplied: what is usually observed is the result of the operation of the market. The simplest way to close the model is to assume that the market is cleared by the equalization of supply and demand and, in this case, there is a third equation in the model, to represent the identity between Q^s and Q^d. If the market clearing quantity is Q, the third equation can be written as

$$Q_t^d = Q_t^s = Q_t; t = 1, 2, \ldots, n \qquad (6.2.3)$$

To obtain a version of the model involving only observable variables, equation 6.2.3 is used to eliminate Q^s and Q^d, giving

$$Q_t = \alpha + \beta P_t + u_t; t = 1, 2, \ldots, n \qquad (6.2.4)$$
$$Q_t = \gamma + \delta P_t + v_t; t = 1, 2, \ldots, n \qquad (6.2.5)$$

The model now involves two relationships between the same two variables, it is clearly simultaneous, and it happens to have been normalized by using the same variable on the left of each equation. There are no exogenous variables.

Unfortunately, the equations in the model are now observationally equivalent. To the investigator, who does not know the true parameter values, the demand and supply relationships have exactly the same form

$$Q_t = \text{intercept} + (\text{slope} \times P_t) + \text{disturbance} \qquad (6.2.6)$$

Any attempt to estimate a relationship between quantity and price is futile, because there would be no way of knowing to which set of parameters the estimates refer. There is simply not enough information to identify the equation that is estimated. Hence the name given to this phenomenon, the problem of identification.

There is one piece of information that has not yet been used. It might be said that if the estimated equation slopes downwards it is a demand equation, and conversely if it slopes upwards it is a supply equation. Unfortunately, there are more than two possible lines having the same form as the demand and supply equations. If it is true that

$$Q_t = \alpha + \beta P_t + u_t; t = 1, 2, \ldots, n$$
$$Q_t = \gamma + \delta P_t + v_t; t = 1, 2, \ldots, n$$

then, for any constant value, represented as λ, it must also be true that

$$\lambda Q_t = \lambda \alpha + \lambda \beta P_t + \lambda u_t; t = 1, 2, \ldots, n \qquad (6.2.7)$$

and, for any constant value, represented as μ, that

$$\mu Q_t = \mu \gamma + \mu \delta P_t + \mu v_t; t = 1, 2, \ldots, n \qquad (6.2.8)$$

Again, it must also be true that the sum of equations 6.2.7 and 6.2.8 represents a valid equation, so that

$$(\lambda + \mu)Q_t = (\lambda\alpha + \mu\gamma) + (\lambda\beta + \mu\delta)P_t + (\lambda u_t + \mu v_t); t = 1, 2, \ldots, n \qquad (6.2.9)$$

or

$$Q_t = \frac{(\lambda\alpha + \mu\gamma)}{(\lambda + \mu)} + \frac{(\lambda\beta + \mu\delta)}{(\lambda + \mu)}P_t + \frac{(\lambda u_t + \mu v_t)}{(\lambda + \mu)}; t = 1, 2, \ldots, n \qquad (6.2.10)$$

Equation 6.2.10 looks complicated but, for particular values of λ and μ, the first term on the right hand side represents an unknown intercept, the term attached to P_t represents an unknown slope and the final term represents a random disturbance. In other words, equation 6.2.10 is again of the form

$$Q_t = \text{intercept} + (\text{slope} \times P_t) + \text{disturbance}$$

If $\lambda = 1$ and $\mu = 0$, equation 6.2.10 would be the demand equation. If $\lambda = 0$ and $\mu = 1$, it would represent the supply equation. For nonzero values of both λ and μ, 6.2.9 would be a linear combination of the two equations, with weights λ and μ, and 6.2.10 would represent the same equation normalized on Q. Depending on the values of λ and μ, equation 6.2.10 might slope up or down. Either way, it is indistinguishable, to the observer, from one or other of the original 'true' relationships. So information on the direction of the slope is not sufficient to identify the original equations and, since λ and μ can take any value, the demand and supply equations imply an infinite number of combinations, all indistinguishable, one from another and from the original equations, as far as the observer is concerned.

Now consider a second example, in which we have in mind the market for a farm product. Suppose that supply depends not only on price but also on an exogenous variable, say rainfall R. The new model is

$$Q_t^d = \alpha + \beta P_t + u_t; t = 1, 2, \ldots, n$$
$$Q_t^s = \gamma + \delta P_t + \epsilon R_t + v_t; t = 1, 2, \ldots, n$$
$$Q_t^s = Q_t^d = Q_t; t = 1, 2, \ldots, n$$

As before, the third equation can be used to eliminate Q^s and Q^d, leaving two equations in the endogenous variables Q and P. Any linear combination of the supply and demand equations now contains rainfall as a variable, except in the trivial case in which the weight on supply is zero. But if the weight on supply is zero, the combination reduces to the demand equation, and it is already known that the demand equation does not include rainfall. So the demand equation is distinct from supply and all (nontrivial) combinations and is therefore identified, but the supply equation is indistinguishable from the combinations and is not identified. This example shows that one can consider the identification of individual equations, that the presence of exogenous variables in the model can aid identification, and that it is the information that rainfall does not enter the demand equation which leads to identification in that equation.

A third example is provided by the static version of the consumption–income model. For convenience, the equations are now written as

$$C_t = \alpha + \beta D_t + u_t; t = 1, 2, \ldots, n \qquad (6.2.11)$$
$$C_t = D_t - Z_t; t = 1, 2, \ldots, n \qquad (6.2.12)$$

Any nontrivial linear combination of equations 6.2.11 and 6.2.12 will contain an intercept, a term in Z_t and a disturbance, and the combinations are therefore distinct from both the consumption function and the identity. The key fact in distinguishing between the consumption function and possible combinations is that equation 6.2.11 does not involve Z_t. Because of this, there is just enough information to identify the consumption function, and equation 6.2.11 is said to be *exactly identified* in the context of this particular model. In some other case there might be another variable, besides Z, which must appear in a nontrivial linear combination, but which does not appear in the consumption function: if so, the consumption function would be *overidentified*. Turning now to the identity, we have a known parameter on D_t (the parameter value is 1), a known parameter on Z_t (a value of -1) and no disturbance term. There are therefore several different ways in which one could distinguish the identity from possible combinations, although this is not really important, because one knows in advance that identities are always identified.

The formal analysis of identification can be rather complicated, but the essential nature of the problem is revealed by the approach developed above. In order to identify a particular equation, it must be possible to show that there is no combination of equations in the model that appears, to the observer, to be indistinguishable from the particular equation in question. If the model is linear in endogenous variables, then only linear combinations need be considered, since any nonlinear combination will automatically be distinct from the equations as originally specified. It is the linear case that is usually considered in textbooks and, in this case, there are methods which enable one to check systematically on whether the original equations will be distinct from potential linear combinations. It is the restrictions on individual equations that provide the information necessary to make the distinction between an equation and possible combinations, and there are various types of restriction that may be used. Examples include the exclusion of variables from individual equations, known nonzero parameter values and restrictions on the disturbances. Of these, by far the most common are exclusion restrictions.

If a model involves nonlinearities in the endogenous variables, the usual textbook methods do not apply. The question, in this case, is whether there are either linear or nonlinear combinations which cannot be distinguished from the equations themselves. Fortunately, nonlinearities tend to aid identification, so introducing nonlinearity to a model in which the equations of a linear version are identified is not likely to cause any additional identification problem. A second case in which the 'usual rules' do not necessarily apply is a model which involves both lagged endogenous variables and serially correlated disturbances. In such a model, one may have to consider time dependent combinations of the equations and, in certain circumstances, this can reveal under-identification of equations that would be identified if the disturbances were serially independent. If the disturbances are not serially correlated, lagged endogenous variables are treated in exactly the same way as exogenous variables and their presence may well aid identification in at least some of the equations.

The discussion above suggests that there may be rather considerable difficulties in applying the more formal methods of checking for identification to anything other than simple classroom examples. As it happens, the models used in practice tend, if anything, to be over-identified, although some would argue that this is because too much reliance is placed on exclusion restrictions suggested by conventional economic theory. Others would argue that such restrictions are necessary, not so much to ensure identification, but rather to avoid having to choose between alternative models solely on the basis of imperfect data. When a problem of under-identification does arise, it is often because the initial specification of the model involves unobservable variables. We have come across a similar problem before, in the context of the single equation dynamic model. This may be derived from two equations in unobservables such as desired or expected values and, because these values cannot be observed, the model has to be reduced to a single equation. Unfortunately, this single equation may be consistent with a number of different underlying hypotheses. In a simultaneous equation

model, we consider whether each equation in the observable version
can be identified. This is a slightly different question, but lack of
identification in the model in observables can often be traced back to
the fact that there is an underlying hypothesis involving variables which
cannot be observed.

6.3   The reduced form

A simultaneous equation model is supposed to operate by the solution
of equations in the endogenous variables, for given values of the predetermined variables. It is instructive to carry through the solution
process algebraically and, to illustrate this, we use the static version of
the consumption—income model. The model states that

$$C_t = \alpha + \beta D_t + u_t ; t = 1, 2, \ldots, n \qquad (6.3.1)$$
$$D_t = C_t + Z_t ; t = 1, 2, \ldots, n \qquad (6.3.2)$$

where, as before, C and D are endogenous and Z is exogenous. In this
context, it is convenient to describe Z as autonomous expenditure. If
equation 6.3.2 is used to substitute for D_t in 6.3.1, we obtain

$$C_t = \alpha + \beta(C_t + Z_t) + u_t$$

or

$$(1 - \beta)C_t = \alpha + \beta Z_t + u_t$$

or

$$C_t = [\alpha/(1 - \beta)] + [\beta/(1 - \beta)]Z_t + [u_t/(1 - \beta)] ; t = 1, 2, \ldots, n \qquad (6.3.3)$$

A similar process gives an equation for D_t. Using equation 6.3.1 to
substitute for C_t in 6.3.2,

$$D_t = (\alpha + \beta D_t + u_t) + Z_t$$

or

$$D_t = [\alpha/(1 - \beta)] + [1/(1 - \beta)]Z_t + [u_t/(1 - \beta)] ; t = 1, 2, \ldots, n \qquad (6.3.4)$$

By this stage, the reader should be familiar with the idea that terms
like $\alpha/(1 - \beta)$, $\beta/(1 - \beta)$ and $1/(1 - \beta)$ merely represent different
unknown parameters and that $u_t/(1 - \beta)$ is a random disturbance term.
Equation 6.3.3 is therefore a linear relationship between C and Z,

which is subject to random disturbance. Equation 6.3.4 gives a similar relationship for D and Z. What we have done is to express each endogenous variable in terms of all the predetermined variables in the model. In the example, there are actually two exogenous 'variables', one of which is the artificial variable that allows for an intercept. There are no lagged endogenous variables. In the general case, any linear simultaneous model can be expressed in a similar way, to give what is known as the *reduced form*. In this context, the requirement is for linearity in the endogenous variables, because it is a set of equations in the endogenous variables that we wish to solve. Nonlinear models do not generally have exact analytic reduced forms. We shall return to this point later in the discussion.

If the model can be expressed in terms of reduced form equations, it may be thought that the original specification is redundant, but this is not so. In the example above, the model is expressed in a certain way, because it is the consumption function that is the relationship of interest and because it is the parameters of this relationship that we wish to know. It is certainly true that, having written down the original specification, which is called the *structural form*, one can then derive the reduced form as a mathematical consequence. Indeed, the reduced form parameters do have a useful interpretation. But it is the structural form that is an approximation for relationships that we believe to exist in the real system, and the purpose of any experimentation will be to refine and improve upon the structural specification.

The reduced form parameters can be interpreted in the following way. If we take equation 6.3.4 and ignore the random disturbance, the parameter attached to Z_t measures the effect on income of a unit change in autonomous expenditure. This parameter is $1/(1 - \beta)$, where β is the marginal propensity to consume and, in the terminology of economics, this is a *multiplier*. To be more specific, it is the autonomous expenditure–income multiplier. There is also an autonomous expenditure–consumption multiplier and, in general, there is a multiplier for each exogenous–endogenous pair in a given model. Each of these multipliers shows the effect, on one endogenous variable, of a unit change in one exogenous variable, with all other exogenous variables held constant. The 'true' values of the multipliers are the parameters of the reduced form equations.

If a model involves lagged endogenous variables, each reduced form equation will express the current value of one of the endogenous variables in terms of both exogenous and lagged endogenous variables, and the interpretation of the reduced form parameters has to be slightly modified. To illustrate this point, consider the model

$$C_t = \alpha + \beta D_t + \gamma D_{t-1} + u_t; t = 1, 2, \ldots, n \qquad (6.3.5)$$
$$D_t = C_t + Z_t; t = 1, 2, \ldots, n \qquad (6.3.6)$$

Using the second equation to eliminate D_t from the consumption function, we obtain

$$C_t = [\alpha/(1 - \beta)] + [\beta/(1 - \beta)]Z_t + [\gamma/(1 - \beta)]D_{t-1} + [u_t/(1 - \beta)];$$
$$t: = 1, 2, \ldots, n \quad (6.3.7)$$

The corresponding equation for income would be

$$D_t = [\alpha/(1 - \beta)] + [1/(1 - \beta)]Z_t + [\gamma/(1 - \beta)]D_{t-1} + [u_t/(1 - \beta)];$$
$$t: = 1, 2, \ldots, n \quad (6.3.8)$$

A unit change in Z does have an immediate effect on D, an effect represented by the parameter $1/(1 - \beta)$. This is known as an *impact multiplier*. However, an increment to income in the current period leads to a change in income in the following period and this, in turn, leads to a change in the next period, and so on. If there is a unit change in Z, in a single given period, the total resulting change in income is given by the series

$$1/(1 - \beta) + \gamma/(1 - \beta)^2 + \gamma^2/(1 - \beta)^3 + \ldots$$

Provided that the model is stable, this series will converge, giving a *total* or *long run* multiplier equal to $1/(1 - \beta - \gamma)$. In this particular case, the stability condition is that $\gamma/(1 - \beta)$ should lie between -1 and $+1$, without reaching either extreme value.

In a static model, the reduced form equations show clearly the connection between the endogenous variables and the disturbances. If exogenous variable observations are taken to be nonrandom then, using equation 6.3.3 as an example, it may be seen that C_t does depend on a random disturbance and, since no other term on the right of 6.3.3 could take up the random variation, it does follow that C_t has a random component. Exactly the same argument applies to D_t, using equation 6.3.4. In this particular case, D_t is subject to the same random disturbance as C_t. More generally, for any value of t, each reduced form disturbance involves all the structural form disturbances, but the way in which these are combined differs between the various equations in the reduced form. If the model is dynamic, the reduced form equations involve lagged endogenous variables and, to show properly how the endogenous variables depend on the disturbances, one should really substitute out the lagged endogenous variables, to give what is known as the *final form*. The equations of the final form express each current endogenous variable in terms of current and past values of exogenous variables and disturbances, and this does enable one to see the origin of the random variation in each of the endogenous variables.

We shall refer back to the reduced form at various stages in the discussion which follows, but now we move on to consider the problems of estimation in a simultaneous model. Before we start, it is worth restating the fact that our concern is with the estimation of the parameters of the structural form.

6.4   Estimation: single equation methods

The preceding sections of this chapter contain a liberal scattering of clues to the effect that there are some problems of estimation which are due entirely to the use of a simultaneous model. To see exactly what these problems are, we shall start by considering the application of OLS to a single equation which is taken from a simultaneous model and, once again, we can use the simple consumption–income example to illustrate the argument.

Suppose that we were to apply OLS directly to the consumption function

$$C_t = \alpha + \beta D_t + u_t ; t = 1, 2, \dots , n \qquad (6.4.1)$$

If $E(u_t) = 0; t = 1, 2, \dots , n$ and the observations $D_t; t = 1, 2, \dots , n$ could be considered to be nonrandom, the OLS estimators for α and β would be unbiased. The OLS estimators would also be unbiased if $D_t; t = 1, 2, \dots , n$ were random but completely independent of the disturbances. For the moment we shall assume that the disturbances are well behaved, but the reduced form equations show that the observations on income must be treated as values taken by a set of random variables. What is more, there exists a direct connection between each observation D_t and the corresponding disturbance u_t. Given the similarity between this and the case of a dynamic model with serially correlated disturbances, we might immediately conjecture that the OLS estimators will be inconsistent. Alternatively, we could follow through the type of analysis used in Section 5.4, to make sure that the analogy is appropriate.

Given that there is an intercept in equation 6.4.1, the OLS slope estimator would be

$$\hat{\beta} = \Sigma d_t c_t / \Sigma d_t^2 \qquad (6.4.2)$$

where $c_t, d_t; t = 1, 2, \ldots, n$ represent observations expressed as deviations from the respective sample means. Using the approach first introduced in Section 2.3, one could then express $\hat{\beta}$ as

$$\hat{\beta} = \beta + \Sigma d_t u_t / \Sigma d_t^2 \qquad (6.4.3)$$

The problem with equation 6.4.3 is that the substitution to reveal the influence of the random disturbances is not complete, since d_t is itself a function of u_t. One should therefore use the reduced form equation for income to substitute for $d_t = D_t - \overline{D}; t = 1, 2, \ldots, n$. Having done this, it ought to be possible to find a set of assumptions concerning the exogenous variable observations and the disturbances, which are sufficient to show that

plim $(\Sigma d_t u_t / n)$ exists and is nonzero

and

plim $(\Sigma d_t^2 / n)$ exists and is nonzero

It would then follow that

$$\text{plim} (\hat{\beta}) = \beta + \text{plim} (\Sigma d_t u_t / n) / \text{plim} (\Sigma d_t^2 / n)$$
$$\neq \beta \qquad (6.4.4)$$

This shows that $\hat{\beta}$ is not a consistent estimator, and an equivalent result holds for all OLS estimators relating to the parameters of a single equation, involving at least one current endogenous variable on the right hand side. Note, however, that the method of proof may sometimes have to be modified, to reflect different sets of assumptions concerning the behaviour of predetermined variables and disturbances.

Since we have already made use of the type of argument outlined above, it may be instructive to demonstrate the problem inherent in OLS estimation in a slightly different way. Consider first the hypothetical situation in which income can be treated as an exogenous variable, with nonrandom observations. One could then construct a diagram such as that shown in Figure 13, assuming that D can only take values between D_{min} and D_{max}. The lines AA′ and BB′ are intended to show that, without any connection between the values of D_t and u_t, observed points must lie between the lines drawn above D_{min} and D_{max} and are likely to lie between the lines AA′ and BB′. So we would have a scatter of points which would tend to fall in the area AA′B′B and, for a relatively large number of observations, the scatter of observed points in the area would tend to reproduce that suggested by the disturbance distributions, for given values of D. The

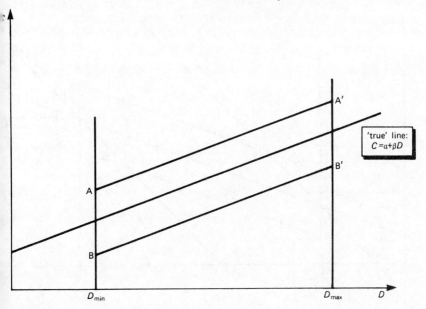

Figure 13

minimization of the sum of squared residuals would then give a line which, with high probability, would be close to the true line.

Now consider the case in which the identity between income and expenditure is explicitly recognized. The identity can be written as

$$D_t = C_t + Z_t; t = 1, 2, \ldots, n$$

or as

$$C_t = D_t - Z_t; t = 1, 2, \ldots, n$$

and all observed values of C and D must satisfy this equation. It can now be assumed that all observations on Z lie between two points Z_{min} and Z_{max} and, in Figure 14, the identity is represented by two lines corresponding to these extreme values of Z. The lines are

$$C = D - Z_{min} \tag{6.4.5}$$
$$C = D - Z_{max} \tag{6.4.6}$$

If the value Z_{min} were actually observed in a given time period, the corresponding observations on C and D would give a point somewhere along the line represented by equation 6.4.5. If the value Z_{max} were observed, the corresponding observations on C and D would give a

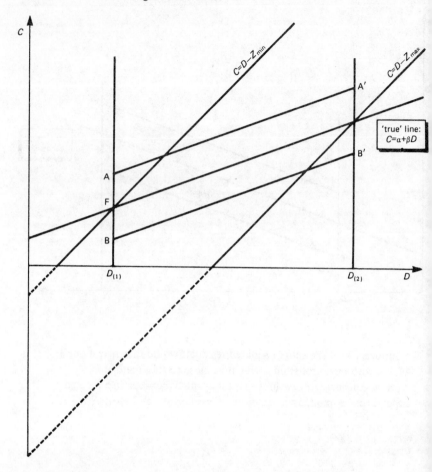

Figure 14

point somewhere along the line represented by equation 6.4.6. Note that equations 6.4.5 and 6.4.6 are both 45 degree lines. All other observed values of C and D must correspond to a point inside the area between these two 45 degree lines.

With the addition of the identity, it is impossible to argue that the area $AA'B'B$ represents the likely scatter of observed points. There is no longer an absolute minimum income value D_{min}, nor is there an absolute maximum value D_{max}. All that we can do is to find two points, $D_{(1)}$ and $D_{(2)}$, which represent the income values that would be generated from the reduced form, by Z_{min} and Z_{max} respectively, for a zero value of the random disturbance

$$D_{(1)} = [\alpha/(1-\beta)] + [1/(1-\beta)]Z_{min} + 0$$
$$D_{(2)} = [\alpha/(1-\beta)] + [1/(1-\beta)]Z_{max} + 0$$

But a negative disturbance could give a value of D to the left of the point $D_{(1)}$ and a positive disturbance could give a value of D to the right of the point $D_{(2)}$. One could therefore have an observed consumption–income point lying outside the lines drawn above $D_{(1)}$ and $D_{(2)}$. The observed points must, however, lie between the extreme 45 degree lines. So the scatter of points represented by the area AA'B'B has now been replaced by a scatter lying between the two 45 degree lines, and this would tend to pull the slope of estimated line up towards that of the 45 degree lines. No matter how many observations there are, it is impossible to generate a 'proper' scatter of points around the true line, and this corresponds to the formal result that the OLS estimators are inconsistent. In the example, the slope of the consumption function is systematically overestimated, which corresponds to a positive inconsistency. But the direction of the inconsistency is specific to the example and, in other cases, simultaneity might lead to negative inconsistency for a given OLS estimator.

It is shown quite clearly, in Figure 14, that it is not possible to obtain a pair of observations on consumption and income that would lead to an observed point directly above the point F. If one were to start with income $D_{(1)}$ and a positive value of the disturbance, then it may seem as though the equation

$$C_t = \alpha + \beta D_t + u_t$$

would suggest an upward shift in the observed point. In fact, this suggestion can be refuted by looking again at the reduced form equation for D. The whole point of our argument is that D_t depends directly on u_t. It is not possible to argue in terms of fixing D_t at $D_{(1)}$ and then choosing a positive value for u_t, since a positive disturbance means that income cannot be at $D_{(1)}$. The point $D_{(1)}$ corresponds to the minimum value of Z and a zero disturbance. A positive disturbance shifts income to the right as well as shifting consumption upwards.

This argument shows why OLS is deficient, at least in terms of lack of consistency, and it also gives some clue as to what may be done to correct the deficiency. If the observations on income could be adjusted in some way, so as to prevent the movement of income values along the horizontal axis, then it would be possible to observe points outside the boundaries imposed by the identity. The identity refers to actual values of income, not to values that have been adjusted. The nature of the adjustment required is also indicated by the argument above. It is the fact that income is random that causes the difficulty. Equation 6.3.4 is the reduced form equation for income, and this states that

$$D_t = [\alpha/(1-\beta)] + [1/(1-\beta)]Z_t + [u_t/(1-\beta)] \, ; t = 1, 2, \ldots, n$$

If the term $u_t/(1-\beta)$ were subtracted from D_t, the result would be a variable that is not influenced by u_t at all. Unfortunately, $u_t/(1-\beta)$ is not observable, so the suggested adjustment cannot be implemented directly. There is, however, a fairly simple approximation that can be used.

The reduced form equation for income can be written more concisely as

$$D_t = \Pi_1 + \Pi_2 Z_t + v_t \, ; t = 1, 2, \ldots, n \tag{6.4.7}$$

where Π_1, Π_2 represent an intercept and slope respectively and v_t; $t = 1, 2, \ldots, n$ represents a set of reduced form disturbances. The disturbances cannot be observed, but the residuals from an estimated line could be obtained. What is more, the variable Z_t is exogenous and OLS, applied to equation 6.4.7, is not subject to the difficulty of having an endogenous variable on the right hand side. If OLS is used to estimate Π_1 and Π_2, we would obtain an estimated equation

$$\hat{D}_t = \hat{\Pi}_1 + \hat{\Pi}_2 Z_t \, ; t = 1, 2, \ldots, n \tag{6.4.8}$$

where the predicted values $\hat{D}_t$; $t = 1, 2, \ldots, n$ differ from the observed values D_t; $t = 1, 2, \ldots, n$ by a set of residuals, which are written as $\hat{v}_t$; $t = 1, 2, \ldots, n$:

$$\hat{D}_t = D_t - \hat{v}_t \, ; t = 1, 2, \ldots, n \tag{6.4.9}$$

The subtraction of the residual from a single observation D_t is thus equivalent to replacing that observation by the corresponding predicted value, determined by equation 6.4.8. This is only an approximation to the subtraction of the true disturbance, which would be the ideal adjustment to income.

The method outlined here is *two stage least squares* (2SLS). This has already been mentioned briefly in the context of the single equation dynamic model: here, the example relates to a single equation taken from a simultaneous model. In the first stage, D_t is regressed on Z_t, to give predicted values $\hat{D}_t$; $t = 1, 2, \ldots, n$. The second stage consists of a regression run on the consumption function, but the values D_t; $t = 1, 2, \ldots, n$ are replaced by $\hat{D}_t$; $t = 1, 2, \ldots, n$. In terms of Figure 14, it can be argued that what we have done is to allow adjusted observations to fall outside the bounds imposed by the identity. For a given value of Z, say Z_{min}, a positive disturbance would move the value of consumption upwards and the value of income to the right. But if income is corrected for the effect of the disturbance, albeit approximately, one could have a case in which consumption is moved upwards, but the corrected income value is not moved to the right. This would give a point $(\hat{D}_t, C_t)$ which lies above the line $C = D - Z_{min}$. To the extent that one can now have a 'proper' scatter of points, this argument suggests that 2SLS does give consistent estimators. We shall shortly consider an algebraic argument in an attempt to reinforce this conclusion, but first consider a possible alternative to two stage least squares.

The first stage of 2SLS consists of an OLS regression run on one of the reduced form equations. In our example, the explanatory variables in the reduced form are exogenous and are assumed to be nonrandom. So the OLS estimators of the reduced form parameters will be consistent and unbiased. Equations 6.3.3 and 6.3.4 show that the reduced form parameters are related to the parameters of the structural form, and so it might be possible to work back to estimates of the structural parameters from estimates obtained from the reduced form regressions. This is a recognized method of estimation, known as *indirect least squares* (ILS), but it does not turn out to be particularly useful. It is only possible to work back to unique estimates of structural form parameters when the equation in question is exactly identified and, when this condition is satisfied, the estimates obtained are identical to those given by 2SLS. This does not mean that the 2SLS estimators are unbiased in the exactly identified case, because the unbiasedness property of the reduced form estimators does not survive the transformation back to the structural form. There is in fact no generally applicable method of obtaining unbiased estimators of the structural parameters of a simultaneous model, and questions of estimator choice are usually resolved by considering asymptotic properties.

Although the idea of working back from reduced form estimates does not produce a generally applicable alternative to 2SLS, we can make use of the fact that the reduced form estimators are consistent in considering an alternative argument for the consistency of 2SLS. In our example, the 2SLS estimators are obtained from an OLS regression of C on $\hat{D}$ and we can write the 2SLS slope estimator as

$$\hat{\beta}_{2SLS} = \Sigma \hat{d}_t c_t / \Sigma \hat{d}_t^2 \tag{6.4.10}$$

In equation 6.4.10 $c_t, \hat{d}_t; t = 1, 2, \ldots, n$ represent the observations $C_t, D_t; t = 1, 2, \ldots, n$, expressed as deviations from the means. The corresponding expression is terms of the structural form disturbances is

$$\hat{\beta}_{2SLS} = \beta + \Sigma \hat{d}_t u_t / \Sigma \hat{d}_t^2 \qquad (6.4.11)$$

This expression is correct, but we shall omit the algebraic detail and concentrate on the interpretation of the expression. The deviations $\hat{d}_t; t = 1, 2, \ldots, n$ are random variables, because they are derived from the predictions of the first stage regressions. These deviations are not independent of $u_t; t = 1, 2, \ldots, n$, because they are indirectly related to the reduced form disturbances. But it is possible to argue that the probability limit of the random term in equation 6.4.11 is zero, for the following reason. If the observations $D_t; t = 1, 2, \ldots, n$ could be adjusted for the true reduced form disturbances, the adjusted values would no longer depend on $u_t; t = 1, 2, \ldots, n$. As it is, we can only adjust the income values by using residuals, taken from a first stage (reduced form) regression. But the OLS estimators of the reduced form parameters are consistent, which suggests that, as the number of observations is increased, the reduced form estimates do tend to get closer to the true values and the reduced form residuals tend to get closer to the reduced form disturbances. In a limiting sense the income observations are correctly adjusted to remove the effect of the random disturbances and, in this same sense, there is no longer a connection between the adjusted income values and the random disturbances. This does suggest that, in equation 6.4.11, the probability limit of the random term is likely to be zero and, if this is the case, the two stage least squares estimator is consistent.

Neither of the arguments that we have used is, in any sense, a formal proof of the consistency of the 2SLS estimators, but the reader may find one or other of the arguments to be helpful in understanding what the use of 2SLS achieves.

Before moving on, we restate the 2SLS method in a more general form. A single structural equation in a simultaneous model may have more than one endogenous variable on the right hand side. Each of these right hand side endogenous variables has to be replaced by a corresponding variable, the values of which are the predictions from the relevant reduced form regression. In the general case, each reduced form equation will express a single endogenous variable in terms of all the predetermined variables in the model. So the first stage consists of as many regressions as there are right hand side endogenous variables. Each of these regressions has a different dependent variable (one of the endogenous variables on the right of the structural equation), but the explanatory variables would typically be the same in each case (all the predetermined variables in the model). The second stage consists of a single regression, on the chosen structural equation, in which right hand side endogenous variable observations are replaced by the predicted values generated in the first stage.

There are other methods of estimation which can be applied to a single equation taken from a simultaneous model and which, like 2SLS, give rise to consistent estimators. But 2SLS is the most widely used of the possible methods and, as there is no unambiguous ranking that would lead to the choice of a 'better' single equation approach, the question of alternatives is not pursued here. The comparison between OLS and 2SLS shows that the latter gives consistent estimators whereas the former does not. It is very difficult to analyse the behaviour of the estimators for a relatively small number of observations, but there is evidence from simulation experiments which suggests that there is less systematic distortion inherent in using 2SLS. On the other hand, the estimator variances appear to increase *vis-à-vis* OLS. This is not surprising: by using predicted values for right hand side endogenous variables, we are using only those parts of the variation that can be explained in terms of the predetermined variables in the model. Thus, for each right hand endogenous variable, we are discarding some of the observed variation, and our earlier discussions would suggest that this would tend to increase the corresponding estimator variances. Although the earlier results do not apply directly to this case, it is certainly true that the asymptotic variances of the 2SLS estimators are at least as large, and typically larger, than those that would be obtained for OLS estimators, if the OLS estimators were consistent. This seems a very curious way of stating the result, but there is a problem of definition associated with the asymptotic variance of an inconsistent estimator. The important lesson is that there is likely to be a cost associated with achieving consistency.

Given the context in which 2SLS was first suggested in Chapter 5, it should come as no surprise to find that 2SLS is, in fact, an instrumental variable method. To show that this is so, we shall express the 2SLS slope estimator from the consumption–income model in a form that we can recognize as an IV estimator. In any standard regression calculation, the sum of cross-products between predicted values and residuals is always zero. If the regression involves an intercept, a similar result holds for predicted values expressed in deviation form. Hence, we may write

$$\hat{d}_t = d_t - \hat{v}_t; t = 1, 2, \ldots, n$$

where $\hat{v}_t$; $t = 1, 2, \ldots, n$ represents a set of residuals from OLS estimation of the reduced form and

$$\Sigma \hat{d}_t^2 = \Sigma \hat{d}_t(d_t - \hat{v}_t) = \Sigma \hat{d}_t d_t \qquad (6.4.12)$$

It follows that equation 6.4.10 may be expressed as

$$\hat{\beta}_{2SLS} = \Sigma \hat{d}_t c_t / \Sigma \hat{d}_t d_t \qquad (6.4.13)$$

A comparison with equation 5.4.11 will show that 6.4.13 is in the form of a IV estimator, the difference here being that it is possible to express the observations as deviations from the means because there is an intercept in the consumption function. The instrumental variable is $\hat{D}$, which is used as an instrument for D. This is clearly a case in which it is possible to find an instrument that is correlated with the original variable, while at the same time satisfying the requirements for consistency. It is also interesting to note that, in Section 5.4, it was suggested that the IV method would generally involve an increase in variance as compared with OLS, and this reinforces our suggestion concerning 2SLS.

Given that 2SLS is a widely used method for obtaining consistent estimates of structural parameters, we conclude this section with some practical details. Typically, one would use a computer program which has facilities for generating 2SLS estimates. Presumably, such a program would also generate other information, such as standard errors, test statistics and some measure of goodness of fit. Since the only generally applicable statistical properties are those derived as asymptotic results, the standard errors would be based on asymptotic variances. The general form for the (asymptotic) standard error of a 2SLS estimator can be written as

$$\text{se } [\hat{\beta}_{j(2SLS)}] = \hat{\sigma} \sqrt{a_{jj}} \qquad (6.4.14)$$

where β_j is a typical parameter, a_{jj} is a quantity that would be correctly computed by treating the second stage regression in exactly the same way as any other regression calculation, and $\hat{\sigma}^2$ is a consistent estimator for the disturbance variance of the structural equation. In the consumption function example, a_{jj} would be computed as

$$a_{jj} = 1/\Sigma \hat{d}_t^2$$

and the estimator $\hat{\sigma}^2$ would be defined in terms of the 2SLS residuals, which we write as

$$\hat{u}_t = C_t - \hat{\alpha}_{2SLS} - \hat{\beta}_{2SLS} D_t; t = 1, 2, \ldots, n \qquad (6.4.15)$$

Specifically, we would have

$$\hat{\sigma}^2 = \Sigma \hat{u}_t^2 / n \tag{6.4.16}$$

or

$$\hat{\sigma}^2 = \Sigma \hat{u}_t^2 / (n - k) \tag{6.4.17}$$

where k is the total number of variables (including any artificial variable) on the right of the structural equation. In the example, $k = 2$. Equation 6.4.16 may be used because there is no longer any very clear theoretical justification for division by $n - k$. Equation 6.4.17 does not define an unbiased estimator, and the difference between n and $n - k$ is irrelevant in considering the consistency property.

Once the standard errors have been obtained, the significance of individual parameters can be tested by computing 'asymptotic t ratios' and either using the t distribution or, since there is only a large sample justification for such a procedure, by using the standard normal distribution. If the sample size is large enough to warrant the use of an asymptotic approximation, there will be virtually no difference between the two procedures.

Finally, a measure of goodness of fit can be obtained: in the consumption function example, this would be

$$R^2_{2SLS} = 1 - \Sigma \hat{u}_t^2 / \Sigma c_t^2 \tag{6.4.18}$$

where $c_t; t = 1, 2, \ldots, n$ are observations on consumption (the left hand side endogenous variable), expressed as deviations from the sample mean. This statistic necessarily takes a lower value than that for OLS applied to an equivalent model, since OLS, by definition, minimizes the sum of squared residuals. It is important to note that, if 2SLS is performed by literally applying an OLS program to the two distinct stages, the residuals, standard errors, t ratios and measure of fit will all be incorrectly computed, because the second stage regression will automatically generate the residuals as

$$\hat{u}_t^* = C_t - \hat{\alpha}_{2SLS} - \hat{\beta}_{2SLS}\hat{D}_t; t = 1, 2, \ldots, n \tag{6.4.19}$$

The difference between equation 6.4.19 and the correct expression 6.4.15 is that 6.4.19 has predicted income values on the right hand side, because predicted values would be supplied as input to the second stage regression. A properly designed IV or 2SLS program would avoid this error.

6.5   Estimation: complete system methods

In each of the consumption—income examples there is only one behavioural equation, and the estimation of this equation corresponds to the
estimation of all the structural parameters in the model. More generally,
in constructing a model of the complete economy, there would be several
behavioural equations. At the most highly aggregate level, the endogenous
variables might include components of expenditure such as consumption
and investment; components of income, such as wage payments and
profits; employment and output; and prices, including wage rates and
interest rates. There might also be variables relating to foreign trade as
well as additional monetary and fiscal variables. In putting the model
together there must be an equation, or set of equations, representing a
theory of the determination of each endogenous variable, and there
must be as many equations as there are endogenous variables. When one
starts to disaggregate, the number of equations can become very large
indeed, and there are constructed econometric models involving hun-
dreds of equations. Very large models do lead to particular problems of
estimation, but we shall not pursue this point. We shall take as typical
the small to medium sized model, in which the list of endogenous
variables would include at least some of those mentioned above.

To illustrate the discussion which follows, a new example is introduced. Again, it must be emphasized that this is not intended to be
'realistic'. In modelling a given system, a great deal of effort is needed
to achieve an appropriate specification, and one cannot expect a textbook example to be directly applicable. But our examples do illustrate
methods that can be used in a serious attempt at model construction.

With this in mind, consider the following equations:

$$C_t = \alpha + \beta D_t + u_t$$
$$I_t = \gamma + \delta R_t + v_t$$
$$R_t = \epsilon D_t + \theta M_t + w_t$$
$$D_t = C_t + I_t + Z_t; t = 1, 2, \ldots, n \qquad (6.5.1)$$

The new variables are real investment I, interest rate R and real money
stock M, and u, v and w are now used to represent the different structural form disturbances. As written, the model suggests that the endogenous variables are C, I, R and D, with M and Z exogenous. The third
equation may look a little curious, but 6.5.1 is based on a textbook
model which is often used, without disturbances, to show how C, I, R
and D could be determined from given values of M and Z. If there were

no disturbances, the third equation could be written as

$$M_t = \lambda D_t + \mu R_t \tag{6.5.2}$$

where

$$\lambda = -\epsilon/\theta \text{ and } \mu = 1/\theta$$

But if M is to be exogenous in an 'econometric' formulation, it would violate our usual convention to write M on the left hand side. We shall therefore assume that ϵ and θ represent parameters of interest, and we shall proceed accordingly.

One could estimate the parameters of 6.5.1 by applying 2SLS to each behavioural equation in turn. An alternative approach is to apply a *complete system* method, in which the parameters of all behavioural equations are estimated in one operation. In Section 4.7 this possibility was discussed in the context of a multiple equation model in which no equation had an endogenous variable on the right hand side. The reasons for considering the complete system approach were first, that there might be explicit cross-equation restrictions, and second that there might be contemporaneous correlation of the disturbances to the individual equations. In 6.5.1 there are no cross-equation restrictions, but it is usually accepted that there can be contemporaneous correlation of the disturbances to a simultaneous model. If the analogy with our earlier argument is valid and if contemporaneous correlation does occur, one would expect a possible gain in efficiency from using a suitable complete system method.

It is worth restating briefly what is meant by contemporaneous correlation. In each time period, the value of the disturbance to each equation can be thought of as being generated according to the rules of a probability distribution. In a simultaneous model, there are several distributions for a single time period, corresponding to the different disturbance terms on the individual structural equations. The existence of contemporaneous correlation means that these distributions are not independent and that there will be some definite association between the values taken by the different disturbance terms. Typically, we would assume that each pair of disturbances has a covariance that may well be nonzero, but which does not vary with time. Thus, for the consumption and investment functions in 6.5.1, we would have

$$\text{cov}\,(u_t, v_t) = \sigma_{uv}; t = 1, 2, \ldots, n$$

To accept contemporaneous correlation as a general characteristic of simultaneous models may seem to be a violation of the principle of simplicity first. However, given that a simultaneous model is a representation for a highly interdependent system and that the disturbances are a summary representation for all the factors that are not explicitly included in the model, it is perhaps sensible to allow for the fact that there may be connections between the disturbances to the individual equations.

It is possible to construct a complete system method by putting together various ideas taken from earlier discussions. The method that we shall describe is *three stage least squares* (3SLS). In taking all the equations together, there is still the problem of having endogenous variables on the right hand side and, to overcome this, we use the same technique as in 2SLS. Each set of right hand side endogenous variable observations is replaced by the set of values predicted from the reduced form regressions. This represents the first stage of the process and we see that, in the first stage, the equations are still considered to be separate. Having taken this first step, let us consider how the equations could be combined.

The method is very similar to that described in the context of a nonsimultaneous multiple equation model. To create a single set of 'dependent' variable observations, each left hand side endogenous variable is taken in turn and the observations are 'stacked' to give a single sequence of values. In our example, with R taken to be endogenous, this would give observations C_t; $t = 1, 2, \ldots, n$ followed by I_t; $t = 1, 2, \ldots, n$ followed by R_t; $t = 1, 2, \ldots, n$. Notice that D_t; $t = 1, 2, \ldots, n$ does not appear in this sequence, because we do not have to estimate the parameters of the identity. In fact all identities are removed before the equations are combined. The 'explanatory' variable observations are entered in a different way. Given that income appears in the first equation, with parameter β, and that income does not appear elsewhere with this parameter, we need a constructed set of observations $\hat{D}_t$; $t = 1, 2, \ldots, n$ followed by two sequences, each consisting of n zeros. Notice that, since income is used here as a right hand side endogenous variable, the predicted values are used in place of the original observations. So the complete set of observations on the constructed variable can be written as $\hat{D}_t$; $t = 1, 2, \ldots, n$ followed by 0; $t = 1, 2, \ldots, n$ followed by 0; $t = 1, 2, \ldots, n$, where 0; $t = 1, 2, \ldots, n$ represents a sequence of n zeros. Income appears again in the third equation, but with a different parameter ϵ. So another of the constructed 'explanatory' variables would have observations 0; $t = 1, 2, \ldots, n$ followed by 0; $t = 1, 2, \ldots, n$ followed by $\hat{D}_t$; $t = 1, 2, \ldots, n$. We can summarize this description by presenting the complete set of data for the combined equation in Table 4.

Table 4

Left hand side		Right hand side				
C_1	1	$\hat{D}_1$	0	0	0	0
.	.	.	.	.	.	.
.	.	.	.	.	.	.
.	.	.	.	.	.	.
C_n	1	$\hat{D}_n$	0	0	0	0
I_1	0	0	1	$\hat{R}_1$	0	0
.	.	.	.	.	.	.
.	.	.	.	.	.	.
.	.	.	.	.	.	.
I_n	0	0	1	$\hat{R}_n$	0	0
R_1	0	0	0	0	$\hat{D}_1$	M_1
.	.	.	.	.	.	.
.	.	.	.	.	.	.
.	.	.	.	.	.	.
R_n	0	0	0	0	$\hat{D}_n$	M_n
Associated parameter	α	β	γ	δ	ϵ	θ

Once the observations have been combined in this way, we effectively
have a single equation in the variables defined by the 'stacking process'.
A complete system method is then equivalent to a single equation
approach applied to the derived equation. By using predicted values for
right hand side endogenous variables, we have allowed for the simultaneity problem. However, having stacked the equations, we have
implicitly stacked the disturbances and, if there is contemporaneous
correlation between the disturbances to the original structural equations,
there will be correlations between the individual disturbances to the
derived equation.

Suppose, for example, that there is contemporaneous correlation
between the disturbances to the consumption function and those to the
investment function. There will then be correlation between u_1 and
v_1, u_2 and v_2, and so on. But these disturbances now appear in the
derived single equation: to be specific, u_1 appears in the first disturbance and v_1 in disturbance $n + 1$, u_2 in the second disturbance and v_2
in disturbance $n + 2$ and so on. The use of predicted values on the right
hand side does modify the disturbances, but not in any fundamental
way. So we do not have independent disturbances in the derived equation, and the estimation procedure should be chosen accordingly.

Given that we have taken care of the simultaneity problem by using predicted values for right hand side endogenous variables, one might think in terms of using OLS, just as OLS is used in the second stage of 2SLS. But if the disturbances are not independent, the obvious strategy would be to apply GLS instead. As before, the use of GLS is equivalent to a further transformation of the equation, after which OLS can be applied. Unfortunately it is not possible to describe this transformation in simple terms and, in fact, it would be difficult to carry out the calculation without a specially designed computer program. But the principles underlying the method do follow from our earlier discussions, and it has been possible to explain the essential nature of the complete system approach.

There is still one remaining problem. In practice, it is not possible to use the correct GLS transformation, as this requires that certain disturbance parameters be known. As before, it is necessary to use estimates in place of the true values. The unknown parameters are the disturbance variances for each structural equation and also the covariances, which measure the extent to which there is contemporaneous correlation. We have already seen how the disturbance variance for a single structural equation can be estimated from 2SLS residuals. After 2SLS estimation of the parameters of the consumption function, the estimate of the disturbance variance can be obtained as

$$\hat\sigma_u^2 = \Sigma \hat u_t^2/n \ [\text{or } \Sigma \hat u_t^2/(n-2)] \qquad (6.5.3)$$

The subscript u has been added to signify that this estimate refers to the disturbances to the consumption function, which are written as $u_t; t = 1, 2, \ldots, n$. Similarly, for the investment function, we would have

$$\hat\sigma_v^2 = \Sigma \hat v_t^2/n \ [\text{or } \Sigma \hat v_t^2/(n-2)] \qquad (6.5.4)$$

and, for the covariance between the disturbances to the consumption function and those for the investment function,

$$\hat\sigma_{uv} = \Sigma \hat u_t \hat v_t/n \ [\text{or } \Sigma \hat u_t \hat v_t/(n-2)] \qquad (6.5.5)$$

The usual approach here is to divide by n: this avoids any difficulty caused by the fact that two different equations may not have the same number of variables on the right hand side.

It is now possible to explain the three stages which go to make up 3SLS. The first stage consists of reduced form regressions, used to obtain predicted values for the right hand side endogenous variables. The second stage consists of 2SLS estimation, applied to each behavioural equation: the residuals from this stage are used to generate estimates of the disturbance parameters. The third stage is an approximation to GLS estimation of the derived single equation. If there is contemporaneous correlation of the disturbances, the 3SLS estimators are more efficient than the corresponding 2SLS estimators, in the sense that the asymptotic variances are generally lower in the 3SLS case.

Three stage least squares is not the only complete system method that is available. An alternative is to apply the maximum likelihood principle, which leads to *full information maximum likelihood* (FIML) estimates of the model parameters. Whereas the 3SLS method uses preliminary estimates of the disturbance parameters, which are then used to generate estimates of the remaining parameters in the model, the FIML method generates both sets of estimates simultaneously. Beyond this, there is little that we can say about FIML. The technical details are complicated and, as the equations defining the estimators are highly nonlinear, an iterative solution procedure has to be used. One cannot possibly attempt FIML estimation unless a suitable computer program is available.

The example considered in this section does not involve any lagged endogenous variables. Had it done so, we would have treated lagged endogenous variables in exactly the same way as exogenous variables. The final step in our analysis of estimator properties considers the extent to which such a procedure is valid, in the context of both single equation and complete system methods of estimation.

6.6 Simultaneous dynamic models

Although we have certainly considered the possibility that the predetermined variables in a model may include lagged endogenous variables, as well as exogenous variables, we have not asked whether this will lead to any additional problems of estimation over and above those that already exist because of simultaneity. To pursue this question, consider again the example first introduced in Section 6.1, the simultaneous dynamic model

$$C_t = \alpha + \beta D_t + \gamma D_{t-1} + u_t$$
$$D_t = C_t + Z_t ; t = 1, 2, \ldots, n \tag{6.6.1}$$

In Section 6.3 we showed that the reduced form corresponding to 6.6.1 is

$$C_t = [\alpha/(1-\beta)] + [\beta/(1-\beta)]Z_t + [\gamma/(1-\beta)]D_{t-1} + [u_t/(1-\beta)] ;$$
$$t := 1, 2, \ldots, n$$

and

$$D_t = [\alpha/(1-\beta)] + [1/(1-\beta)]Z_t + [\gamma/(1-\beta)]D_{t-1} + [u_t/(1-\beta)];$$
$$t := 1, 2, \ldots, n \quad (6.6.2)$$

Given that the predetermined variable observations are Z_t and D_{t-1}; $t = 1, 2, \ldots, n$, the application of 2SLS would suggest first regressing D_t on Z_t and D_{t-1}, with an intercept, to produce predicted values $\hat{D}_t$; $t = 1, 2, \ldots, n$ and then regressing C_t on $\hat{D}_t$ and D_{t-1}, again with an intercept, to produce 2SLS estimates of α, β and γ. We have argued that 2SLS estimators are consistent, but we did so in a case in which the predetermined variables were all exogenous. The question now is whether this is also true when there are lagged endogenous variables in the model and, if so, whether there are additional conditions that must be satisfied.

To start with, consider the use of OLS in estimating the parameters of the reduced form equation for income. It is immediately apparent that this is similar to the use of OLS in estimating the parameters of a single equation dynamic model. If the disturbances u_t; $t = 1, 2, \ldots, n$ are serially independent, so too are the disturbances $u_t/(1-\beta)$; $t = 1, 2, \ldots, n$, and the OLS estimators will not be unbiased but they will be consistent. The same analysis would apply to the reduced form equation for consumption: in this case, the lagged endogenous variable is not the same economic variable as that on the left of the equation, but the nature of the estimation problem will be the same. We can then consider 2SLS estimation of the structural form. Our arguments for the consistency of 2SLS require that the reduced form estimators should be consistent: it is not necessary that they should be unbiased. So it is reasonable to suppose that, in a dynamic model, the 2SLS estimators will be consistent in those cases in which the reduced form parameters are consistently estimated by OLS.

Before proceeding further, we should mention the role of stability conditions. The essential meaning of such conditions is that if we ignore the random disturbances and consider the effect of an initial shock, in the form of a once and for all change in one exogenous variable, then if the stability conditions are satisfied, the endogenous variables would eventually attain values which no longer exhibit any discernible change from one period to the next. In the single equation dynamic model, with serially independent disturbances, a proof of consistency of the OLS estimators will typically involve stability conditions, if only to ensure that other asymptotic properties can be obtained without too much difficulty. Similar arguments apply to the

use of both 2SLS and 3SLS in a simultaneous dynamic model.
Although it is not true that stability is strictly necessary to a proof of
consistency, such quantities as asymptotic standard errors and
asymptotic test statistics are invariably derived on the basis of stability
assumptions. It is therefore wrong to assume that one can apply the
resulting formulae uncritically to a model which is not stable.

Despite the problems associated with stability conditions, the
conclusion to be drawn from the discussion above is that the introduction of lagged endogenous variables does not fundamentally alter
our approach to estimation, so long as there is no serial correlation.
If this condition is violated, it is necessary to alter the estimation procedures. As in the single equation case, there are two basic approaches
to the problem. The first is to extend the use of instrumental variables
to the lagged endogenous variables in the model, and the second is to
use a two step or iterative procedure, which may well involve instrumental variables, but which also recognizes the existence of a disturbance problem and aims for improvements in asymptotic efficiency, as
well as for consistency. These ideas may be applied to a single equation
taken from a simultaneous model or, alternatively, as part of a complete system approach.

This account of the use of a simultaneous dynamic model has been
very brief, but it does cover the essential points to emerge from a
combination of simultaneity and dynamic behaviour. The vast majority
of constructed econometric models do in fact involve lagged endogenous variables, and this is the final stage in our development of
estimation methods for models of the economic system. What we
should say, however, is that constructed econometric models are also
almost invariably nonlinear in endogenous variables. In a single equation
model this would not be a problem but, in a system context, nonlinearity in endogenous variables does require some modification of
estimation methods.

6.7   Forecasting and policy simulation

The estimation phase of the model building process may involve several
stages of testing and revision, but the end product will be a set of
equations in which the unknown parameter values are replaced by
estimates. If the intention is simply to assign values to key economic
parameters, the exercise is then complete. However, models are usually
constructed with some specific application in mind and, if this is the

case, the estimated version of the model will be used to generate forecasts or to conduct various experiments which obviously cannot be performed on the real system.

Suppose first that we wished to generate forecasts from the simplest version of the consumption—income model

$$C_t = \alpha + \beta D_t + u_t$$
$$D_t = C_t + Z_t; t = 1, 2, \ldots, n \qquad (6.7.1)$$

At the end of the estimation process, we would have

$$C_t = \hat{\alpha} + \hat{\beta} D_t + \hat{u}_t$$
$$D_t = C_t + Z_t; t = 1, 2, \ldots, n \qquad (6.7.2)$$

where $\hat{\alpha}$ and $\hat{\beta}$ are now taken to refer to specific point estimates, obtained by any chosen method of estimation, and where $\hat{u}_t; t = 1, 2, \ldots, n$ are the residuals corresponding to the particular estimates obtained. Now suppose that we require forecasts for period $n + 1$. If the model still holds in period $n + 1$, it would be true that

$$C_{n+1} = \alpha + \beta D_{n+1} + u_{n+1}$$
$$D_{n+1} = C_{n+1} + Z_{n+1} \qquad (6.7.3)$$

and, for given values of α and β, Z_{n+1} and u_{n+1}, these equations would produce values for C_{n+1} and D_{n+1}. We have estimates of α and β, but if the forecast is made at the end of period n, the value of Z_{n+1} would be unknown and the value of u_{n+1} can never be observed. So, before a forecast can be made, it is necessary to set some value for Z_{n+1} and to decide what to do about forecasting the behaviour of u_{n+1}. Unless one has evidence of serial correlation, or some other reason for predicting a nonzero value for u_{n+1}, all that one can do is to set the implicit prediction of u_{n+1} to zero. The predictions for C_{n+1} and D_{n+1} would then be given as the solution to the equations

$$\hat{C}_{n+1} = \hat{\alpha} + \hat{\beta} \hat{D}_{n+1}$$
$$\hat{D}_{n+1} = \hat{C}_{n+1} + Z_{n+1} \qquad (6.7.4)$$

The solutions are

$$\hat{C}_{n+1} = \hat{\alpha}/(1 - \hat{\beta}) + \hat{\beta}/(1 - \hat{\beta})Z_{n+1}$$
$$\hat{D}_{n+1} = \hat{\alpha}/(1 - \hat{\beta}) + 1/(1 - \hat{\beta})Z_{n+1} \qquad (6.7.5)$$

These are reduced form equations, in which the disturbance term is set to zero and in which the components of the reduced form parameters are replaced by estimates taken from the structural form. Depending on the method of estimation and on the properties of the model, it can happen that the resulting estimates of the reduced form parameters are exactly the same as those obtained by direct estimation of the reduced form equations, but this is not generally true.

Predictions that are generated in this way are, in formal terms, particular values taken by a set of random variables. The statistical properties of these random variables are not exactly the same as those described in Section 2.9 in the context of a single equation, because the properties of the estimators used in defining the prediction rule are now rather different. But the most important conclusion drawn from our earlier discussion is still relevant. Even when the model is 'true', one cannot expect to obtain perfectly accurate point forecasts.

Before a forecast can be generated, it is necessary to supply values for all the predetermined variables. So, for the model

$$C_t = \alpha + \gamma D_{t-1} + u_t$$
$$D_t = C_t + Z_t ; t = 1, 2, \ldots, n \tag{6.7.6}$$

the predictions for period $n + 1$ would be determined as

$$\hat{C}_{n+1} = \hat{\alpha} + \hat{\gamma} D_n$$
$$\hat{D}_{n+1} = \hat{C}_{n+1} + Z_{n+1} \tag{6.7.7}$$

for given values of Z_{n+1} and D_n. In practice there are lags in the production of data and in the construction of the model and, if $n + 1$ is taken to refer to the period immediately after the data period, a more realistic situation would be that in which the model construction is completed during some later period, say $n + 2$, and in which the model is to be used to generate forecasts for period $n + 3$. The input required would be the values for D_{n+2} and Z_{n+3}. But the actual value of D_{n+2} would not be available until some time after the end of period $n + 2$, and Z_{n+3} relates to the forecast period. So one would have to make subsidiary forecasts for each of these values. In the case of the exogenous variable the forecast value is generated outside the model but, given that the model is dynamic, it is possible to make forecasts of endogenous variable values over two or more periods. Assuming that D_{n+1} is actually available and that values can be assigned to Z_{n+2} and Z_{n+3}, the two period forecast would be generated as

$$\hat{C}_{n+2} = \hat{\alpha} + \hat{\gamma} D_{n+1}$$
$$\hat{D}_{n+2} = \hat{C}_{n+2} + Z_{n+2}$$
$$\hat{C}_{n+3} = \hat{\alpha} + \hat{\gamma} \hat{D}_{n+2}$$
$$\hat{D}_{n+3} = \hat{C}_{n+3} + Z_{n+3}$$

In this way the forecasts can be carried forward to periods $n + 4$, $n + 5$ and so on, but the values of the exogenous variable do have to be supplied at each stage.

As described here the exercise is very mechanical, but if one is faced with the problem of having to make the best possible point forecast, the approach may be rather different. The formal model will usually play an important part, but the forecasts may be adjusted to take account of any new information that is available at the time at which the forecast is made. Suppose that one had reason to anticipate a change in government policy. Ideally, all that one would have to do is to revise a subsidiary forecast for one of the exogenous variables. However, the expected policy change may indicate a changed environment, unlike that operating during the period covered by the data used for estimation. Under these circumstances, one might decide to adjust parameter estimates, or to use a nonzero value in place of the disturbance to a particular structural equation. The model could then be used to work the implications of any adjustment through to all the endogenous variables in the system. Whatever form these adjustments may take, it is clear that it is unrealistic to suppose that a model is used as a forecasting machine, producing numbers which are untouched by human hand.

If one is not confident of the accuracy of the subsidiary forecasts for the exogenous variables, a range of possible values may have to be used to generate conditional predictions for the endogenous variables. Alternatively, one might use exogenous variable values that are not necessarily considered to be forecasts, to see what would happen under certain alternative sets of assumptions. This is essentially what happens when the model is used for policy simulation. The underlying idea is that there are certain exogenous variables to which values are assigned by policy decision. These are the *policy instruments*. The model can be used to show how a change in policy is transmitted to one or more of the endogenous variables, these being the *policy objectives*. If the model does not involve lags, a change in policy will have a once and for all effect on the endogenous variables. If there are finite lags in the exogenous variables, the full impact of the policy change may only be apparent after a certain delay. Finally, if the model is dynamic, a once and for all change in a single exogenous variable can generate a complete time path for the endogenous variables. This type of experimentation is usually performed by using the estimated version of the model as a deterministic equation system, although one could also consider generating artificial disturbances, to allow for the fact that the underlying model does not assume exact relationships between the variables.

In both forecasting and policy simulation, each set of values for the endogenous variables is obtained by solving the equations of the estimated version of the model. In the examples that we have used it is very simple to do this, but our examples have special characteristics. The number of equations is small and the equations are linear in the endogenous variables. In practice, the equations used may be linear in the parameters, but there will often be nonlinearities in the endogenous variables. To illustrate this point, consider an equation taken from the model shown in 6.5.1. The equation states that

$$R_t = \epsilon D_t + \theta M_t + w_t; t = 1, 2, \ldots, n \qquad (6.7.8)$$

In fact, it is much more likely that this equation would be linear in the logarithms of the variables. If the variables appear only in logarithmic form, there is no problem: one can treat $\log R$ and $\log M$ in exactly the same way as any other variable in the model. But if we had used logarithms in the third equation of 6.5.1, the interest rate would have appeared as $\log R$ in this equation and as R in the investment function. Similarly, D would appear as $\log D$ in the third equation but as D in the consumption function and the identity. If there are nonlinearities in endogenous variables, an additional problem occurs when the estimated version of the model is used for forecasting or for policy simulation, because one then has to solve equations which are nonlinear in the variables for which solutions are required. In this situation, an iterative solution procedure has to be used to generate the predictions for a single time period. For a large model, the solution process can represent a significant computational task.

6.8 Finale

The final version of our representation for an economic system is a set of simultaneous dynamic equations, with random disturbances. In practice, it is likely that the equation system will also be nonlinear in endogenous variables. Thus we have an 'econometric' formulation which corresponds to a wide class of economic models. It is obvious that there are difficulties in using this representation. It is easy to point to the statistical problems of estimation and to the deficiencies of available data. It is easy to find examples of constructed econometric models in which there are exogenous variables that ought not to be exogenous and policy instruments that are not really instruments. Above all, it is easy to point to the fact that forecasts obtained from econometric models are sometimes less accurate than one would wish them to be. Forecasting is by far the most public manifestation of the use of econometric methods and is therefore the target on which criticism is most likely to focus. But if we are to criticize in this way, we should have a clear idea as to what it is that we are attacking. It is not surprising that there are practical difficulties in model construction, given the quite staggering complexity of 'real' economic systems. Nor is it surprising that forecasts are subject to error: even with an 'ideal' set of assumptions there is a random component in the predictions from an econometric model, and the implied statistical properties of the forecasts from large scale models are far more complicated than those for the ideal case. Finally, one does have to contend with 'the data problem', under which the order of magnitude of error, or at least of data revision, is often greater than that of the changes that one is trying to predict. What one can say, in defence of the econometric approach, is that there is at least an attempt to come to terms with the complexity of the interactions between economic variables and to understand the way in which real systems do operate.

6.9   Exercises (solutions on p. 284)

6.1 Consider the model

$$C_t = \alpha + \beta Y_t + u_t$$
$$I_t = \gamma + \delta Y_{t-1} + v_t$$
$$Y_t = C_t + I_t + Z_t; t = 1, 2, \ldots, n$$

where C is consumers' expenditure, Y is income, I is investment and Z is autonomous expenditure. C, I and Y are endogenous. Find the reduced form equation for consumers' expenditure. Do you think that the consumption function is identified?

6.2 Consider the model

$$Q_t^d = \alpha + \beta P_t + u_t$$
$$Q_t^s = \gamma + \delta R_t + v_t$$
$$Q_t^d = Q_t^s; t = 1, 2, \ldots, n$$

where Q^d is the demand for wheat, Q^s is the supply of wheat, P is the price of wheat and R is a variable relating to climate. Which variables would you consider to be endogenous? Do you notice any special feature of this model?

6.3 How might you obtain 2SLS (instrumental variable) estimates of the parameters of a consumption function, if it is recognized that this is part of a simultaneous model, but you do not know the specification of the other equations?

Suggestions for further reading

There are several excellent texts which offer a more formal approach to the topics described in this book. See, for example:

Christ, C. F., *Econometric Models and Methods*, Wiley, 1966

Harvey, A. C., *Econometric Analysis of Time Series*, Philip Allan, 1981

Johnston, J., *Econometric Methods*, 2nd ed., McGraw-Hill, 1972

Judge, G. G. *et al., The Theory and Practice of Econometrics*, Wiley, 1980

Maddala, G. S., *Econometrics*, McGraw-Hill, 1977

Pindyck, R. S., and Rubinfeld, D. L., *Econometric Models and Economic Forecasts*, 2nd ed., McGraw-Hill, 1981

For the statistical background to econometrics, see, for example:

Hey, J. D., *Statistics in Economics*, Martin Robertson, 1974

or, at a more formal level,

Mendenhall, W., Scheaffer, R. L., and Wackerly, D. D., *Mathematical Statistics with Applications*, 2nd ed., Wadsworth, 1981

A comprehensive introduction to the mathematics needed in many branches of economics is:

Chiang, A. C., *Fundamental Methods of Mathematical Economics*, 2nd ed., McGraw-Hill, 1974

For a recent discussion of the problems of model specification and use, see:

Arestis, P., and Hadjimatheou, G., *Introducing Macroeconomic Modelling: An Econometric Study of the United Kingdom*, Macmillan, 1982

Statistical tables

Tables A, B and D are extracted from more comprehensive tabulations prepared by the Research Support Unit, Faculty of Economic and Social Studies, University of Manchester.

Table C is extracted from tables prepared by R. P. Thompson, Department of Econometrics, University of Manchester.

Table E is extracted from tables prepared by R. W. Farebrother, Department of Econometrics, University of Manchester.

The author gratefully acknowledges permission to reprint extracts from these tables.

Table A *Critical values for the standard normal distribution*

The table gives critical values c for chosen values of $\Pr(-c < Z < +c)$ (or for equivalent values of $\Pr(Z > +c)$), where Z is a standard normal variable. The table can also be used in reverse, to obtain exact probabilities for $c = 0.5, 1.0, 1.5, 2.0, 2.5$ and 3.0.

$\Pr(-c < Z < +c)$	$\Pr(Z > +c)$	c
0·0000	0·5000	0·00
0·3830	0·3085	0·50
0·5000	0·2500	0·67
0·6826	0·1587	1·00
0·8000	0·1000	1·28
0·8664	0·0668	1·50
0·9000	0·0500	1·64
0·9500	0·0250	1·96
0·9544	0·0228	2·00
0·9800	0·0100	2·33
0·9876	0·0062	2·50
0·9900	0·0050	2·58
0·9974	0·0013	3·00
0·9990	0·0005	3·29

Table B (p. 269)   *Critical values for the t distribution*

The table gives critical values c for chosen values of $\Pr(-c < t < +c)$ (or the equivalent values of $\Pr(t > +c)$), where t is a random variable having a t distribution with df degrees of freedom.

Table C (p. 270)   *Critical values for the F distribution*

The table gives critical values c such that $\Pr(F > c) = 0\cdot05$, where F is a random variable having an F distribution with df_1 and df_2 degrees of freedom.

Table B *Critical values for the t distribution*

df	$\Pr(-c < t < +c) = 0.90$ or $\Pr(t > +c) = 0.05$ $c = t_{df}^{0.05}$	$\Pr(-c < t < +c) = 0.95$ or $\Pr(t > +c) = 0.025$ $c = t_{df}^{0.025}$	$\Pr(-c < t < +c) = 0.98$ or $\Pr(t > +c) = 0.01$ $c = t_{df}^{0.01}$	$\Pr(-c < t < +c) = 0.99$ or $\Pr(t > +c) = 0.005$ $c = t_{df}^{0.005}$
3	2·35	3·18	4·54	5·84
5	2·01	2·57	3·36	4·03
6	1·94	2·45	3·14	3·71
7	1·89	2·36	3·00	3·50
8	1·86	2·31	2·90	3·35
9	1·83	2·26	2·82	3·25
10	1·81	2·23	2·76	3·16
12	1·78	2·18	2·68	3·05
14	1·76	2·14	2·62	2·98
16	1·75	2·12	2·58	2·92
18	1·73	2·10	2·55	2·88
20	1·72	2·09	2·53	2·84
22	1·72	2·07	2·51	2·82
24	1·71	2·06	2·49	2·80
26	1·71	2·06	2·48	2·78
28	1·70	2·05	2·47	2·76
30	1·70	2·04	2·46	2·75
40	1·68	2·02	2·42	2·70
60	1·67	2·00	2·39	2·66
∞	1·64	1·96	2·33	2·58

Table C   *Critical values for the F distribution*

$$c = F^{0.05}_{df_1, df_2}$$

df_2 \ df_1	1	2	3	4	6	8	10	24
3	10.13	9.55	9.28	9.12	8.94	8.84	8.79	8.64
5	6.61	5.79	5.41	5.19	4.95	4.82	4.73	4.53
6	5.99	5.14	4.76	4.53	4.28	4.15	4.06	3.84
7	5.59	4.74	4.35	4.12	3.87	3.73	3.64	3.41
8	5.32	4.46	4.07	3.84	3.58	3.44	3.35	3.11
9	5.12	4.26	3.86	3.63	3.37	3.23	3.14	2.90
10	4.96	4.10	3.71	3.48	3.22	3.07	2.98	2.74
12	4.75	3.88	3.49	3.26	3.00	2.85	2.75	2.51
14	4.60	3.74	3.34	3.11	2.85	2.70	2.60	2.35
16	4.49	3.63	3.24	3.01	2.74	2.59	2.49	2.23
18	4.41	3.55	3.16	2.93	2.66	2.51	2.41	2.15
20	4.35	3.49	3.10	2.87	2.60	2.45	2.35	2.08
22	4.30	3.44	3.05	2.82	2.55	2.40	2.30	2.03
24	4.26	3.40	3.01	2.78	2.51	2.35	2.25	1.98
26	4.22	3.37	2.97	2.74	2.47	2.32	2.22	1.95
28	4.20	3.34	2.95	2.71	2.44	2.29	2.19	1.91
30	4.17	3.32	2.92	2.69	2.42	2.27	2.16	1.89
40	4.08	3.23	2.84	2.61	2.34	2.18	2.07	1.79
60	4.00	3.15	2.76	2.52	2.25	2.10	1.99	1.70
∞	3.84	3.00	2.60	2.37	2.10	1.94	1.83	1.52

Table D *Critical values for the χ^2 distribution*

The table gives critical values c for chosen values of Pr $(\chi^2 > c)$, where χ^2 is a variable having a χ^2 distribution with df degrees of freedom.

df	Pr $(\chi^2 > c) = 0.10$ $c = \chi^{2(0.10)}_{df}$	Pr $(\chi^2 > c) = 0.05$ $c = \chi^{2(0.05)}_{df}$	Pr $(\chi^2 > c) = 0.01$ $c = \chi^{2(0.01)}_{df}$
1	2·71	3·84	6·64
2	4·61	5·99	9·21
3	6·25	7·81	11·34
4	7·78	9·49	13·28
5	9·24	11·07	15·09
6	10·64	12·59	16·81
7	12·02	14·07	18·47
8	13·36	15·51	20·09
9	14·68	16·92	21·67
10	15·99	18·31	23·21
11	17·27	19·68	24·72
12	18·55	21·03	26·22
13	19·81	22·36	27·69
14	21·06	23·68	29·14
15	22·31	25·00	30·58
16	23·54	26·30	32·00
17	24·77	27·59	33·41
18	25·99	28·87	34·81
19	27·20	30·14	36·19
20	28·41	31·41	37·57
22	30·81	33·92	40·29
24	33·20	36·42	42·98
26	35·56	38·89	45·64
28	37·92	41·34	48·28
30	40·26	43·77	50·89
40	51·80	55·76	63·69
50	63·17	67·50	76·15
60	74·40	79·08	88·38
80	96·58	101·98	112·33
100	118·50	124·34	135·81

Table E   *Lower and upper bounds for critical values in the Durbin-Watson test*

The table gives lower d_L and upper d_U bounds for critical values c, such that $\Pr(d < c) = 0.05$, under the null hypothesis of no serial correlation.

n	k = 2		k = 3		k = 4		k = 6		k = 10	
	d_L	d_U	d_L	d_U	d_L	d_U	d_L	d_U	d_L	d_U
15	1.08	1.36	0.95	1.54	0.81	1.75	0.56	2.22	0.17	3.22
16	1.11	1.37	0.98	1.54	0.86	1.73	0.61	2.16	0.22	3.09
17	1.13	1.38	1.01	1.54	0.90	1.71	0.66	2.10	0.27	2.97
18	1.16	1.39	1.05	1.53	0.93	1.70	0.71	2.06	0.32	2.87
19	1.18	1.40	1.07	1.54	0.97	1.68	0.75	2.02	0.37	2.78
20	1.20	1.41	1.10	1.54	1.00	1.68	0.79	1.99	0.42	2.70
22	1.24	1.43	1.15	1.54	1.05	1.66	0.86	1.94	0.50	2.57
24	1.27	1.45	1.19	1.55	1.10	1.66	0.92	1.90	0.58	2.46
26	1.30	1.46	1.22	1.55	1.14	1.65	0.98	1.87	0.66	2.38
28	1.33	1.48	1.25	1.56	1.18	1.65	1.03	1.85	0.72	2.31
30	1.35	1.49	1.28	1.57	1.21	1.65	1.07	1.83	0.78	2.25
35	1.40	1.52	1.34	1.58	1.28	1.65	1.16	1.80	0.91	2.14
40	1.44	1.54	1.39	1.60	1.34	1.66	1.23	1.79	1.01	2.07
50	1.50	1.58	1.46	1.63	1.42	1.67	1.33	1.77	1.16	1.99
75	1.58	1.65	1.57	1.68	1.54	1.71	1.45	1.77	1.37	1.90
100	1.65	1.69	1.63	1.71	1.61	1.74	1.57	1.78	1.48	1.87
200	1.76	1.78	1.75	1.79	1.74	1.80	1.72	1.82	1.67	1.86

Solutions to exercises

Chapter 1

1.1 (a) Let Y be the random variable for the modified game and note that $Y = V + 6$, where V is the random variable for the original game. The probability for each value of Y is $1/6$ and so

$$E(Y) = (1/6)(7) + (1/6)(8) + (1/6)(9) + (1/6)(10)$$
$$+ (1/6)(11) + (1/6)(12) = 9 \cdot 5$$
$$\text{var}(Y) = (1/6)(7 - 9 \cdot 5)^2 + (1/6)(8 - 9 \cdot 5)^2 + (1/6)(9 - 9 \cdot 5)^2$$
$$+ (1/6)(10 - 9 \cdot 5)^2 + (1/6)(11 - 9 \cdot 5)^2$$
$$+ (1/6)(12 - 9 \cdot 5)^2 = 2 \cdot 917$$

In comparison with the original game, the expectation has increased by 6 but the variance has not changed. The general rules for this case are that if $Y = V + c$, where c is constant, then

$$E(Y) = E(V + c) = E(V) + c$$
$$\text{var}(Y) = \text{var}(V + c) = \text{var}(V)$$

(b) Again, let Y be the random variable for the modified game and note that now $Y = 2V$. The probability for each value of Y is still $1/6$, and so

$$E(Y) = (1/6)(2) + (1/6)(4) + (1/6)(6) + (1/6)(8)$$
$$+ (1/6)(10) + (1/6)(12) = 7$$

$$\text{var}(Y) = (1/6)(2 - 7)^2 + (1/6)(4 - 7)^2 + (1/6)(6 - 7)^2$$
$$+ (1/6)(8 - 7)^2 + (1/6)(10 - 7)^2$$
$$+ (1/6)(12 - 7)^2 = 11 \cdot 67$$

In comparison with the original game, the expectation has been multiplied by 2, but the variance is multiplied by 4. The general rules in this case are that if $Y = cV$, where c is constant, then

$$E(Y) = E(cV) = cE(V)$$
$$\text{var}(cV) = c^2 \text{var}(V)$$

1.2 The rules from exercise 1.1 can be combined to give

$$E(c + dV) = c + dE(V)$$
$$\text{var}(c + dV) = d^2 \text{ var}(V)$$

where c and d are constants. Hence

$$E(F) = 32 + 1 \cdot 8E(V) = 32 + 1 \cdot 8(15) = 59$$
$$\text{var}(F) = (1 \cdot 8)^2 \text{ var}(V) = 3 \cdot 24(9) = 29.16$$

1.3 (a) $\displaystyle\sum_{t=1}^{t=n}(10) = 10 + 10 + \ldots + 10 = n(10)$

(b) $\Sigma(cX_t) = 10(1) + 10(2) + 10(3) = 60 = 10(1 + 2 + 3) = c\Sigma X_t$

(c) $\Sigma(X_t + Y_t) = (1 + 2) + (2 + 4) + (3 + 6) = 18$
$\qquad\qquad = (1 + 2 + 3) + (2 + 4 + 6) = \Sigma X_t + \Sigma Y_t$

Note, however, that $\Sigma X_t Y_t$ is not the same as $\Sigma X_t \Sigma Y_t$:

$$\Sigma X_t Y_t = 1(2) + 2(4) + 3(6) = 28$$
$$\Sigma X_t \Sigma Y_t = (1 + 2 + 3)(2 + 4 + 6) = 72$$

1.4 The formula for the sample mean of C is $\overline{C} = \Sigma C_t / n$. By summing the values of C and dividing the result by 11, we obtain $\Sigma C_t = 717 \cdot 44$ and $\overline{C} = 65 \cdot 2218$. Then

t	$C_t - \overline{C}$	$(C_t - \overline{C})^2$
1	$-7 \cdot 4118$	$54 \cdot 9350$
2	$-5 \cdot 5018$	$30 \cdot 2700$
3	$-1 \cdot 9518$	$3 \cdot 8096$
4	$1 \cdot 1082$	$1 \cdot 2281$
5	$-0 \cdot 1718$	$0 \cdot 0295$
6	$-0 \cdot 5718$	$0 \cdot 3270$
7	$-0 \cdot 5118$	$0 \cdot 2620$
8	$-0 \cdot 7018$	$0 \cdot 4925$
9	$3 \cdot 0082$	$9 \cdot 0492$
10	$6 \cdot 3782$	$40 \cdot 6812$
11	$6 \cdot 3282$	$40 \cdot 0459$
	$0 \cdot 000$	$181 \cdot 130$

Alternatively, one can form the sum ΣC_t^2 and use the 'short cut' formula

$$\Sigma(C_t - \overline{C})^2 = \Sigma C_t^2 - (\Sigma C_t)^2/n$$

Either way, we obtain

$$\Sigma(C_t - \overline{C})^2 = 181 \cdot 130$$

So the sample variance is

$$s_C^2 = 181 \cdot 130/11 = 16 \cdot 466$$

and the sample standard deviation is the square root of this quantity

$$s_C = 4 \cdot 058$$

In a similar fashion, it can be shown that $\Sigma D_t = 814 \cdot 03$, $\overline{D} = 74 \cdot 0027$, $\Sigma(D_t - \overline{D})^2 = 441 \cdot 136$ and $s_D = 6 \cdot 333$. Note that solutions may vary slightly, because of different degrees of rounding error. Note also that division by $n - 1$ produces different values for standard deviations.

Chapter 2

2.1 The values of L are as follows:

if $V_1 = 0$ and $V_2 = 0$, then $L = 0$
if $V_1 = 0$ and $V_2 = 1$, then $L = 0 \cdot 8$
if $V_1 = 1$ and $V_2 = 0$, then $L = 0 \cdot 2$
if $V_1 = 1$ and $V_2 = 1$, then $L = 1$

Since each value for L is associated with a probability of 1/4,

$$E(L) = (1/4)(0) + (1/4)(0 \cdot 8) + (1/4)(0 \cdot 2) + (1/4)(1) = 0 \cdot 5$$
$$\begin{aligned} \text{var}(L) &= (1/4)(0 - 0 \cdot 5)^2 + (1/4)(0 \cdot 8 - 0 \cdot 5)^2 \\ &\quad + (1/4)(0 \cdot 2 - 0 \cdot 5)^2 + (1/4)(1 - 0 \cdot 5)^2 = 0 \cdot 17 \end{aligned}$$

Now consider the random variable V_1. This has two outcomes, each with a probability of 1/2. So

$$E(V_1) = (1/2)(0) + (1/2)(1) = 0 \cdot 5$$
$$\text{var}(V_1) = (1/2)(0 - 0 \cdot 5)^2 + (1/2)(1 - 0 \cdot 5)^2 = 0 \cdot 25$$

Similarly, $E(V_2) = 0 \cdot 5$ and var $(V_2) = 0 \cdot 25$. Then

$$0 \cdot 2E(V_1) + 0 \cdot 8E(V_2) = 0 \cdot 5$$

which is the value of $E(L)$ and

$$0.04 \text{ var } (V_1) + 0.64 \text{ var } (V_2) = 0.17$$

which is the value of var (L). These results demonstrate the validity of the rules

$$E(L) = a_1 E(V_1) + a_2 E(V_2)$$
$$\text{var } (L) = a_1^2 \text{ var } (V_1) + a_2^2 \text{ var } (V_2)$$

where L is the linear function

$$L = a_1 V_1 + a_2 V_2$$

and V_1 and V_2 are independent or at least uncorrelated random variables.

2.2 (a) In this application of the two variable model, C is equivalent to Y and D is equivalent to X. Hence, $\Sigma x_t y_t = \Sigma(D_t - \bar{D})(C_t - \bar{C})$, $\Sigma x_t^2 = \Sigma(D_t - D)^2$ and

$$\hat{\beta} = \Sigma x_t y_t / \Sigma x_t^2 = 280.789/441.136 = 0.6365$$

and

$$\hat{\alpha} = \bar{Y} - \hat{\beta}\bar{X} = 65.2218 - (0.6365)74.0027 = 18.118$$

The estimated line is therefore

$$\hat{C} = 18.118 + 0.6365D; \quad 1970–1980$$

(b)
$$\Sigma e_t^2 = \Sigma y_t^2 - \hat{\beta}\Sigma x_t y_t = \Sigma(C_t - \bar{C})^2 - \hat{\beta}\Sigma(D_t - \bar{D})(C_t - \bar{C})$$
$$= 181.130 - (0.6365)280.789$$
$$= 2.4078$$
$$\hat{\sigma}^2 = \Sigma e_t^2/(n-2) = 2.4078/9 = 0.2675$$
$$\text{se } (\hat{\beta}) = \hat{\sigma}/\sqrt{\Sigma x_t^2} = \hat{\sigma}/\sqrt{\Sigma(D_t - \bar{D})^2} = 0.5172/\sqrt{441.136}$$
$$= 0.0246$$

Note that solutions may vary somewhat, because of different degrees of rounding error.

Solutions 2.3 to 2.5 make use of the rules of summation given in Section 1.6. A line which uses these rules is signified by an asterisk (*).

2.3
$$\Sigma e_t^2 = \Sigma(Y_t - \hat{\alpha} - \hat{\beta}X_t)^2$$
$$\partial(\Sigma e_t^2)/\partial\hat{\alpha} = \Sigma[2(Y_t - \hat{\alpha} - \hat{\beta}X_t)(-1)]$$
$$= -2\Sigma(Y_t - \hat{\alpha} - \hat{\beta}X_t) \qquad *$$
$$= -2(\Sigma Y_t - n\hat{\alpha} - \hat{\beta}\Sigma X_t) \qquad *$$
$$\partial(\Sigma e_t^2)/\partial\hat{\beta} = \Sigma[2(Y_t - \hat{\alpha} - \hat{\beta}X_t)(-X_t)]$$
$$= -2\Sigma X_t(Y_t - \hat{\alpha} - \hat{\beta}X_t) \qquad *$$
$$= -2(\Sigma X_t Y_t - \hat{\alpha}\Sigma X_t - \hat{\beta}\Sigma X_t^2) \qquad *$$

For a turning point, $\partial(\Sigma e_t^2)/\partial\hat{\alpha} = 0$ and $\partial(\Sigma e_t^2)/\partial\hat{\beta} = 0$. So

$$-2(\Sigma Y_t - n\hat{\alpha} - \hat{\beta}\Sigma X_t) = 0$$
$$-2(\Sigma X_t Y_t - \hat{\alpha}\Sigma X_t - \hat{\beta}\Sigma X_t^2) = 0$$

or

$$\hat{\alpha}n + \hat{\beta}\Sigma X_t = \Sigma Y_t \qquad *$$
$$\hat{\alpha}\Sigma X_t + \hat{\beta}\Sigma X_t^2 = \Sigma X_t Y_t \qquad *$$

The second order conditions show that this solution is indeed the minimum of Σe_t^2.

2.4
$$\Sigma x_t y_t = \Sigma(X_t - \bar{X})(Y_t - \bar{Y}) = \Sigma(X_t Y_t - X_t \bar{Y} - \bar{X}Y_t + \bar{X}\bar{Y})$$
$$= \Sigma X_t Y_t - \bar{Y}\Sigma X_t - \bar{X}\Sigma Y_t + n\bar{X}\bar{Y} \quad *$$

where $\bar{X}$ and $\bar{Y}$ do not vary with t and so are treated as constants in applying the rules of summation. Now

$$\bar{Y}\Sigma X_t = (\Sigma Y_t/n)\Sigma X_t = (\Sigma X_t/n)\Sigma Y_t$$

and

$$n\bar{X}\bar{Y} = n(\Sigma X_t/n)(\Sigma Y_t/n) = (\Sigma X_t/n)\Sigma Y_t$$

So

$$\Sigma x_t y_t = \Sigma X_t Y_t - (\Sigma X_t/n)\Sigma Y_t$$

Similarly it can be shown that

$$\Sigma x_t^2 = \Sigma X_t^2 - (\Sigma X_t/n)\Sigma X_t$$

and the required result then follows.

2.5 First note the following

(a) $\quad \Sigma x_t = \Sigma(X_t - \bar{X}) = \Sigma X_t - n\bar{X} = \Sigma X_t - \Sigma X_t = 0 \qquad *$

(b) $\Sigma x_t y_t = \Sigma x_t (Y_t - \overline{Y}) = \Sigma x_t Y_t - \overline{Y} \Sigma x_t$ *

   $= \Sigma x_t Y_t$, since $\Sigma x_t = 0$

(c) $\Sigma x_t^2 = \Sigma x_t (X_t - \overline{X}) = \Sigma x_t X_t - \overline{X} \Sigma x_t$ *

   $= \Sigma x_t X_t$, since $\Sigma x_t = 0$

(d) $Y_t = \alpha + \beta X_t + u_t$

Then

$$\begin{aligned}
\hat{\beta} &= \Sigma x_t y_t / \Sigma x_t^2 \\
&= \Sigma x_t Y_t / \Sigma x_t^2, \text{ using } (b) \\
&= \Sigma x_t (\alpha + \beta X_t + u_t) / \Sigma x_t^2, \text{ using } (d) \\
&= (\alpha \Sigma x_t + \beta \Sigma x_t X_t + \Sigma x_t u_t) / \Sigma x_t^2 \qquad * \\
&= (\alpha \cdot 0 + \beta \Sigma x_t^2 + \Sigma x_t u_t) / \Sigma x_t^2, \text{ using } (a) \text{ and } (c) \\
&= \beta + \Sigma x_t u_t / \Sigma x_t^2
\end{aligned}$$

2.6 From equation 2.3.5 we have

$$\begin{aligned}
\hat{\beta} - E(\hat{\beta}) &= \hat{\beta} - \beta = \Sigma w_t u_t \\
[\hat{\beta} - E(\hat{\beta})]^2 &= [\Sigma w_t u_t]^2 \\
&= w_1^2 u_1^2 + w_2^2 u_2^2 + \ldots + w_n^2 u_n^2 + \text{cross-products}
\end{aligned}$$

The cross-products are of the form $w_t w_s u_t u_s$ and, if

$$\text{cov}(u_t, u_s) = E([u_t - E(u_t)][u_s - E(u_s)]) = E(u_t u_s) = 0; s \neq t$$

then

$$E(w_t w_s u_t u_s) = w_t w_s E(u_t u_s) = 0; s \neq t$$

(Note that we have used $E(u_t) = E(u_s) = 0$; for all s, t.) Hence

$$\begin{aligned}
\text{var}(\hat{\beta}) &= E([\hat{\beta} - E(\hat{\beta})]^2) = E([\Sigma w_t u_t]^2) \\
&= E(w_1^2 u_1^2 + w_2^2 u_2^2 + \ldots + w_n^2 u_n^2 + \text{cross products}) \\
&= E(w_1^2 u_1^2) + E(w_2^2 u_2^2) + \ldots + E(w_n^2 u_n^2) \\
&\qquad + E(\text{cross-products}) \\
&= w_1^2 E(u_1^2) + w_2^2 E(u_2^2) + \ldots + w_n^2 E(u_n^2) + 0
\end{aligned}$$

Finally, if

$$\text{var}(u_t) = E([u_t - E(u_t)]^2) = E(u_t^2) = \sigma^2; t = 1, 2, \ldots, n$$

then

$$\text{var}(\hat{\beta}) = \Sigma w_t^2 \sigma^2 = \sigma^2 \Sigma w_t^2$$

It is shown above equation 2.4.7 that $\Sigma w_t^2 = 1/\Sigma x_t^2$. Hence var $(\hat{\beta}) = \sigma^2/\Sigma x_t^2$.

Chapter 3

3.1
$$e_t = Y_t - \hat{\beta}_1 - \hat{\beta}_2 X_{2t} - \ldots - \hat{\beta}_j X_{jt} - \ldots - \hat{\beta}_k X_{kt};$$
$$t = 1, 2, \ldots, n$$

$$\partial(\Sigma_t e_t^2)/\partial\hat{\beta}_j = \Sigma_t(\partial e_t^2/\partial\hat{\beta}_j) = \Sigma_t(\partial e_t^2/\partial e_t)(\partial e_t/\partial\hat{\beta}_j)$$
$$= \Sigma_t(2e_t)(-X_{jt}) = -2\Sigma_t X_{jt} e_t; j = 1, 2, \ldots, k$$

For a turning point

$$\partial(\Sigma_t e_t^2)/\partial\hat{\beta}_j = 0; j = 1, 2, \ldots, k$$

So

$$-2\Sigma_t X_{jt} e_t = 0$$

or

$$\Sigma_t X_{jt} e_t = 0; j = 1, 2, \ldots, k$$

Substitution for e_t leads to the normal equations 3.2.1. For example, when $j = 2$, we have

$$\Sigma X_{2t}(Y_t - \hat{\beta}_1 - \hat{\beta}_2 X_{2t} - \ldots - \hat{\beta}_k X_{kt}) = 0$$

or

$$\hat{\beta}_1 \Sigma X_{2t} + \hat{\beta}_2 \Sigma X_{2t}^2 + \ldots + \hat{\beta}_k \Sigma X_{2t} X_{kt} = \Sigma X_{2t} Y_t$$

3.2 From the data given in Section 3.2, compute $\bar{X}_2 = 5$, $\bar{X}_3 = 9.6$ and $\bar{Y} = 8$. Then express the data in deviation form and proceed as follows:

x_{2t}	x_{3t}	y_t	$x_{2t}x_{3t}$	$x_{2t}y_t$	x_{2t}^2	$x_{3t}y_t$	x_{3t}^2
2	−3.6	−3	−7.2	−6	4	10.8	12.96
1	−2.6	−2	−2.6	−2	1	5.2	6.76
−1	−0.6	0	0.6	0	1	0.0	0.36
0	6.4	3	0.0	0	0	19.2	40.96
−2	0.4	2	−0.8	−4	4	0.8	0.16
0	0.0	0	−10.0	−12	10	36.0	61.20

Using these values in the equations

$$\hat{\beta}_2 \Sigma x_{2t}^2 + \hat{\beta}_3 \Sigma x_{2t} x_{3t} = \Sigma x_{2t} y_t$$
$$\hat{\beta}_2 \Sigma x_{3t} x_{2t} + \hat{\beta}_3 \Sigma x_{3t}^2 = \Sigma x_{3t} y_t$$

This gives

$$10\hat{\beta}_2 - 10\hat{\beta}_3 = -12$$
$$-10\hat{\beta}_2 + 61{\cdot}2\hat{\beta}_3 = 36$$

Since these equations are identical to equations 3.2.5 the solutions for $\hat{\beta}_2$ and $\hat{\beta}_3$ are identical to those obtained by direct solution of the normal equations in original form.

3.3 There is no single solution to this exercise, but see the results reported in Sections 3.3, 3.5, 3.6 and 3.7.

3.4 The suggested form leads to the estimated equation

$$\log \hat{M}1 = -0{\cdot}86 - 0{\cdot}24 \log (r - 2) + 1{\cdot}02 \log Y - 0{\cdot}18 \log P;$$
$$\quad\quad (1{\cdot}22) \ (0{\cdot}05) \quad\quad\quad (0{\cdot}20) \quad\quad (0{\cdot}22)$$
$$\quad\quad\quad\quad\quad\quad\quad\quad\quad\quad\quad\quad\quad\quad\quad\quad 1964{-}80$$

$$\text{RSS} = 0{\cdot}010 \quad \text{VAR} = 0{\cdot}0008 \quad R^2 = 0{\cdot}997$$
$$(\text{DW} = 2{\cdot}108 - \text{see Section 4.5})$$

3.5 The estimator $\hat{\beta} = \Sigma X_t Y_t / \Sigma X_t^2$ would be biased.

$$\hat{\beta} = \Sigma X_t (\alpha + \beta X_t + u_t) / \Sigma X_t^2$$
$$= (\alpha \Sigma X_t + \beta \Sigma X_t^2 + \Sigma X_t u_t) / \Sigma X_t^2$$
$$E(\hat{\beta}) = \alpha \Sigma X_t / \Sigma X_t^2 + \beta \Sigma X_t^2 / \Sigma X_t^2 + E(\Sigma X_t u_t / \Sigma X_t^2)$$
$$= \alpha \Sigma X_t / \Sigma X_t^2 + \beta + 0$$

The bias, $E(\hat{\beta}) - \beta$, is $\alpha \Sigma X_t / \Sigma X_t^2$. Since α is not zero (by assumption), the bias can only be zero if $\Sigma X_t = 0$.

3.6 (a) Let $\beta_6, \beta_7, \beta_8$ be the parameters associated with $Q_2 D, Q_3 D$ and $Q_4 D$. Then H_0 is $\beta_6 = \beta_7 = \beta_8 = 0$. H_a is that at least one of $\beta_6, \beta_7, \beta_8$ is nonzero. From the information given, $S_R = 13{\cdot}485, S = 2{\cdot}581$, $n = 72, k = 8, g = 3$. Hence

$$F = [(13{\cdot}485 - 2{\cdot}581)/3] \, / \, [2{\cdot}581/(72 - 8)] = 90{\cdot}13$$

We require $F_{3,64}^{0{\cdot}05}$: from Table C. This is somewhat less than $2{\cdot}76$. Hence H_0 is strongly rejected. The seasonal effect takes the form of shifts in the income parameter between quarters.

(b) This enables us to test H_0: all parameters the same between subsamples, against H_a: at least one parameter is different between subsamples. This is a Chow test (see Section 3.11). From the information provided, $S_R = 2 \cdot 581$, $S = S_1 + S_2 = 0 \cdot 485 + 1 \cdot 575 = 2 \cdot 060$, $n = 72$, $k = 16$ (8 parameters, in each of two subperiods) and $g = 8$. Hence

$$F = [(2 \cdot 581 - 2 \cdot 060)/8] / [2 \cdot 060/(72 - 16)] = 1 \cdot 77$$

We require $F_{8,56}^{0 \cdot 05}$: from Table C. This is slightly greater than $2 \cdot 10$. Hence H_0 is not rejected and, on the basis of this test, there is no clear indication of structural change between subperiods.

(c) In this case, the null hypothesis of an unchanged model for 1977–80 corresponds to 16 stochastic restrictions. $S_R = 2 \cdot 581$, $S = 1 \cdot 793$, $n = 56$, $k = 8$ and $g = 16$. Hence,

$$F = [(2 \cdot 581 - 1 \cdot 793)/16] / [1 \cdot 793/(56 - 8)] = 1 \cdot 32$$

We require $F_{16,48}^{0 \cdot 05}$. This is difficult to interpolate accurately from Table C, but is not less than $1 \cdot 70$. So H_0 is not rejected. This type of test is also sometimes called a Chow test, but it is different from (b) above. In (b), we test a set of exact restrictions. In (c), we test a set of stochastic restrictions.

Chapter 4

4.1 (a) The disturbance would become $u_t P_t$; $t = 1, 2, \ldots, n$ and var $(u_t P_t)$ would be $\sigma^2 P_t^2$. Hence one would expect to observe heteroscedasticity.

(b) To the extent that multiplying by price approximates fitting in current price terms, one should test for heteroscedasticity in the current price version of the consumption function. If $\sigma_t^2 = \exp(\delta_1 + \delta_2 \log P_t^2)$, then H_0: $\delta_2 = 0$ implies no heteroscedasticity. H_a: $\delta_2 \neq 0$ implies heteroscedasticity and, if δ_2 were actually equal to 1, then σ_t^2 would be proportional to P_t^2. The Breusch-Pagan test statistic is calculated as shown in equation 4.3.8, with $S_R - S = 0 \cdot 0928$, $\Sigma e_t^2 = 2 \cdot 635$, $n = 72$, $k = 8$, $p = 2$ $(p - 1 = 1)$. Hence

$$\chi^2 = 0 \cdot 0928 / [2(2 \cdot 635/72)^2] = 34 \cdot 64$$

Since $\chi_1^2 (0 \cdot 05) = 3 \cdot 84$, H_0 is convincingly rejected. Moreover, the second residual regression does suggest that δ_2 is fairly close to 1. (The standard errors reported are merely indicative.) The results for part (b) thus confirm the suggestion made in the solution to (a).

4.2 (*a*) The problems here are (i) $n = 24$, which is small for a test based on the asymptotic distribution of the test statistic (ii) χ^2 is not much greater than the critical value (iii) the value of the Durbin-Watson statistic. Since this is a cross-section there is no serial correlation through time, but the residuals are picking up some systematic influence and strongly indicate at least one missing variable. Hence, the conclusion drawn is not justified: if anything the Breusch-Pagan test is picking up the effects of misspecification. (*b*) This is confirmed on adding X_3. Both DW and R^2 are 'improved' and β_3 appears to be significantly different from 0. The Breusch-Pagan test now gives no evidence of heteroscedasticity. Although one might have expected both income and grouping effects to have caused heteroscedasticity, this is not revealed in the chosen data set. Income related heteroscedasticity might be obscured by grouping, or by using total expenditure instead of income, but this is highly speculative, without further analysis, preferably on a larger data set.

4.3 Write the constraint as

$$0.5 = \alpha(0) + \beta(1) + v$$

This suggests adding 0·5 as an extra observation on the dependent variable and 1 as an extra observation on the explanatory variable. But note that the 'observation' attached to α is 0, not 1, so the artificial variable observations in the augmented model consist of n 1s and one 0. The variance v is known to be 0·1, and this is unlikely to be the same as the disturbance variance in the main part of the model. So one would have to perform a transformation to allow for heteroscedasticity. The transformation would be based on an estimate of the disturbance variance, obtained from a preliminary regression on the unrestricted model.

4.4 $$Y_t - \rho Y_{t-4} = \alpha(1 - \rho) + \beta(X_t - \rho X_{t-4}) + u_t - \rho u_{t-4};$$
$$t = 5, 6, \ldots, n$$

Note that the disturbances are now independent, but four observations are lost. OLS applied to this equation approximates the best linear unbiased estimator, but it is not exactly best linear unbiased, because of the lost observations.

Chapter 5

5.1 $$Y_t = \delta Y_t^* + (1 - \delta)Y_{t-1} + u_t$$
$$= \delta\beta X_{t+1}^* + (1 - \delta)Y_{t-1} + u_t$$

X_{t+1}^* can be expressed as

$$X_{t+1}^* = (1 - \lambda)\,[X_t + \lambda X_{t-1} + \lambda^2 X_{t-2} + \ldots\,]$$

So

$$Y_t = \delta\beta(1 - \lambda)\,[X_t + \lambda X_{t-1} + \lambda^2 X_{t-2} + \ldots\,] + (1 - \delta)Y_{t-1} + u_t$$
$$\lambda Y_{t-1} = \delta\beta(1 - \delta)\,[\lambda X_{t-1} + \lambda^2 X_{t-2} + \ldots\,] + \lambda(1 - \delta)Y_{t-2} + \lambda u_{t-1}$$

By subtraction, writing $\lambda = 1 - (1 - \lambda)$ to show the form of the equation,

$$Y_t = \delta\beta(1 - \lambda)X_t + [(1 - \delta) + (1 - (1 - \lambda))]\,Y_{t-1}$$
$$- (1 - \delta)(1 - (1 - \lambda))Y_{t-2} + u_t - \lambda u_{t-1}$$

Problems:

(a) The parameters of interest are δ, β and $1 - \lambda$, and there are three composite parameters. But δ and $1 - \lambda$ enter the composite parameters in a symmetrical fashion and, from estimates of the composite parameters alone, it is impossible to assign unique estimates to δ and $(1 - \lambda)$.

(b) OLS estimation would lead to inconsistent estimates, since there are lagged dependent variables on the right, together with a moving average error.

5.2 $$Y_t = \beta_1 Y_{t-1} + \beta_2 X_t + u_t\,; t = 1, 2, \ldots, n$$
$$u_t = \rho u_{t-1} + v_t\,; t = 1, 2, \ldots, n$$
$$Y_{t-1} = \beta_1 Y_{t-2} + \beta_2 X_{t-1} + u_{t-1}\,;$$
$$Y_t - \rho Y_{t-1} = \beta_1 Y_{t-1} - \beta_1 \rho Y_{t-2} + \beta_2 X_t - \beta_2 \rho X_{t-1} + u_t - \rho u_{t-1}\,;$$
$$Y_t = (\beta_1 + \rho)Y_{t-1} - \beta_1 \rho Y_{t-2} + \beta_2 X_t - \beta_2 \rho X_{t-1} + v_t\,; t = 2, 3, \ldots, n$$

5.3 (a) At a 0·05 significance level, $n = 17$ and $k = 4$, $4 - d_U = 2·29$, and DW = 2·026. But there is a lagged dependent variable here, so the Durbin-Watson test is not appropriate. Since $n = 17$, the h test procedure is also somewhat dubious, but there is little else that we can do on the basis of the information provided. Hence

$$h = [1 - 0·5(2·026)]\,\sqrt{(17/[1 - 17(0·099)^2])} = -0·059$$

In a one tailed test against negative first order serial correlation, the critical value is $-1·64$. Since h is much greater (closer to 0) than this, there is no evidence of first order serial correlation.

(b) In the absence of serial correlation, the OLS estimators are consistent and the 'usual' test procedures are justified in a large sample: otherwise, the OLS estimators are not consistent. In this example $n = 17$, and there will be some small sample bias even though there does not appear to be evidence of serial correlation. (*c*) As shown in Section 5.5, there are various ways of arriving at this type of equation. It might be chosen directly, or imply partial adjustment, or a distributed lag. If this were a geometric lag, the implied lag distributions on Y and r would be identical and one might expect moving average disturbances to show up as negative first order serial correlation. Given the results in (*a*), it might be more reasonable to view this equation as consistent with a partial adjustment model. If so, the one period adjustment coefficient is 0·569 and the long run income and interest rate parameters are 0·27 and −0·34, respectively.

5.4 In solving these equations, the first equation can be replaced by a new equation, defined as

$$\text{new equation} = a_1 \,(\text{equation } 1) + a_2 \,(\text{equation } 2)$$

for any $a_1 \neq 0$ and any a_2. Since the definition of Z affects only the first equation, only this equation differs between cases. In case (*a*),

$$\hat{\beta}_{I1} \Sigma X_{t-1} Y_{t-1} + \hat{\beta}_{I2} \Sigma X_{t-1} X_t = \Sigma X_{t-1} Y_t$$

In case (*b*), there is an additional constant a which appears in each term, but cancels from both sides of the equation. In case (*c*) we obtain an equation which is actually a_1 (equation 1) $+ a_2$ (equation 2). Hence all three cases give the same solution. Case (*a*) is the 'simple' IV procedure, case (*c*) is the suggested two stage least squares procedure, and both are equivalent to (*b*).

Chapter 6

6.1
$$
\begin{aligned}
C_t &= \alpha + \beta(C_t + I_t + Z_t) + u_t \\
&= \alpha/(1 - \beta) + [\beta/(1 - \beta)](I_t + Z_t) + u_t/(1 - \beta) \\
&= \alpha/(1 - \beta) + [\beta/(1 - \beta)](\gamma + \delta D_{t-1} + v_t) + [\beta/(1 - \beta)]Z_t \\
&\quad + u_t/(1 - \beta) \\
&= (\alpha + \beta\gamma)/(1 - \beta) + [\beta\delta/(1 - \beta)]D_{t-1} \\
&\quad + [\beta/(1 - \beta)]Z_t + (u_t + \beta v_t)/(1 - \beta)
\end{aligned}
$$

A linear combination of equations involving the identity would contain Z_t. A linear combination involving the investment function would contain D_{t-1}. The consumption function is therefore identified: in fact it is over-identified.

6.2 Climate is clearly exogenous and this leaves Q^d, Q^s and P as endogenous variables. Eliminating Q^d and Q^s leaves

$$Q_t = \alpha + \beta P_t + u_t$$
$$Q_t = \gamma + \delta R_t + v_t$$

and the model is no longer simultaneous. In fact R determines Q and Q determines P, despite the way in which the first equation is written. Provided that u_t and v_t are not correlated, this is a recursive model.

6.3 The answer would be to select variables which would appear in a macromodel, but which could reasonably be taken as exogenous. One might also add some lagged variables to this list. These variables would then be used as explanatory variables in first stage regressions, designed to generate predicted values of variables which (1) appear on the right of the consumption function and (2) would be endogenous in a complete model. The predicted values then replace the observed values of the right hand endogenous variables in the second stage regressions. In conventional usage, there is confusion as to whether instrumental variables are the predicted values, or the variables used to generate the predicted values. We have tended to use the former, but in describing more general procedures the latter use is common.

Index